AFGHANISTAN: INSIDE A REBEL STRONGHOLD

AFGHANISTAN: INSIDE A REBEL STRONGHOLD

JOURNEYS WITH THE MUJAHIDDIN

MIKE MARTIN

BLANDFORD PRESS
POOLE · DORSET

First published in the UK 1984 by Blandford Press,
Link House, West Street, Poole, Dorset BH15 1LL

Distributed in the United States by
Sterling Publishing Co., Inc.,
2 Park Avenue, New York, N.Y. 10016

British Library Cataloguing in Publication Data

Martin, Mike
  Afghanistan.
  1. Afghanistan—Politics and government
  —1973-
  I. Title
  958'.1044'0924   DS369.5

ISBN 0 7137 1388 7

Typeset by Poole Typesetting (Wessex) Ltd., Bournemouth

Printed in Spain by Grijelmo Bilbao

Contents

For Afghanistan, for freedom

Acknowledgements

I owe a debt of gratitude to many people in Britain, the Middle East, Pakistan and Afghanistan who helped make this book, though I will name just a few. To Dr. Armanyar for his hospitality and the doors he opened; to Karim, whose attempts to teach me some elementary Pushtu was but one of many favours though I dare say the most exhausting; to the officials and the unofficials; to the hundreds of Afghans for their hospitality against all odds; to Gill, Peter and Maggie for the St. Christophers; and to my family and friends who bought the beer when the cash ran dry . . . thankyou.

The publishers would like to thank Anita Lawrence for drawing the maps, based on original drawings by Gill Hewitt.

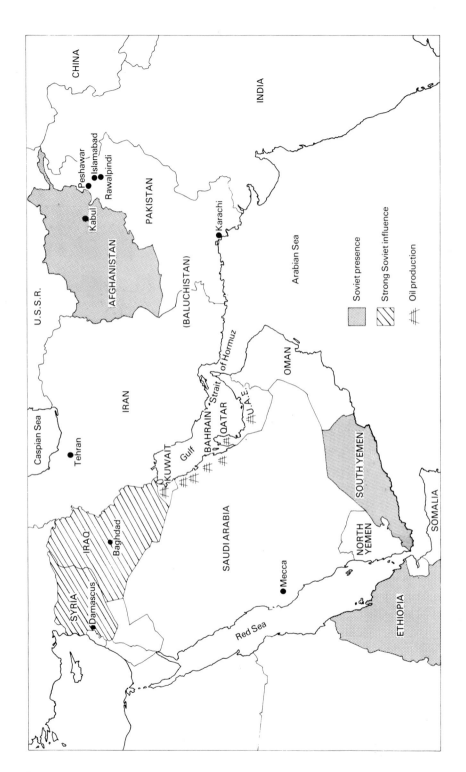

CHINA

INDIA

Peshawar
Islamabad
Rawalpindi
PAKISTAN
Kabul
AFGHANISTAN
Karachi

U.S.S.R.

(BALUCHISTAN)

Arabian Sea

Soviet presence

Strong Soviet influence

Oil production

Caspian Sea

IRAN

Tehran

Strait of Hormuz

OMAN

BAHRAIN
QATAR
U.A.E.
Gulf
KUWAIT

SOUTH YEMEN

SYRIA
IRAQ
Baghdad
Damascus

SAUDI ARABIA

Mecca

NORTH
YEMEN

SOMALIA

ETHIOPIA

Red Sea

The Region

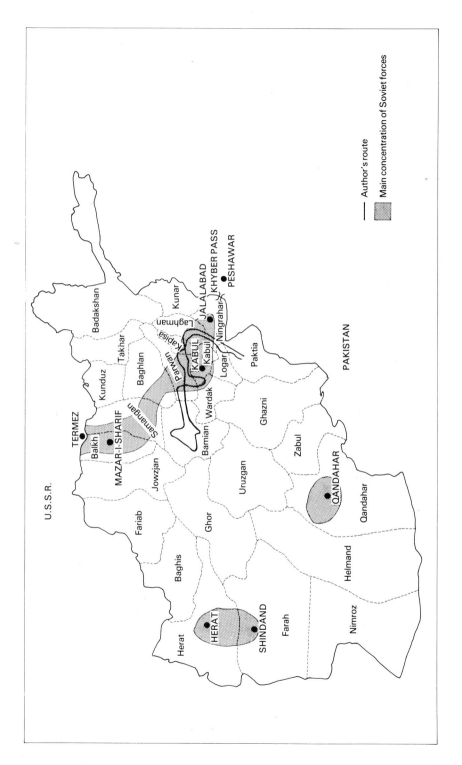

Afghanistan

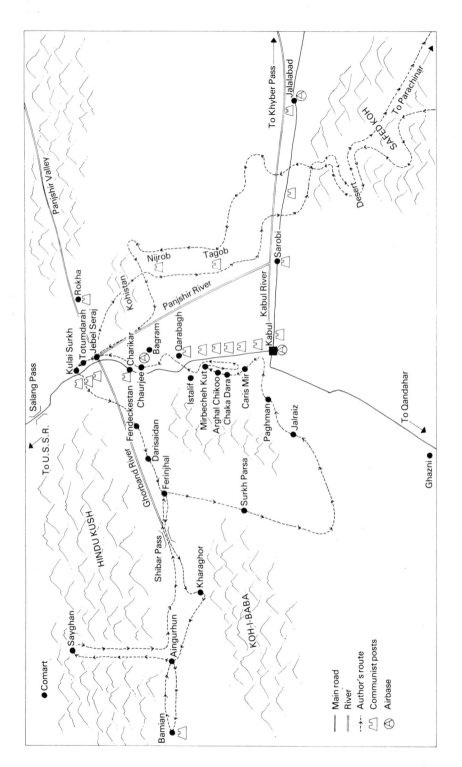

10

The Author's Route (not to scale)

1

Flight to a Cauldron

I had expected to begin this narrative with words like 'The flight from London to Pakistan was boring as long journeys by plane tend to be,' or 'The flight was uneventful.' It was not. Tribal war broke out as the aircraft was being refuelled at Dubai.

There is a sense of the surreal in awakening to the glare of the sun in the Arabian Gulf after twelve hours' travelling. The beer I had drunk in the transit lounge at Cairo Airport was to be the last beer for six months and it had been that one beer too many: the joker in the six-pack which added to the sense of incoherence in the bright dawn after the night made short by eastward flight. But then the tangible world itself seemed barely real as it shimmered in the heat haze. A distant cityscape of towers, rotundas, ziggurats, projecting balconies, arches and concrete and steel follies shifted in the watery light. It is not just the distortion of heat and humidity that has produced the strange skylines of the Gulf. Some of the buildings were made that way. Countless millions of petrodollars were spent during the boom decade of the 1970s to bring Western architects to the Gulf to design banks, hotels and office blocks for the civil servants and the great trading houses. The arks and thrones of a brave new world. For years these architects had been frustrated by cost-conscious accountants who virtually determined design by their precise knowledge of floor space return on a given investment. There was little money left with which the designer could exercise his or her creativity and the result in so many Western cities is a skyline filled with filing cabinet architecture.

There were no such constraints in the Gulf and, if at times the result seems to have more to do with hallucinogenic drugs than architecture, well why not? Those who see the Dubai Sheraton for the first time tend to gasp, then laugh. It looks like an erupting star arrested in cosmic flight by the imagination of its creator Rader Mileto. Its bright red atrium which soars from the reception area to the roof, with the rooms arranged on galleries open to public view, is a source of visual wonder and lewd innuendo. The world can see exactly who you are taking into your room. In a part of the world where most of the landscape is desert, a flourish of drama or the absurd or just fun is a tonic. Many of the modernistic structures suffer from

11

a lack of architectural context, but history had not seen such a colossal transfer of wealth. Strange things were bound to happen.

While these thoughts occupied a mind slowly coming back to life, the young man sat down in the empty seat next to me. I did not notice him at first. Why should I? The art of air travel is mutual anonymity. It is a silent costume ball for which we dress in our best disguises and let our fellow passengers invent who we are. He said nothing but there was something intense radiating from the young Pathan in the dark suit which made me look up from the out-of-date copy of *The Times*. Blood trickled from his nose and he sat with a grim expression focused on the in-flight magazine held in clenched fists.

Excuse me, you appear to be bleeding over an article about the rich Islamic heritage of the region.

I did not articulate the thought, partly because it seemed like stating the obvious and partly because my attention was diverted by events in the aisle. A brawl had broken out and from the rear door to the first class compartment Afghan and Pakistani Pathans were trading blows. Non-combatant passengers looked on. At each end of the aisle members of the Egyptian crew looked on with expressions of impassivity redolent of the Sphynx. Perhaps it was the collective will of the few Britons on board whose determination to ignore the unpleasant resulted in a subsidence of the action. The dictum 'ignore it and it will go away' still enables the British to pass through the excitable corners of the world with an air somewhere between serenity and oblivion. That it was an 'uneasy peace' I could sense as I turned again to *The Times*. (An uneasy peace is what journalists write into their copy to encourage news editors to keep them on the spot where they can continue to develop the creative side of their writing in the submission of expenses claims.)

My companion continued to bleed quietly into the magazine. Outside airport workers spread their prayer mats on the tarmac and submitted to the call of Mecca. Others watched the dials on the tanker as tons of aviation fuel were pumped through the umbilical into our plane. European expatriates edged up the steps of a plane bound for London. They had expressions of people who have completed some great journey or who have survived an adventure and are going home: by turns excited and deeply content. The men involved in the fight were expatriates too; Pathans from the tribal region that straddles the frontier between Afghanistan and Pakistan. They had been working in Nigeria. They wore shiny suits, the style of which was conceived in the 1950s, and their hair had the opaque brilliance of patent leather. Each carried an enormous new radio cassette player. It was not the style of the Pathans on the North West Frontier.

But the superficialities of dress and modern gadgets could not conceal deeper cultural traditions like the blood feud. Round two began with shrill insults being traded between half a dozen women from each camp. Their squabbling reached a pitch of squealing malevolence which could be heard a kilometre away, though they were separated by just three rows of seats and, with the grace of a cohort of Billingsgate fish wives, they harangued each other, their men and most of the passengers. There was a minor skirmish between rows 9 and 14 and everyone landed in a heap on the floor. More Sphynx stares from the crew. Two men rolled into that secret, curtained place where only the crew are admitted and where the hostesses conjure up meals. There was a great crash from within and they rolled out the other side, still locked in the embrace of combat.

Violence gave way to bitter argument for a time and I resumed my reverie, peering through the window at a world grown as evanescent as the one within was chaotic. The temperature was in the middle 30s centigrade and rising. Buildings seemed to vanish, blasted away in the intense, brilliant light. Three years earlier the Gulf had been my home, and I remembered day after incandescent day in which the tangible world was bleached away by the sun. Social and political events in the region added to the sense of failure of the real world as perceived by the Western mind. There was too much room for those with the power of imagination to conceive of fantastic worlds all of their own to replace the one distorted through the prism of heat. Most expatriates left after a year or two with a suntan and a buoyant bank balance, but some stayed much longer. Some of these became immune to the deceptions of the imagination which eventually withered in the remorseless heat. But in others that same heat inflamed the imagination to psychotic levels.

The querulous nature of the Pathans had been inflamed by generous libations of Scotch at Cairo Airport and, for all I knew, ever since they left Nigeria. Their celebrations at the prospect of returning home after years abroad had degenerated into recriminations over some distant dispute. The Pathans cannot let sleeping dogs lie. Like malaria, such feuds are conducted in recurring and often deadly cycles of vengeance. The brawl erupted with renewed intensity. My companion was still staring dolefully at the magazine when the attack came. The assailant clambered over the back of our seats, grabbing my neck for support. Thus perched, he began to pummel the young man with his free fist. Partly because I had come to the conclusion that such behaviour was a shade excessive before breakfast, but also because the character astride the seats had stuck his foot through the cricket page of *The Times,* I decided I had had enough. I dislodged the one from his perch and restrained the other who, seeing the change in their relative fortunes, was about to stamp on his head. Then I set off through the maelstrom of battling men and women, their arms flailing like demented tick-tack men. Such a manoeuvre was neither brave nor rash. Honour among the Pathans is such that they would not allow an outsider to come to harm. Like Moses at the parting of the waters I passed through the fray. The air hostess continued to look on with glassy disdain as I suggested she call a policeman. Or a battalion of policemen.

'What do you expect? They are Pathans,' she said with that air of sophisticated immobility affected by girls in that trade who have been accorded a social status out of all proportion to the work they do. I wanted to tell her that from Pathans you could expect many rich and diverse things. I wanted an end to the brawling more, however, so I said nothing. She did nothing, so I left the plane and found a policeman. He was a diminutive Baluch from Pakistan and he took his gun from his holster as we climbed the steps of the plane. I suggested diplomatically that the proximity of so much aviation fuel made wielding a gun hazardous. He agreed, turned and tossed the weapon down to a colleague who would never have made a fielder in cricket. The gun clattered across the tarmac.

While the plucky Baluch dealt with the Pathans I sank back into my seat. The ringleaders were led away and the rest returned to their seats bearing expressions of sullen vengeance that seemed to point a way to the dark side of the region.

The plane banked over the blue of the Gulf. Events in the aircraft might have been a microcosm of a part of the world more complex and mystifying than any other. From Rabat to Islamabad a score of nations are bound in the unity of the Islamic faith, yet no region is more divided by schism, ideology, tribal or personal rivalry. Oil, wealth almost beyond measure, the fragile security of Western interests and the rise of militant Islam were but some of the explosive issues that prompted President Carter's National Security Adviser Zbigniew Brzezinski in early 1979 to call the region an 'arc of crisis'.

The events of 1979 proved him right. No prophecy would prove too dark as one crisis followed another until it seemed the region would fly apart. What were those centrifugal forces that threatened to undermine the fabric of half a dozen countries? Oil. The very word takes us to the heart of global relationships. Israel, the unruly cuckoo state of the Middle East, inspired even noble in its genesis, remained apparently blind to the trials of those displaced Palestinians about its borders. The West, in seeking to assuage the guilt of history, collaborates in the sins of the present. The rise of fundamentalist Islam found the West wanting, not only in answers to the phenomenon but in a basic understanding of it. What of exotic hybrids like Colonel Gaddafi of Libya whose eclectic philosophy attempted to weld the irreconcileable forces of Islam and Marxism? The instrument of terror was a commonplace. The Russians had bridgeheads to the oil states in South Yemen and Ethiopia, influence in Syria and Iraq.

Some of the expatriates on the island of Bahrain where I lived started to leave at the time of the Iranian revolution in 1978. Ayatollah Khomeini arrived in early 1979. The United States' ambassador to Afghanistan was killed in Kabul. Afghanistan's communist rulers had held power for less than a year but popular resistance to the regime was already widespread. Even in Bahrain, one of the Gulf's more progressive and liberal sheikhdoms, there was unrest. Riots were started by the Shi'ite minority, inspired by the Iranian theocracy. More expatriates left the Gulf as concern about the stability of the region increased. In November forty-eight people were seized and held

14

hostage at the United States embassy in Tehran. If this was an attack on 'Western imperialism' or 'the Great Satan', the next outrage struck at the very heart of Islam. The Grand Mosque in Mecca, Saudi Arabia, was overrun by terrorists. Many died before they were prized out of Islam's holiest shrine. More died when a mob burned the American embassy in Islamabad, Pakistan.

They were ugly days. Political choice in the region seemed to be polarised between the anarchy of the mob and tyranny. The United States aircraft carriers *Kitty Hawk* and *Midway,* with a dozen support ships, were sailing just outside the Arabian Gulf. But President James Carter was at bay, ultimately to become the political victim of his tendency to trust others. The Iranian revolution destroyed American policy in the region which had been forged under President Richard Nixon. The idealism generated by the Carter administration came to be seen as a liability. At the time these incidents seemed to be the anarchic manifestation of a region which suffers from collective schizophrenia, caught between a desire for religious, even political, unity and its tendency to fragmentation. Hindsight and investigation suggests there was a common thread running through these events. Worse, they were but the sound of the leper's bell heralding worse to come. When the cataclysm came it would leave 1979 as the year historians might point to as the one in which the axis of global power shifted, perhaps irrevocably, against the West.

There is a story, possibly apocryphal, that in the closing months of 1979 Russian agents scoured second-hand book shops in London and bought up books covering the period of the British Empire's involvement in Afghanistan. Just as the borders of the land of the Afghans were defined by foreigners, so too is much of their history illuminated by outsiders. Was it not ironic that the scourge of imperialism should take such an interest in the dusty catalogue of British adventures in that remote and mountainous land? Not at all. The world's last empire was on the move.

At Christmas, 1979, the Russians made their move against Afghanistan. They flew in an airborne division to Kabul airport and Bagram airbase 40 kilometres north of the capital. Hundreds of Antonov transport planes flew in between Christmas Day and 27 December. On that day crack Russian troops stormed the palace of President Hafizullah Amin and killed him. Their former ally became an unperson: the Kremlin now called him a CIA agent. Two Russian motorised divisions crossed the border and within two days had secured the principal cities: Herat, Qandahar, Kabul. The world knew these places as history and romance. Now they were front page news. At the start of the new decade the Russians had overrun Afghanistan just as they had overrun Hungary and Czechoslovakia.

This is a book about Afghanistan, but events in the country cannot be seen in isolation. Historically Afghanistan has been the crossroads for invaders and for the great trade routes. The view from the West is of a remote and hostile land visited only by the adventurous. Kipling is still our guide. But the

Author Mike Martin with Afghan Mujahiddin during an earlier journey.

invasion transformed Afghanistan into the crucible in which the future of the struggle between East and West, not to mention the role that Islam is to play in the world, will be decided. At the time of the invasion I wrote:

Islam is the only currently effective form of opposition to Soviet expansion plans in the region and it is on the defensive in Afghanistan . . . The new leader, Babrak Karmal, a hardline Marxist, has been brought to power by the Soviets and his justification for that power will lie only in their continued support. The furtherance of world communism is a long-held aim of the Kremlin, a fact which may please the new regime but it should remember that the Soviet presence in Afghanistan is part of a larger scheme whose manifestations can also be seen in the Horn of Africa and South Yemen. President Karmal's authority will exist only as long as his Soviet masters feel it serves their ambitions for a warm water port or what appears to be a regional pincer movement with the Gulf as its objective.

Now, as the plane traced the desolate Makran coast of southern Pakistan, I was travelling back to Afghanistan. It was three years since my first journey with the Afghan resistance fighters. My intention was to find out what power it was that made the people of one of the world's poorest countries fight the armed tyranny of the communist super-power. I asked one of the Pathans if the dispute had been resolved. He made no reply but gave me an enigmatic smile. This much I already knew: the Pathan is a gracious host and a loyal ally but when offended he is utterly unforgiving. History shows this, but perhaps the Russians who received the books from London did not read that chapter.

2

Where Empires Yield

Afghanistan is a place where the history of others goes to be acted out. The Achaemenids, the Mongols, the British. Empires come this way on their way to the past. It is a conduit for invading forces and the pivot of their fortunes. To the Afghans history or, more properly, folklore is a living process which cannot be divorced from the present. Genghis Khan and Alexander the Great are the currency of everyday conversation. More than a score of dynasties ruled over part or all of what we now call Afghanistan. Civilisations burned for a short time and disappeared. This Ozymandian transience left its mark on the people rather than on the landscape. Their wariness of foreigners probably has its roots in the experiences of the past. The sense of fatalism too. Afghan history is alive in the people rather than in monuments.

If history has left a profound mark on the people then an equally important element in the forging of the Afghan character is landscape. It is a beautiful and savage country and survival has dictated a temperament as uncompromising as the environment. The country lies within parallels 29 30' and 38 35' latitude and 60 50' and 74 50' longitude. With a land area of 650,000 square kilometres it is about the size of Texas. To the north lies the Soviet Union, to the north-east China, to the east is Pakistan and to the west is Iran. Desert and mountain dominate the land. The country is virtually divided by the Hindu Kush (Hindu killer) range which runs for 950 kilometres from the north-east to the south-west, with peaks soaring to more than 5,000 metres. In the extreme north-east is the Pamir Knot of towering peaks from which radiates the Hindu Kush and the Karakorams and Himalayas to the east. The Turkestan Plains run from the northern slopes of the Hindu Kush to the River Amu Darya (Oxus) which forms the border with the Soviet Union. To the south and south-west desert and semi-desert constitute the bleak vistas to the Iranian border. Great rivers tumble out of the central mountain ranges. The mainly agrarian population is perennially occupied with the problem of how to control the water supply. They face extremes like spring when melting snows lead to flooding and summer when many rivers dry up, and the ingenuity of many individual irrigation systems suffer from a lack of coordination. The climate is as extreme and varied as the landscape, with blistering heat in summer and bitter cold in winter. Even

18

in summer it can be very cold in the mountains at night, and the higher peaks are capped with snow throughout the year. Rainfall is limited and sporadic.

It was through such terrain that a chain of invaders passed. The origins of the Afghans remains obscure. Early Stone Age man probably lived in caves in the north and archaeological work has revealed Neolithic, Iron and Bronze Age sites. Folklore suggests that the Pathans, who make up nearly half of the estimated sixteen million population, can trace their origins to the tribes of ancient Israel. However, there is little evidence to show that the lost tribes of Judaic legend ever crossed the Hindu Kush.

Persia and Islam have been the abiding influences in Afghanistan. In 559 BC Cyrus established the Achaemenid Empire from the Mediterranean to the Indus. The eastern satrapies incorporated what is now Afghanistan: Aria (Herat), Bactria (Balkh), Arachosia (Qandahar). North of Balkh, Cyrus died at the hands of the Massagatae. In his campaign against Tomyris, she had addressed him before the battle: 'Rule your own people and try to bear the sight of me ruling mine.' The military abilities of Cyrus were matched by Darius in administration. He reorganised the empire and introduced laws underpinned by equitable taxation and sound money. The empire flourished under this early monetarist.

Darius was beaten by the Greeks at Marathon and Xerxes, his son, was similarly defeated at sea and on land. However, the Achaemenid Empire remained impregnable to the threat of Greek invasion until the time of Alexander. The Greek commander is still remembered in Afghanistan as Sikander. After defeating the Achaemenid armies at Gaugamela, Alexander led his armies through Afghanistan and across the Hindu Kush. He established many cities in the east but the unity of the empire passed with his death. The Hellenes who ruled the old Persian satrapies fought each other but none prevailed. The pattern of periods of stability and unity followed by internal feuding would be maintained for centuries.

The next influence of importance came from the east. The Maurya Empire of Chandragupta replaced the Macedonians and, under Asoka, there began the spread of Buddhism. There is physical evidence of this westward movement in the chain of Buddhist cells still to be found carved into cliff faces and which end at the colossal statues of Buddha recessed into the cliffs at Bamian. Hellenic civilisation flourished on the plain of present-day Peshawar with its heart at Taxila but it fell around 97 BC to the Sakas.

In AD 75 the Kushans crossed the River Oxus (Amu Darya) and swept through what is now Afghanistan and north India. The greatest of the Kushan kings was Kanishka who reigned in the second century from his northern capital of Purushapura (Peshawar). Kanishka embraced Buddhism and, largely as a result, there was a rich flowering of what came to be known as Gandharan art. The Kushans were overrun by the Sasanian dynasty which had succeeded the Parthians in Persia.

Law and order collapsed in the fifth century when the region was again invaded from the north, this time by the White Huns. A century later the

Sasanians had extended Persian control once again over modern Afghanistan.

Internal rivalries had so weakened the Sasanian state that when the Arabs appeared under the banner of Islam, the armies of the empire crumbled in two decisive battles. Sasanian power was broken at Qadisiya in AD 637 and buried forever at Nihawand in 642. Just ten years after the death of the Prophet Mohammed the word of Islam, the third of the great monotheistic religions, was at the frontier of present-day Afghanistan. Islam took far longer to become established east of Herat than most Afghans will admit today though the Afghan is as assiduous in his devotions as any Muslim. The Arabs' eastward thrust passed by the central mountains of Afghanistan and struck north and south. The heartlands of the country remained untouched by the faith for a long time. Abdullah ibn Amir captured Herat, Merv and Balkh in 650 and for sixty years the thrust of the Arabs in the east was towards Bokhara and Samarkand, finally captured in 710. The southward route through Seistan brought the Arabs as far as Kabul but the impact of Islam remained small.

Ghazni is a modest, dusty town today but in the early eleventh century it was a great centre of art and learning. In the previous century it had been the south-eastern outpost of the Samanid Empire based on Bokhara. A former slave called Sabuktagin seized the office of governor and founded the Ghaznavid dynasty of which the Afghans are still justly proud. Sabuktagin launched attacks on the Hindus living in the Kabul valley and twice defeated the Hindu king Jaipal at Laghman and Ningrahar.

But it was his son Mahmud who transformed Ghazni into legend and himself into the first Afghan folk hero. He launched campaigns west into Persia, north against Balkh and east into the Punjab. Magnificent architecture flourished at Ghazni and its court attracted scholars, poets including Persia's greatest, Firdausi, and scientists such as Al-Biruni. This efflorescence of science and the arts was fuelled by wealth from Hindu temples sacked by Mahmud in more than a dozen strikes to the east.

Ghazni was a cultural lamp that burned brightly and briefly: Mahmud died in 1030 and 120 years later his city was razed and 70,000 people slaughtered. The man responsible was a Tadjik from Ghor (the Hazarajat of present-day Afghanistan) called Jahansoz the World Burner. This act of barbarism was a forerunner of worse to come: the onslaught of Genghis Khan. The Mongols brought destruction on a cataclysmic scale but it was not paralleled by a distinctive and enduring civilisation. Their destructive impact on the political, social and religious lives of others was total, yet they left little of substance with which we can identity them. One is tempted to speculate on the impact that the barbarism of the Mongols has had on the collective psychology of the Afghans.

'The greatest joy is to conquer one's enemies, to pursue them, to seize their property, to see their family in tears, to ride their horses, to possess their daughters and wives.' Thus spoke Genghis Khan. In 1219 he devastated the

20

great cities of Samarkand and Bokhara, butchering the populations. In 1220 he sacked Ghazni and Herat and later destroyed Balkh so completely that a hundred years later a traveller would record that the once great city was still a ruin. He built no great palaces from which to launch these journeys of destruction: he lived in a tent. The achievement of Genghis Khan was to lay waste the work of others.

The tradition continued with his son Chagatai who in 1240 penetrated as far as Lahore and destroyed it. Within a century the lands of Transoxiana had fallen to Timur who, while often as ruthless as his forbears, would go some way towards assuaging the destructive legacy of the Mongols. He gave his name to the splendours of the architecture which adorned his capital at Samarkand. On his way to India, Timur captured Herat and Qandahar and, in the former, some of the finest Timurid art and architecture flourished. Timur's son Shah Rukh ruled from Herat in the early fifteenth century and his wife Gohar Shad commissioned many fine buildings, the remains of which still stand. The latter part of the century saw a cultural renaissance as poets and scholars were drawn to Afghanistan's westernmost city.

Like the rise and fall of Ghazni, however, Herat too leaves one with a sense of transience. It would be left to Babur to establish an enduring dynasty – the Mughals. Though this great empire was based in north India, Babur's heart remained in Kabul and that is where his tomb is. He wrote of the city: 'The climate is extremely delightful, and there is no such place in the known world.' He also wrote that Kabul was to be governed by the sword, not the pen. He should know: he had taken it by force in 1504. Babur faced the problem which has dogged invaders from antiquity to the present: how to stabilise your base inside Afghanistan in the face of tribal hostility? His inability to subdue the Pathans may well have prompted his decision to establish his empire in India. This he succeeded in doing in 1525 when, after the battle of Panipat, he claimed the throne in Delhi. The result was that Afghanistan came to be on the periphery of the great Mughal Empire. To the west the Safavid dynasty, established in 1501, sought to reassert Persian dominance over the mountainous land. Until the eighteenth century when Afghanistan took on the rough semblance of a nation state, the Mughals and the Persians struggled to dominate the land. Afghanistan fell increasingly under the influence of the Persians and, by the end of the sixteenth century, most of western Afghanistan was under Safavid rule. There was a third element – the Uzbeks from the north. During the seventeenth century, Mughal, Safavid and Uzbek fought over Afghan cities.

The Afghan tribes remained largely independent of these dynastic forces. Their preoccupations were best expressed by the seventeenth-century Pathan poet Khushal Khan Khattack.

The dogs of the Mohmands are better than the Bangash,
Though the Mohmands themselves are a thousand times worse than the dogs,
The Warrakzais are the scavengers of the Afridis,
Though the Afridis, one and all, are but scavengers themselves.

Only at the end of the poem does he refer to the Mughals. Within the land of the Afghans feuding and parochialism reigned. But a piece of inspired opportunism by an Afghan warrior was about to change that. The Persian leader Nadir Khan's cruelties led to frequent outbreaks of rebellion and he was constantly on the move seeking to quell uprisings. He and his men were camped near Meshed in north Persia one night in 1747. The Afghan contingent of the Persian army was led by Ahmed Khan of the Abdali tribe which had been defeated by Nadir Khan's legions. The internecine strife generated by Nadir Khan led to his murder that night and, indirectly, to the establishment of the Durrani Empire, the first true Afghan state.

Many legends surround the crowning of Ahmed Khan as shah of Afghanistan at Qandahar where he had fled with 4,000 men from the slaughter at Meshed. At a jirgah (gathering of chiefs) it is said that Ahmed Khan alone remained silent when each candidate grew voluble as to why he should be elected shah. A holy man is said to have observed that Ahmed Khan alone had proved, by declining to add to the dissent, that he was fit to govern. He was crowned Ahmed Shah and took the title Durr-i-Durran (Pearl of Pearls) and the Abdalis became known as the Durranis. He was just 24, able and backed by outstanding troops. From his campaigns with Nadir Khan he knew the weaknesses of the Mughal Empire. He subdued Kabul and Ghazni and then began the first of eight expeditions across the Indus to ravage the Punjab as far as Delhi. Initially the campaigns were to claim in his own name from the Mughal emperor Peshawar and the districts which had been ceded to Nadir Khan. But then the ambitious and talented ruler took Lahore and the western Punjab in 1752. In the same year he conquered Kashmir, the seductive land that Afghans yearn for to this day.

Ahmed Shah died in 1773 leaving an empire which stretched from Lahore in the east to beyond Meshed in the west and from the Amu Darya in the north through Baluchistan to the Makran Coast in the south. It was an empire which covered all of present-day Afghanistan. The decline of both the Mughal and Safavid empires enabled him to consolidate power in the acquired lands. But the familiar cycle of consolidation and disintegration was to return to the nadir of the wheel after his death. Internecine strife dominated the next few decades as men of lesser abilities fought over the empire.

In 1600 an Englishman, Captain William Hawkins, met with the Mughal emperor Jahangir at the imperial court in Delhi. He was a representative of the East India Company which, he said, was interested in 'trade not territory'. Two centuries later the picture was quite different. Afghanistan was about to find itself not only pressed by a great European empire from the east but a second from the north. The history of Afghanistan to the present day is inextricably bound up with the fate of those two empires.

The Orchard at the Edge of War

Rawalpindi and Islamabad are two cities separated by a twenty-minute bus ride and centuries, just as if York and Milton Keynes were neighbours. Rawalpindi is a great ramshackle city full of colour and smells. Each building adds to the concatenation which takes you through time as well as space. Islamabad is stately and bureaucratic. The streets are aligned on a grid system understood best by residents and the bright minds of children. The city was expressly built as the capital for the new state of Pakistan and it is a singular place, fashionable for visitors to decry for its modernism. Here the engines of government, embassies and office blocks are located between parks where the air is full of the scent of jasmine and rose. The wide boulevards are lined with jacaranda trees in full bloom, the mauve sprays with the quality of lace. Through the luxuriant growth go tiny sleek black bee-eaters, fastidious about their work. It is too peaceful for a capital city. Everyone knows that the metropolitan heart of Pakistan is Karachi. The government, ever-sensitive to this suggestion, ruled that foreign correspondents should be based in Islamabad and not the great southern port. To listen to the voice of the nation, not its heart.

The little bus raced through the wild lands of the North West Frontier Province to the provincial capital of Peshawar. It was hot and uncomfortable as you tried to doze against the metal clatter of the engine. At Attock and afterwards you no longer dozed as the drama of the town and then the beauty of the Peshawar plain took your mind off the discomfort. In 1581 Akbar, heir to Babur and one of the greatest Mughal emperors, gave the order to build the huge fort that sits squat and glowering over the River Indus at Attock. The broad river gave its name to India yet runs through Pakistan. Some still maintain that it is the natural border between the Afghans and the Pakistanis. Beyond the huge and sluggish river we were in Pathan country where history gave way to legend.

The vale of Peshawar is like a great orchard radiating in all directions from the city. Babur wrote: 'As far as the eye could reach were flower gardens. In the neighbourhood of Peshawar in spring-tide, the flowers are exquisitely lovely.'

Peshawar is not lovely but it has the style developed by a woman whom fortune has not favoured with beauty. It is a frontier town full of vitality and expectation, beyond which lies uncertainty. The meek shall not inherit such places. There is a new town, built in the time of the empire, and where the smart – that means usually the military in Pakistan – live now; and an old town at the heart of which is the Bazaar of the Story Tellers. The professional spinners of yarns are no more but it is still where you find out what is going on. And the hotels are cheaper.

The hotel was a formless building wedged between a hessian warehouse and a garage. Beyond the glow of the restaurant windows on the first floor, you had to imagine its lost shape. You climbed a flight of steps past the restaurant windows and a midget sitting in the doorway behind a potted plant, and walked a long corridor to reception. It was cheap and there were no other Europeans staying there. The manager was a dapper Punjabi with a casual smile and a love of cricket, the acceptable legacy of empire. He insisted that the room was not 'achieving European standard'. I took it and he shrugged his shoulders. Once they had put up Europeans he said, but they had been hippies. He thought they were rather like the holy men who once drifted through the region in large numbers on esoteric business. Neither hippies nor holy men liked cricket and they did not come that way any more.

An ancient fan turned the hot air in the room and a single window afforded a view of the corridor. The room was full of black, metallic cockroaches. Despite my familiarity with these insects I had never overcome an irrational loathing for them. The best part of the hotel was the flat roof from where you could look across the old town or west to the mountains where, in the evening, the sun smoked in a red sky. The mountains were the ancient home of the Mohmands, Shinwaris and Afridis, warrior tribes who retain their independence despite the blandishments of central governments on both sides of the border. The border: nearly 1,500 kilometres and following a line drawn up by the British at the end of the last century. The line – named after Durand who drew it – is actually painted in white on some of the mountains.

And beyond it, Afghanistan. To look up at those mountains which usurped the sky was to be on the edge of eternity or a dream. Afghanistan. It sits on the periphery of the Western consciousness. It is the remote and extravagant land that the British warred in and Kipling romanticised. Trusty Watson had just returned from Afghanistan when he met Holmes. Alexander, Genghis Khan and Timur passed his way: it was the place for the man who would be king. But, surely, when the British Empire went home did not Afghanistan really cease to exist?

The heat and the sound of the faithful being called to prayer woke me well before 5 am. In the summer there is no respite from the heat on the plain and yet in Peshawar there is not the torpor to be found in other hotlands. Part of the town's rough vitality is in the sense of endeavour, almost of mission, on faces in the crowded streets. Expectancy too. Expressions suggest that events are afoot that it would be worth knowing about.

I washed the sweat from my body, drank some tea and walked into the

24

blinding sun. The midget – I called him Majid – was perched on the steps and he called out 'salaam alaikum' in a strange and husky voice. I replied to the Muslim greeting 'alaikum salaam'.

In the bazaar I bought some cockroach spray. Perhaps they were the spectre of some suppressed fear. All I knew was that they cost me sleep as a sighting – they gambol at night – demanded ceaseless chase until it was trapped and destroyed. Then the next one appeared . . . and so on. Little boys whispered 'Mista, mista, eh mista,' in conspiratorial tones and then rolled their tongues to make a sound like grasshoppers. The smells were everywhere: woodsmoke, shit, cooking oil, fruit, kebabs, rotting meat and incense. The latter is associated with things spiritual and mystical. I was reminded of the flats of chic couples in north London where, after a hard day at the Covent Garden bead emporium, they would slip incense into a small vase and light it in order to transcend the early evening news. Its real function in the east is more prosaic: it is used to disguise the pervasive smell of shit.

I sat with my knees under my chin in the back of the motor-rickshaw as the driver weaved through the chaotic traffic on GT Road. Against a pall of dust and fumes a crowded tapestry had come to life: brightly painted lorries sandwiched British saloon cars of 1950s vintage, cycles and bullock carts. The ubiquitous blue motor-rickshaws, whose drivers treat each fare like a life or death race, buzzed through the traffic with engines at the pitch of chainsaws. Pathans, from both sides of the border, sauntered by with expressions that suggested freedom and its conviction. Robert Byron said it best on entering Afghanistan in the 1930s. 'Here at last was Asia without an inferiority complex.' Their free and easy gait suggested a people in harmony with the world yet who had retained their sense of delight at it. They strode independently along, each a master of his fate and none fool enough to think himself more than a man.

All frontier towns have a sense of the merry-go-round; in the streets of Peshawar there were Tadjiks, Uzbeks and Nuristanis from Afghanistan, Punjabis, Sindis and Baluch from Pakistan. a few Hindus, Europeans and Americans. You wondered where they came from and where they were going. It was bad form to ask. Destinations were your own business.

The driver swerved to avoid the lunatic, dressed only in baggy trousers, who lurched into the road. His eyes were fastened on forefingers pushed together in an arch and he uttered inaudible imprecations which were lost in the roar. Gibberish or some great truth. 'Crazy man,' cried the driver.

The bazaars were lined with barrows: bright yellow mangoes, plums, apricots and peaches. The sellers weighed the fruit in hand-held scales and carefully arranged the luscious mounds. As art. The monotonous jumble of streets was brought alive by the people. They were the keepers of the legends and mysteries of a turbulent past which exercises an enduring fascination. The future is the anticipation of some exotic event.

The Islamic Unity of Afghanistan Mujahiddin was formed in 1982, only the latest attempt to co-ordinate the war effort. The Afghans are given to grandiloquent titles, the extravagant gesture. The headquarters of the Unity was a low anonymous building with guards outside rusted metal doors. They sat with Kalashnikov rifles across their laps and looked at you with affected suspicion before letting you pass on the recitation of their leaders' names. Exiled Afghans milled about the courtyard listening to the gossip. Here they might find out how the war was going. What was the news from their province, their village? Badakshan, Laghman, Kunar. The parochial questions suggested the atomic nature of the conflict. From a room above the courtyard came the slow tap-tap of a typewriter and in the next room the whirr and rasp of a stencilling machine. News of the war, for dissemination in the English-speaking world. The Afghans came by their news differently. They gathered in the rooms off the courtyard, drinking green tea and listening to the tales told by fighters lately returned from the front. That was how it had always been.

I was shown to a cool room stacked with bundles of magazines. The resistance had learned the value of propaganda but had yet to learn the art of subtle presentation. The Russians were 'monsters' and the resistance 'heroic'. This may well have been true but such adjectival simplifications tended to excite torpor in news editors who are fussy about the clichés they work to death. From the Mujahiddin they sought facts which were a rare commodity in a war obscured by the repressive secrecy of the Russians and the rigours of geography. You wondered if there was a more depressing element in this equation, which would ultimately favour the invader: did the people in the West care about the fate of Afghanistan anyway?

Mujahid means warrior of God. They rose as Ali Ansari, one of their leaders, walked in. In their robes they seemed to float up into the air and then sink as the tall, grave man bade us sit with a slight wave of his hand. Courtesy dictated that we did not get to the point of our meeting before exchanging pleasantries: I commented on the air of activity at the headquarters and he asked me how I liked Peshawar. We talked of Afghan exiles we knew in London. I commented on the heat and chilled water was brought in an aluminium beaker.

Only then did we touch on the matter in hand. Ali Ansari sat with his hands palm down on his lap as I made my speech. Illiteracy in Afghanistan means that the culture is still largely oral and oratory valued. With his long beard and serene manner, I might have been a supplicant before a bishop in the old times. Each word was listened to carefully and every point weighed. I said that I wanted to travel through the heartlands of Afghanistan, at least as far as Bamian; to see the fighting and to understand a little of the struggle. Ali Ansari nodded, then spoke in Dari, the Afghan variant of Persian, to the others before looking at me with steady eyes.

'You will go to Afghanistan,' he said as if the very name were an inspiration or some dark secret to which he held the key. Then he rose and left. I asked when I could expect to cross the border and I was told that someone would contact me. When? 'Inshallah,' he replied, which means

26

'God willing,' and has the same connotations as manana. An Afghan with a turban and a wild smile thrust his Kalashnikov into my hands.

'We go to Afghanistan. We kill Russians,' he said cheerfully. I said that my immediate destination was more prosaic; the hotel. He looked disappointed for a moment, then brightened.

'OK my friend. We go to hotel. Drink tea. Then we go to Afghanistan and kill Russians.'

We settled for tea at his home and set off by motor-rickshaw. We rattled by under the colossal ramparts of the Bala Hisar fort commissioned by Babur and rebuilt by the Sikhs in the nineteenth century. A structure so gross and intimidating was, I suppose, necessary for a strategic town like Peshawar which has been fought over so many times and been a capital for a host of rulers. Peshawar retains its strategic significance at the mouth of the Khyber Pass and the daunting battlements of the Bala Hisar now conceal the headquarters of Pakistan's Frontier Corps. Those troops were facing directly what the armies of the British Empire never had to – confrontation with the Russian army. Whatever the destiny of the region, Peshawar, you feel, will survive. A new style of architecture might be added to the Mughal red stone, the colonial spacious and the modern bland. But the heart of the city will remain its people and they will continue to know something the outsider never can.

Past Dean's Hotel, with its neat lawns and sofas into which guests sink without trace. It retains the standards and manners of colonial days so that the guest is not only served well but stylishly intimidated. Such was the horror among staff when a guest discovered a foreign body in his soft drink that the brand was banished forever from the hotel and the name never mentioned again. Above a nest of traffic lights at the crossroads a neon light advertised a rival hotel. It was shaped like an Edwardian gas lamp and tilted at a crazy angle, just as it had been three years before. On the corner was Dervish Motors who would take you for a whirl in a new Japanese model. At the Post Office there was a crisis. The makers of postage stamps were putting insufficient gum on the back so that stamps fell off and letters arrived everywhere with 'postage due' marked on them. There were letters – with 'postage due' on them – to the *Pakistan Times* and heated debates in the long queues in the hot and shabby hall. At the counter marked 'arms permits' there was no queue. The Pathans do not pay much heed to such formalities; to bear a gun is a mark of their freedom. My companion laughed.

'My father taught me how to shoot the gun but not how to ask someone if I can use it.'

Mohammed was an intense wiry man from Badakshan who had been fighting the Russians for three years and the communists for longer. He had been wounded twice and had come to Pakistan to work. Over tea in the spartan room lined with cushions, he asked me about the scar on my wrist received in a fight years before.

'And you kill this man?' he asked.

He was puzzled when I said no. Puzzlement and generosity arose from the same well-springs; the Pushtunwali or 'Way of the Pathans'. It is the code these men live and die by. Its tenets were forged in the savage and spectacular terrain that is the home of the Pathans and which demands uncompromising rules as a framework for survival. Its main features are vengeance (badal), being a good host to all-comers (melmestia) and the giving of asylum (nanawati). Wherever I would travel I was to encounter extraordinary hospitality, the more remarkable for the shortages caused by the war. Hospitality means giving the guest whatever he asks for and, if necessary, defending his life and honour. Hezb-i-Islami, the party which would guide me, had not merely agreed to take me on a tour of the war front; they had taken responsibility for my safety and bound up in that commitment was honour, duty and a rigid code evolved over centuries. No law made in Parliament or imposed by autocracy touches a people as the Pushtunwali does the Pathans. What comfort there was to be found in the coming months would emanate from the Pushtunwali. On one occasion it saved my life.

I walked through the crowded bazaars where humanity flies at a furious pace and where passage through the protean mass seems impossible. It is an illusion, for the sea of humanity will swallow you up and expel you. If you have eyes to see there is room to pass. This multitude of options in a crowded world is to be found in human relationships too. A stranger will invite you to tea, out of curiosity and a quest for new worlds. Options and roads are constantly opening, despite the appearance of a suffocating mass. I would have to wait many days before my contact turned up and I filled the time, when I was not talking to the resistance parties and government officials, with walks in the bazaars. The crafts were grouped together: coppersmiths, leather workers, jewellers. Drug companies and chemical firms had followed this tradition and were clustered together. In the labyrinth of the cloth bazaar where the dyed satins and cottons were rolled on giant bobbins, the ice vendor manoeuvred his cart, piled high with milky blocks, to avoid a horse and cart and, in so doing, crushed a cycle. Collision is rare. The art of this restless life is to maintain motion without physical contact.

And all as if the world were a normal place. Yet Peshawar lay less than 80 kilometres from the war. In the papers there was news of attacks on Russian forces in Kabul. But it was old news and it warranted only a short piece. More was given over to Pakistan's diplomatic efforts for peace. In the chai khanas (tea houses) the emphasis was exactly reversed: you could listen to long stories about the fighting and the occasional dismissal of the talks with a clearing of the throat and a gobbet deposited in the street. Contempt. Despite this, I retained faith in Pakistan, an idea as much as a country. In Pakistan I had never been left with that feeling of resignation that can afflict the visitor to Asia. Thanks to Islam there are fewer beggars to leave the visitor stricken with guilt. The burden of oppression lifts in the country founded by Qaid-i-Azam Mohammed Ali Jinnah. Democratic instincts suggest that this should not be so in a country ruled too many years since

Street bazaar in Peshawar.

Tradition and technology meet in the street where carpet sellers display their wares.

independence by the military. But it is. Pakistan has faced hostility from within and beyond its borders. India to the east and now the Red Army to the north-west. More than 3½ million Afghan refugees were camped on this side of the border. Yet the economy of the country had performed well and the confidence of the people was abundant. Eating a mango in the shade of a livid green minaret you forgot the war over the border.

I was contacted at last. He was young and shy, an agricultural expert with broad features scattered over a flat face too big to contain them. Despite the mournful effect he was friendly and we drank cups of green tea in the hotel. But he had merely come out of courtesy, so that I did not feel I had been forgotten. He was not to be my guide. I asked him to arrange a visit to one of the remoter refugee camps. He was about to leave for England and was worried how his wife, whose only experience was the closed world of an Afghan village, would adjust to London. With great difficulty, I said, and gave him the address of Afghan friends in London. I wished him luck and asked him when I would meet my guide. Inshallah.

So I continued to visit the crowded offices of the parties which were scattered throughout the city. There were about six principal parties and perhaps a dozen lesser organisations for whom a hatred of communism was all they had in common. Most were orientated about Islam as a political force, although Muslims do not make the distinction between faith and politics that we do in the West. This is a difficult concept for Westerners to understand and one which led to the diplomatic blunders over the Iranian revolution. Within the Islamic faith, which defines not only man's relationship to God but his day-to-day actions, the business of government is but an extension of the faith. I asked myself why, if this was the case, was the Islamic dimension of the resistance so fragmented and hoped to find the answer across the border.

'Unity' was imposed on the major Islamic parties by influential Arab supporters of the resistance who, exasperated by the fragmentary tendencies of the parties, decided that he who pays the piper can occasionally call the tune. Reluctantly the parties were brought under the umbrella of the Unity, whose first president was Professor Abdur Rasool Sayyaf. The internal machinery of the Unity was a delicate balance of power between the key parties: Gulbuddin Hekmatyar of Hezb-i-Islami became vice-president of the consultative committee 'war cabinet', while his arch-rival Professor Burhanuddin Rabbani of Jamiat-i-Islami was appointed chairman of the defence committee. In 1984, Sayyaf tried to consolidate his power and strengthen the Unity by sending Hekmatyar and Rabbani overseas as heads of 'diplomatic' missions.

Party workers spoke earnestly of the Unity, except in private where they only spoke of their own party. If the concept of the Unity had crossed into Afghanistan . . . it had gone as a joke. To complicate matters there was a second 'Unity' which contained groups a shade more sympathetic to the ideals of Western democracy. It also boasted a Maoist party. The parties had connections with factions in the Arab world, Pakistan, Iran and the West. Political fission, rivalries and loyalties, which overlay traditional tribal loyalties, made for a body politic both Byzantine and Machiavellian. The fragmented nature of the resistance might have been disastrous but the Afghans thrived on it and, paradoxically, it was one of their strengths. The party I was to travel with, Hezb, was the most radical and austere group, which advocated a return to the fundamental precepts of Islam. Its inspiration came from radical Muslim philosophers and the Iranian revolution. Under the uncompromising leadership of Hekmatyar, the party was the least interested in cooperation with other groups though it did reluctantly join the Unity. I had chosen this most fundamentalist of groups because of my interest in the impact of the Islamic renaissance on global politics.

Abdul Ghafoor appeared and announced he was to be my guide and interpreter. He showed little enthusiasm for the expedition but the party had sent him so he had to obey. When would we leave? Inshallah, he said. He would drop in every few days and we would drink tea while he explained why I had to wait a few more days. It was clear that his comfortable sinecure at the party headquarters lent contentment to his life. He would bring each meeting to a close by saying vaguely but importantly that I would have to excuse him as he had some business to attend to and that he would call again. Inshallah.

The sky over Peshawar was filled with eagles, circling slowly down invisible helter-skelters of air. A fitting symbol for a city of warriors. You could watch the eagles wheeling over the Bala Hisar from the roof of the hotel, where at dusk a great neon sign came to gaudy life with a hiss. Neon speaks of passage and alienation, the twin psychoses of the Western world, yet we gathered happily in the ruby glow to watch the sunset. There was Majid the midget, a round-faced Turkoman from north Afghanistan and a young Pakistani couple. There was also a one-legged crow whose life was devoted to trying to stay upright when it alighted on the roof. It was a place to meet people with better stories than Pakistan television.

A youth, whose sincerity disguised his nervousness, said he had run away from home to join the resistance. It was his duty as a Muslim to join the Jehad (it means to exert oneself in the name of Islam and includes war as a last resort), but he wanted to cross the border quickly before his father caught up with him. I told him I thought it unlikely that the resistance would take on a Pakistani, but he was undeterred until the Afghans told him the same. When I saw him again he seemed faintly relieved.

I hoped that he would not turn out like the slick and sententious party man from one of Pakistan's banned political organisations who knocked on my door. He had heard there was a European at the hotel (everyone had heard: I was an oddity) and said he wanted to talk politics. In truth he wanted to deliver a monologue against General Zia ul Haq and the military regime and for me to acquiesce in his assumptions. I listened, without enthusiasm, as he recited the litany of sins perpetrated by the regime and how only his party could restore justice in Pakistan. Not democracy, his party. Democracy was important he added hastily and then told me how opposition groups would incite trouble on the anniversary of Pakistan's independence. The clean-cut party hack was assiduously organising blood on the streets for August. He seemed rather pleased with himself. I wondered if he would be around when they started cracking heads.

I left him and went up on the roof. The crow was there. So were the couple, as always gentle, very much in love and appalled at the world about them. You always hoped that some of their tenderness might stay with you. Ahmed, one of the room boys at the hotel, was a mean character whose eyes followed you everywhere. He ordered all the men off the roof when the couple were there. Under Islam it is unseemly for men and women to mingle. The girl scolded him and said I should stay and if Ahmed wished to press the issue they would claim I was a relative. That might have been a hard case to make but Ahmed retreated scowling.

Islam sets the rhythm of life. You wake to the sound of the faithful being called to prayer each day and every day. The fasting month of Ramadan began and the rhythm changed. Now a siren woke you at 3 am so that the Muslims could eat before dawn when the fast began. Life slowed down as people refrained from food, drink and cigarettes. The drink was the hardest as the days grew hotter. Only the sick, pregnant women, travellers and warriors are exempt from the fast. Peshawar grew sleepy by the middle of the afternoon and a hush fell over the bazaars. An hour before dusk, and the end of the day's fast, crowds gathered in the restaurants. The fast is a reaffirmation of faith: it steels the body and purifies the mind. Always you are left with the feeling that this is a religion with a dynamic mission. The hotel manager said that as a non-Muslim I would be served meals in my room. Ahmed – the evil – did not agree. He refused to bring me food or water.

I walked out of Peshawar museum into the blazing sun. Inside an ancient slab of stone bore an inscription to the effect that the world is unstable and that fame alone can make you immortal. A testament to the ambitions of the resistance leaders, thrown up by a turbulent tradition, seeing an opportunity in one Afghanistan's lawless periods. Ramadan had made Abdul Ghafoor's appearances even less frequent and Afghanistan seem more elusive. (Only when you cross the border do you realise how truly chimerical the country is.) Then Engineer Imran appeared, looking crazed and distracted and friendly at the wheel of a battered Hillman with its windscreen missing.

'Hello. Get in. Where are you going?' We lurched off through the traffic. 'You are British. Marvellous people, by God. They were the best of rulers. I am thinking your Queen is a wonderful lady. British better than those damn Italians. What is your name? Aaah. Sir Mike. That is a damn wonderful name Sir Mike.'

And all in a breath as we barrelled along with hot blasts of air in our faces. His florid, exasperated face suggested that he was out of tune with most worlds but happy in his and eager to share it. He dropped me off and called out that he would visit me to talk about 'important matters, by God'. Then he disappeared into the mêlée. I had little doubt that he would show up again.

Once I caught Majid the midget peering down to the streets, lost in thought. Gone was his chuckling demeanour out of a cheerful heart and in its place was an implacable sadness. All the griefs of a man bound up in the body of a boy. Usually he played the boy: his favourite sport was to hide behind a rubber plant and launch himself at the legs of members of staff and friendly guests. The air was filled with shrieks until he was caught and swung by the arms like a child. I do not think he had a God: rather the world was filled with gods whose feet of clay he delighted in exposing. He was a mischievous spirit. Afghanistan and the rest of the adult world were not his concern.

A Russian attempt to recover territory in Qandahar province had been beaten off. The newspaper carried few details. They rarely did but you bought them in case, and from habit and to ease the boredom. There were odd incidents at the hotel: a mad dog held guests at bay on the first floor and had to be shot; wrangling Afghans were led away by taciturn police after a fight; Ahmed – the stupid – dropped the television which exploded all over the restaurant. And all the time there was a war going on across the border and Abdul Ghafoor did not appear.

Engineer Imran did. 'My friend Sir Mike,' he cried and slapped me on the shoulder. From a brown paper bag he pulled a *Qoran,* kissed it and passed it to me. 'To bring one heart to Islam is better than making the Hajj to Mecca.' I thanked the engineer but observed gently that I did not have conversion in mind. 'No matter Sir Mike,' he cried. Engineer Imran grew voluble, then frenzied, banging the table to make a point and thumping my back to reinforce it. His expression changed from wild smiles to stylised calm. He was middle-aged, bald with grey sideburns and a black moustache that constantly twitched.

The world according to Engineer Imran: 'There were many great prophets and Isa (Jesus) was the greatest for the Christians. But Isa went to God, who is lovely, and said: "They think I am your son. I am not. Please make me a follower of Mohammed." Isa will come back, but he will follow Mohammed and all Christians will be Muslims. Isa will come to Jerusalem and I will say "this is my friend Sir Mike".'

It was a wild world, peopled with saints and sinners. He spoke of Islam in China for a moment then his conviction that World War 3 was at hand.

'Islam tranquillises. You can convert today but do not listen to those holy men with beards. They are frauds like General Zia. Those men will all go to hell.' Now the engineer's monologue was unstoppable. Majid the midget and Ahmed – the speechless – stood staring at this performance from behind the rubber plants. 'I tell you Sir Mike, Isa will return and he will be a Muslim and all the Christians will be Muslims and then all the Jews will be slaughtered, the bastards. They killed your Isa. Hitler knew they were bastards so he killed six million. They are bastards Sir Mike.'

The darkness descended. I felt sick and angry at the rush to totality and the dead end. Where was the reason, compassion? I called him an ass and left him looking perplexed. He did not know why I was offended.

That evening I went for a meal in a restaurant in the bazaar, reflecting on fanaticism. In a frontier town the world changes swiftly. The chai khana was crowded and the din was punctuated by the sound of plates of kebab and tikka being slammed on bare wooden tables along with the flat discs of bread called nan. I was reading a book about Baluchistan when a toothless old man took it and began to look at the pictures. Three Punjabis seized it, snorted angrily about the Baluch, and one spat into the pages. The old man protested at which one of the Punjabis tore the book in half and began a tirade about the trouble-making Baluch. I said he had caused trouble and demanded the price of the book. A hush fell over the chai khana as they refused. Why should they pay for destroying seditious literature? Several Pathans had gathered between us and the door, their faces wreathed in smiles beneath magnificent loose turbans. The Punjabis turned to leave but their way was barred by two Pathans who pulled knives from beneath embroidered waistcoats. Their smiles broadened as they invited the Punjabis to pay up. A fifty-rupee note was thrown on my table. Outside I thanked the Pathans who shook their heads as if to dismiss the gesture.

'They are bad men. You are guest in Peshawar,' one said cheerily and waved goodnight before sauntering away in the light of a dozen hurricane lamps dangling in the street.

That night I received a telephone call from the office of one of the parties. It was 2 am and the voice whispered: 'My friend you go to Kabul tonight.' I declined. The next day a newspaper carried a piece about how a Mujahid had been killed tinkering with a mine at one of the party HQs. I used the newspaper to wrap the skins of the fruit I ate in my room during Ramadan. There was nothing to do but pace out each day and be patient. It had been five weeks now. Sometimes I would sit with other journalists who were covering the Afghan war or waiting to go into Afghanistan. We would swap stories but Pakistan is dry and journalists' anecdotes tend to go down better with a beer. Inverted snobbery combined with professional secrecy produced the 'I'm not a journalist' syndrome. Reporters scurried from place to place as usual but it had become chic for newcomers to deny their trade and everyone sat around and engaged in pained conversation about anything but newspapers. Then they retired and all along the corridors of Dean's you heard the furtive tapping of typewriters.

One afternoon in the lounge at Dean's a noisy and thirsty Italian combat film crew spotted the young man in the white blazer and demanded cold drinks. The 'waiter' was a French reporter who shouted a lot and stormed out. It was getting crowded in Peshawar and still Abdul Ghafoor did not appear.

All sorts of carpetbaggers appeared, each with their own interpretation of the war and its meaning. One of the oddest was the American woman whose presence kept the town buzzing for weeks. She was blonde and brassy and her ebullient manner defied her advancing years. She came to sell radio-controlled model aircraft which, she explained, could be packed with explosives and used by the Mujahiddin to bomb Russian positions. While she conducted an affair with a local hotelier, the Mujahiddin pondered the possibilities of aerial warfare.

'Nothing is ordinary in Peshawar,' said the manager of my hotel.

Or Asia for that matter. Before it gives it unmakes all your assumptions. I had ceased to believe that I would actually cross the border and had come to exist in a world full of disparate and vivid images.

It grew hotter and summer storms darkened the sky early like spilled ink but it did not rain. The nights were full of exotic distortion. A boy singing for hours somewhere in the depths of the hotel. Power cuts every night at dinner time and Ahmed standing next to my table with a torch while I ate. Outside the storm raged, lightning flashing in mute anger, but there was no rain. In the morning a great white horse lay dead outside the hotel, its heart having given out. Majid sat watching it from behind his plants. I spent some time watching the little songbirds in wooden cages in the bazaar and when I returned to the hotel Majid was still staring at the carcass, now bloated. We went to the roof and he produced mangoes. They were overripe – the taste was heady and perfumed – and we slobbered the juice down our chins. I have yet to meet the person who can peel and eat a mango and retain their dignity. Majid told me that Younis Khalis, one of the resistance leaders of advancing years, had just married a 15-year-old girl. Still he reckoned the dead horse was the most interesting thing to have happened for a while and he keeled over several times in imitation of its death throes.

On Jamrud Road there were several Mujahiddin hospitals. I was walking past one at the end of the day when a young Afghan with a wooden leg hailed me. We sat and talked as he showed me his limb and sundry scars of battle.

'You go to Afghanistan,' he said.

'That was rather the plan,' I said ruefully.

'When you go to Afghanistan it is soon enough,' he said and tapped his leg.

The lorries and buses painted in heroic themes roared by: fierce-eyed warriors, soaring eagles, volcanoes and alpine scenes. Blues, greens, yellows and reds. The motor-rickshaw screeched to a halt and Majid and Ahmed – the bearer of tidings – tumbled out.

'Mista. Man come to hotel. You go Afghanistan now,' cried the midget.

4

The Great Game

India has exerted a power over the imagination throughout history: it was the goal for the invaders who passed through Afghanistan. The struggle between the British and Russian empires in the nineteenth century affected the entire region but had India at its heart. In the words of Lord Curzon, Viceroy of India: 'Turkistan, Afghanistan, Transcaspia, Persia – to many these words breathe only a sense of utter remoteness or a memory of strange vicissitudes and moribund romance. To me, I confess they are the pieces on a chessboard upon which is being played out a game for the dominance of the world.'

In 1600 Queen Elizabeth granted a charter to the East India Company which signalled the beginning of British involvement in the sub-continent. The French, the Dutch and the Portuguese too sailed to India for trade but, until the end of the seventeenth century, the Mughal Empire had been able to retain control over the Europeans. The passing of Aurangzeb led to the rapid decline of the empire. European rivalries were matched by those of the Indian princes who fell to warring. Alliances between the European powers and the princes were forged but, by the middle of the eighteenth century, the British, inspired by Robert Clive, had destroyed the power of France in India and had become the pre-eminent European power.

The British saw a threat to India from Napoleon. Dominance of mainland Europe and success in Egypt prompted fears of a strike against India. Such an attack would come through Persia and Afghanistan. Of necessity, Afghanistan was about to come into focus for the Europeans. But it was not armies that were sent to the north west in the beginning. It was gifted individuals. If military prowess and organisational flair were one side of the empire, then these hardy adventurers who drifted into exotic and uncharted territory were the other. Together they represented a formidable combination.

Mountstuart Elphinstone was dispatched in 1809 to Peshawar to treat with Shah Shuja the ruler of Kabul. He secured a mutual defence treaty but accomplished something of greater value: his extensive observations and study of this territory. His *An Account of the Kingdom of Caubul* (London, Longman, Hurst and John Murray, 1815) remains one of the most remarkable books written about the lands between the Indus and the Hindu

Kush. Nothing escapes the eye and inquisitive mind of Elphinstone: he is natural historian, geographer and genealogist. His description of the characteristics of the Afghans has never been bettered. 'Their vices are revenge, envy, avarice, rapacity and obstinacy. On the other hand, they are fond of liberty, faithful to their friends, kind to their dependents, hospitable, brave, hardy, frugal, laborious and prudent, and they are less disposed than the nations in the neighbourhood to falsehood, intrigue and deceit.' He describes a sumptuous dinner: 'Here fruit was brought to us and we spent our time in reading the numerous Persian verses that were written on the walls: most of them alluded to the instability of fortune and some were very applicable to the king's actual condition.' He reports an old man as saying: 'We are content with discord, we are content with alarms, we are content with blood, but we will never be content with a master.' Such insights are still true and are clues as to why the Afghans are prepared to make great sacrifices in the fight against the Russians. Elphinstone's experiences, he would say later, cured him of ambition.

Elphinstone's assessment of the instability of Shah Shuja was correct. The king went into exile. The Napoleonic threat receded but a new and more formidable power was on the horizon. Russia would preoccupy the planners of the British Empire for much of the nineteenth century.

Between the domains of Britain and Russia there were two minor empires in the 1830s: that of the Sikhs as well as the Afghans under Dost Mohammed who followed Shah Shuja. Dost Mohammed sought help from the British against the Sikhs who were occupying Peshawar and the Afghan ruler wrote to the Governor General of India Lord Auckland to this end. Auckland replied that British government policy was one of non-interference in the affairs of independent nations. This was not the most ingenuous statement in the history of diplomacy but it was not just such agile interpretations of the truth which led to the catastrophe of the first Afghan War. Worse, was a fundamental lack of understanding of the Afghans. Captain Alexander Burnes, who had established himself as a traveller of distinction after his wanderings in central Asia, was sent by Auckland to Kabul to amplify the 1809 agreement between Shah Shuja and Elphinstone. Tension increased when a Persian army, backed by Russian military advisers, besieged Herat and in Kabul there appeared a Russian agent to woo Dost Mohammed.

Auckland reasoned that a compliant ruler in Kabul was necessary to counter the perceived Russian threat. An alliance was forged with Ranjit Singh, ruler of the Sikhs, and the exiled Shah Shuja, under which the latter would be restored to the throne with British and Sikh help. The instrument for the enforced restoration was to be the Army of the Indus consisting of some 15,000 troops and 6,000 camp followers. The policy developed its own momentum despite the lifting of the Herat siege and the withdrawal of the Russian agent from Kabul. The subtleties of eastern diplomacy were transcended by the rather more black and white view of the Westerner. The consequences were disastrous.

It has been said that Afghanistan is an easy country to invade but impossible to control afterwards. The Army of the Indus took Qandahar without a fight and defeated the son of Dost Mohammed in a series of engagements near Ghazni. The army was in Kabul by early August, 1839. Dost Mohammed fled north to rally his followers while an apparently quiescent population watched Shah Shuja assume the throne again. The British political envoy with the force was Sir William Macnaghten whose brief was to withdraw the army when Shah Shuja's position was secure. However, it rapidly transpired that the newly-installed king could not survive without the army, a position accurately compared to that of Babrak Karmal and the Russians in the early 1980s. The army settled in. Officers' wives flocked to the capital and single men formed liaisons with Afghan women who gave generously of their favours. There was alcohol in abundance. The strict moral codes of the Pathans were offended at every turn. For the British it was the grandeur of the *Titanic.*

Macnaghten was able to buy off hostile tribes until economies forced the curtailment of such payments. The force could have survived their own lack of cultural tact had they had good leadership. Unfortunately, Macnaghten's optimistic analysis of the situation was dangerously wrong. By 1841 the army was under the command of Major-General William Elphinstone who, because of senility and gout, was hopelessly inadequate. Large sections of the army were camped in a cantonment which was virtually indefensible and they were besieged. Despite bitter arguments, they had not taken up positions at the secure Bala Hisar fort. Tribesmen overran two British outposts in 1841. By the end of the year the British were short of supplies and forced to negotiate. Macnaghten and several of his lieutenants were butchered at a meeting with Afghan chiefs in December. General Elphinstone decided to retreat to Jalalabad, against the advice of his own officers and the Afghan chiefs who counselled delay until an escort could be assembled to guarantee safe passage. Some 16,500 set off on the death march, through bitter winter weather and under constant fire. The tribes were united in their hostility to the feringhi (foreigners) and they waited in the mountains to pick off the soldiers in the valleys below. It has the air of a ghastly surreal fairground shooting gallery. Those who were not shot died from cold and disease. With the exception of a few hostages, only one man survived – Dr. William Brydon who rode into Jalalabad on 13 January. Today there are few Afghans who cannot recite the names of Macnaghten and Brydon and the events of the first Afghan War. An army under Major-General George Pollock exacted what was nothing better than revenge. The bazaar in Kabul and parts of Charikar and Istalif were razed. But Shah Shuja was assassinated and, when the British forces withdrew from Afghanistan, Dost Mohammed was back on the throne.

'Is Dost Mohammed dead that there is no justice in the land?' is a saying in Afghanistan. Dost Mohammed maintained friendly relations with the British who were busy extending the writ of empire over large tracts of India.

He was preoccupied trying to forge a sense of unity in fissile Afghanistan. Just before his death in 1863 he managed to conquer Herat in the West. Yet he failed to promote Afghan claims to Peshawar which would have been a comparatively easy matter at the time of the collapse of the Sikh Empire. Neither did he exploit the difficulties of the British at the time of the Indian Mutiny in 1857 which might have extended Afghanistan's borders to the east. Afghans still point to these 'failures' as having stunted Afghanistan's rightful growth.

Fratricide followed Dost Mohammed's death and it was only after years of civil war that Sher Ali emerged as ruler. British policy during the middle of the century was known as 'masterly inactivity'. But by the third quarter of the century there was growing support for a British 'forward policy' whose advocates called for a more dynamic role in Afghan politics to counter the threat from the north.

The Russian Empire today covers one sixth of the earth's land mass. Expansion began in the sixteenth century under Ivan the Terrible and the invasion of Afghanistan was a continuation of that process. The communist revolution of 1917 transformed this empire into a collection of 'republics' and each has the theoretical right to secede. But the totalitarian habit of rearranging the meaning of language renders such guarantees meaningless. The Union of Soviet Socialist Republics remains at heart the Russian Empire. That empire is aggressive and expansionist.

In the fourteenth and fifteenth centuries the Russians lived under the Tartar yoke. This fact of history – with its cruelties – left the national consciousness deeply affected. It partly explains the Russian justifications for their almost continuous southward and eastward expansion in subsequent centuries: that is, a 'forward policy' was the only way to secure their own frontiers. It may even help explain the psychology behind Sino-Soviet hostility. Ivan the Terrible took Perm in 1542, Kassan in 1552 and fours years later Astrakan in the Volga Delta. In 1581 Siberia was taken by a swashbuckling Cossack Hetman Jermak. Even Alaska was claimed but was sold to the United States in 1867 for ten million roubles, possibly the most significant land deal in history.

Under Catherine the Great an advance on the Caucasus began in 1768. Tribes and khanates were subdued and the incorporation of territory into the empire was followed by Russian colonisation. Afghan leaders looking for precedents to give them hope in their struggle would find a gloomy picture of Russian tenacity and determination in the face of resistance. The extraordinary siege of the mountains of the Caucasus provides an example. A million mountain tribesmen under the charismatic leadership of Muslim Khazi Mullah Mohammed resisted the Russian advance. He defeated them in engagements in the 1820s and died a warrior's death in 1832. Resistance continued for more than twenty years. But the Russians were prepared to spend decades besieging the entire region, raising ever-larger armies and building a massive network of forts. The Russian will prevailed.

In 1775 Peter the Great wrote: 'Approach as near as possible to Constantinople and India. Whoever governs there will be the true sovereign of the world. Consequently, excite continual wars, not only in Turkey but in Persia . . . penetrate as far as the Persian Gulf . . . advance as far as India.' That advance was well under way when, in the middle of the nineteenth century, Prince A. M. Gorchakov, a Russian diplomat, wrote: 'The position of Russia in central Asia is that of all civilised states which are brought into contact with half-savage nomad populations . . . the more civilised state is forced . . . to exercise a certain ascendancy over those whom their turbulent and unsettled character makes undesirable neighbours . . . First the civilised state must put a stop to raids . . . Once the wild tribes are pacified, they acquire a right to protection against their neighbours. The civilised state is hereby impelled to advance deeper into barbarous countries.' Such was the justification for the advances which by the early 1850s had seen Russian hegemony extended over large parts of the Khanate of Khokand. Bokhara fell in 1866 and two years later the Russians moved into Samarkand, once the fabled capital of Timur.

British diplomats in London and Delhi viewed this progress with dismay. The advocates of the forward policy were now in the ascendant and its political voice was found in Benjamin Disraeli when he became Prime Minster in 1874. Two years later the British demanded of Sher Ali that he accept a European-staffed mission in Kabul. The Amir refused. Russian and British rivalries moved to the Bosphorus and the crisis was only resolved by the Congress of Berlin after which Russia left Turkey. Those who support the east-west 'pendulum' theory of Russian territorial ambitions – pressure is increased in one direction in direct proportion to the resistance it meets in the other – point to Russia's next move as evidence. It led to the second Afghan War. The Russians sent their own mission to Kabul against the wishes of Sher Ali. The British demanded equal access. Sher Ali declined to answer as he was in mourning for a son, though the British accused him of procrastination. Once again, insensitivity to the ways of the Afghans would play a part in the outbreak of war.

Again the British army had little difficulty in taking Kabul. This time the British got what they wanted: control of Afghan foreign policy, a mission in Kabul and control of the Khyber Pass. Sher Ali fled and died in Balkh in 1879. The stage was set for the appearance of another of the country's great rulers, Amir Abdur Rahman. But first the British suffered a major military setback. To avenge the humiliation of Maiwand in which more than 1,000 troops died or were wounded, General Sir Frederick Roberts assembled a force of 10,000 men and marched them from Kabul to Qandahar in just twenty days. This astonishing march covered 500 kilometres during the height of the summer and at the end of it the general inflicted a resounding defeat on the Afghans. He was later made Lord Roberts of Qandahar.

Russia continued to move south and east, taking Merv in 1884. The British government was shaken though Members of Parliament were still able to make bad jokes about 'Mervousness'. Britain proposed a commission to define Afghanistan's northern boundary and Russia agreed. But, even as the commission began its work, the Russians moved on Panjdeh which had been historically part of Afghanistan. An Afghan force lost a battle against the Russians at Pul-i-Khisti and it was only war preparations by the British that checked further advances. The northern boundary was agreed in 1885 between the British and Russian empires with the Afghans as bystanders. The eastern Afghan border was drawn by the British in 1893 though the 'Durand Line' was ratified by successive Afghan governments.

While the borders of Afghanistan were being delimited by outside powers, Amir Abdur Rahman was consolidating his power within the country. 'The putting in order (of) hundreds of petty chiefs, plunderers, robbers and cut throats . . . This necessitated breaking down the feudal and tribal system and substituting one grand community under one law and one rule,' wrote the Amir. To break the power of the tribal kingdoms, the Amir ordered forced migrations. In the 1890s the mountain fastness of Kafiristan (Land of the Unbelievers) was stormed and the inhabitants converted to Islam. The region was re-named Nuristan (Land of Light). He founded a civil administration which developed into the ministries of the twentieth century.

Abdur Rahman was succeeded in 1901 by Habibullah who, like his predecessors, was faced with the problem of fending off two competing empires. Defeat at the hands of the Japanese and the rise in Europe of Germany meant that for the time being Russia ceased to be a threat to Afghanistan. In 1907 the Russians and the British carved up neighbouring Persia into spheres of influence and both agreed not to meddle in the affairs of Afghanistan. Habibullah declared the agreement illegal. Once again the Afghans had had no part in deliberations affecting their country. Yet, despite such treatment, Habibullah resisted the blandishments of the Central Powers to side with them in World War 1. It was an affirmation of Afghanistan's 'natural' role as a neutral and non-aligned country. Habibullah was assassinated in 1919.

Amanullah, his successor, began his rule by going to war with the British in May, 1919. The British used planes to bomb Kabul and Jalalabad, but the empire was exhausted after years of war and, despite being in a position to dictate peace terms, the British virtually restored control of its foreign policy to the Afghans. As a symbol of their new-found independence, the Afghans promptly signed a treaty of friendship with the Russians in 1921, the first of many treaties between the two countries. The new communist government in Russia laid telephone lines in Afghanistan and an air route between Moscow and Kabul was inaugurated. Amanullah brought about his own downfall when he tried to introduce liberal reforms. He opened co-educational schools, forced women to remove the veil and instituted programmes of education for nomads. A conservative backlash forced the Amir into exile in 1929.

King Mohammed Zahir Shah came to the throne in 1933 after another interval of intrigue. Great changes were under way in the country. A new class of entrepreneurs emerged in the 1930s who boosted the import/export trade, founded commercial banks and developed industries like cotton. The 1930s were a period when skirmishes on the frontier kept the British and Afghan forces busy but now the British were preoccupied with the rise of Nazi Germany and the threat of war. That war would lead directly to the end of the greatest empire of all. During World War 2 Afghanistan once again adopted a neutral stand.

Then came the momentous change east of Khyber. The British Empire went home and free India and free Pakistan came into being. Afghanistan retained its neutrality. Within the cities a new liberal sentiment emerged towards the end of the 1940s. Newspapers were started which dared to criticise the imams. But it was an urban phenomenon just as the communist movement which began around 15 years later would be. Country people, mostly illiterate, remained untouched by these ideas. Conservative reaction to the liberal sentiment led to the suppression of many of the newspapers in the early 1950s. In 1953 General Mohammed Daoud took power in a bloodless coup. Under his firm rule as prime minister development proceeded apace and roads, irrigation and communications infrastructures were developed. By exploiting the 'Pushtunistan' issue, Daoud was able to gain short-term politcal advantage at the expense of long-term relations with neighbouring Pakistan.

Pushtunistan is the dreamed-of homeland for the Pathans on both sides of the Afghan-Pakistan border. It is an ideal vaguely talked about by the Pathans and it has usually been used by ambitious politicians on both sides of the Durand Line to create unrest among the tribes. Daoud spoke of the aspirations of the Pathans on the Pakistan side of the border without ever hinting that land on the Afghan side would be ceded to an emergent Pushtunistan. His crude manipulation of the issue succeeded only in alienating the Pakistanis and, in the long run, upsetting the delicate neutrality that had been the hallmark of Afghanistan's foreign policy. While it is unlikely that Pushtunistan will exist as an independent (or even federated) homeland for the Pathans, the issue played a pivotal role in forcing Afghanistan off its neutral axis and into the Russian political orbit. In 1955 Daoud asked the Americans for arms and support over Pushtunistan but the United States, anxious not to upset Pakistan, refused. The Russians moved to accommodate the Afghans. That year Khrushchev visited Afghanistan and announced Russian support for his hosts over Pushtunistan.

1955 marked the beginning of Afghanistan's descent into the Russian camp. Afghanistan had played off one side against the other in its quest for aid but a rough parity of influence between the super-powers existed. After 1955 agreement followed agreement between Russia and Afghanistan. Russian investment in its backward southern neighbour suggests an experiment in which the objective was to make Afghanistan's economy dependent on itself. The plan was to 'buy' a government sympathetic to itself and, through long-term penetration of the Afghan economy and government, see the country brought under communist rule. In 1956 a loan agreement worth $100 million was signed, under which the Russians built the airbase at Bagram and the Salang Tunnel through the Hindu Kush. The invading armies of 1979 would make good use of these facilities. Daoud needed arms and these the Russians willingly supplied: MiGs, tanks and light weapons arrived. Advisers followed and a programme of military training in the Soviet Union was initiated. Officers returned with communist ideas which were part of the military curriculum. The Russians gave Daoud modern armed forces but those forces were moulded along ideological lines inimical to the interests of Afghanistan. They would play a crucial role in the country's destiny.

The Pushtunistan issue flared up in 1961 and diplomatic relations between Afghanistan and Pakistan were severed. Pakistan closed the border, a severe blow to land-locked Afghanistan. Russia stepped in and airlifted Afghanistan's crops out of the country. Daoud resigned in 1963.

A new period of liberal experimentation was ushered in with the departure of Daoud and lasted for a decade. But that was not long enough for the new centrist parties to develop roots in the face of hostility from the new urban communists. The communists were grouped in the Khalq and Parcham factions, the latter under Babrak Karmal who was closer to the orthodox ideological line of Moscow. Khalq was under the leadership of Nur Mohammed Taraki and Hafizullah Amin. King Zahir Shah himself initiated the call for a popularly elected Parliament. In 1964 a new constitution was agreed by a Loyah Jirga, a gathering of religious and political leaders. The following year elections were held. Parliamentary deliberations were disrupted by bloody rioting by communist students and agitators led by Karmal. The optimism of the new era was shattered and liberal reforms bogged down by inertia. The expanding middle classes lost faith in the liberal experiment. Disillusioned, some turned to the communists, others to the fundamentalist Islamic groups now emerging. Still others turned to the time-honoured practices of nepotism and corruption.

The country was ripe for takeover and Daoud seized power again in 1973. The King went into exile in Italy. Alliances of convenience have been a tradition of Afghan politics and Daoud saw no danger in using the communists to facilitate his return to power. But the communists were playing a game quite alien to normal Afghan political intrigue. By the time Daoud realised that he was the pawn of the communists and not vice versa it was too late.

Daoud's position was bolstered by the Russians who supported the government with enhanced military and economic aid. Communists moved into key ministries and ambitious reforms were announced. But before long Daoud was forced to try to consolidate his own position at the expense of practical government. The spectacle of an increasingly repressive one-party state riddled with communists drove opponents from the centrist ranks into the arms of the fundamentalist Muslims. Politics and society were being polarised. Leaders of the Islamic movement fled the country to exile in Pakistan.

Daoud realised that not only were his hands tied by communists inside his government, but that Afghanistan's economic dependence on the Soviet Union had become a liability. He began to mend his fences with Pakistan and effectively agreed to bury the issue of Pushtunistan. He turned to Iran and the Shah, long concerned with Afghanistan's drift into the Soviet camp, offered \$2 billion in economic aid. Daoud opened up potentially fruitful dialogues with the oil-rich Arab nations. But it was the last desperate throw of the dice.

The Saur (April) Revolution of 1978 saw the communists take power in a bloody coup backed by the military. Taraki emerged as president of the Democratic Republic of Afghanistan and its prime minister. Amin and Karmal were appointed deputy prime ministers. Revolutionary committees were established and the people waited to see what was in store for them. The coup surprised the Russians as much as anyone: Afghanistan, according to orthodox communist thought, was not ready for communism. The development of communism had been confined to the hybrid atmosphere of the cities. The party had grown outside the mainstream of Afghan life, almost outside of reality. That the early months of communist rule remained quiet probably furthered the self-deception of Taraki and the communists that the people supported them.

The early days of the communist government were characterised by broad statements of policy without any radical substance. The apparent reconciliation between the Parcham and Khalq factions of the People's Democratic Party of Afghanistan (PDPA) collapsed in July when Karmal was forced out of the government and sent to Prague as ambassador. The Khalqis then systematically weeded out their rival Parchamites. Even the new ideology could not escape the Afghan tradition of loyalties to individuals and intrigue.

In the autumn of 1978 the communists changed the national flag from the traditional Islamic green to red. For a people acutely attuned to the symbolic gesture such a sign was unmistakable. The Taraki regime announced great changes: land reforms designed to transfer millions of acres to the poor; the virtual elimination of the bride price; and compulsory education for both sexes modelled on Marxist lines. It is tempting to sympathise with such land reforms and wonder why even the landless revolted against them. The reason lies in the *Qoran* which to the Muslim is the literal word of God. The *Qoran* sanctions the holding of private property and here was a government defying the received word of God. The bride price plays an important role in the economic life of the Afghans; arranged marriages are often used to end feuds and cement alliances. The use of education to indoctrinate young people with ideas directly conflicting with Islam was bound to arouse hostility. The reforms would undermine the social and religious structures of the people. What the people wanted was quite different from what 'the people' ought to have according to the social and political architects of the revolution. Yet still the Afghans remained largely quiescent.

Then the party workers appeared in the countryside armed with the blueprints of the revolution and apparently determined to execute the plans dreamed up in Kabul. There were protests but the government did not back off. Peasants went for their guns. By the winter the level of the armed revolt was such that the reforms were stagnating and by the spring of 1979 the government's preoccupation was with its own survival in the face of widespread insurrection. People realised that the only way to guarantee the survival of their way of life was to remove the communist government. Russia increased arms supplies to the Taraki regime to suppress the uprising and dozens of new agreements were signed.

A major revolt came in Herat in March, when residents turned on the communists and Russian advisers. For three days the rebels controlled the city before a bloody counter-attack returned control to the government. By the summer there were 5,000 Russian advisers in Afghanistan directing government operations against the insurgents. Amin had by now assumed considerable power behind the Taraki 'throne' and he is credited with the most barbaric of the government's acts. His insistence on a ruthless policy of repression to deal with a recalcitrant population had earned him widespread hatred and even a few raised eyebrows in the Kremlim. It is believed that the Russians were urging Taraki to dislodge Amin and to take a more conciliatory line in government policy. This and fears that Amin was making a bid for total power prompted Taraki to try to have him removed in September, 1979. But the slick and Byzantine Amin moved first, seizing power and having Taraki and his family executed. It was officially announced that the former president had died of a mysterious illness.

New campaigns against the rebels were launched but it was already too late for Amin. The army was beginning to disintegrate as troops defected to the rebels. Those who remained were demoralised. The rebels were operating close to Kabul and there appeared to be a real threat to the government itself. By the end of 1979 the future of Afghanistan was being decided in Moscow.

When the new year dawned, Amin was dead, like his two predecessors, and the Russian armies held the cities and were fanning out into the countryside. The history from now on is that of the resistance. The Russians were only a few hundred miles from the oil fields of the Gulf or the warm water port that Peter the Great had dreamed of. The Russian Empire had moved again.

5

Refugees

When the resistance to the communist government of Taraki and Amin began, so did the migration of Afghans across the mountains to become refugees in Pakistan. When the Russians invaded the stream became a flood. Old men, women and children walked from all parts of Afghanistan, bringing their animals with them. Goats, sheep, a chicken tied by the feet to a bundle lashed to a donkey. They would walk for eighteen hours a day through boulder-strewn valleys and over freezing mountain passes, resting only long enough to eat some nan and drink some tea. Their villages had been bombed by the Russians and their crops burned. Old men walked bent double beneath huge bundles of belongings wrapped and knotted in cloth, a bag of food in one hand and a stick in the other to drive the donkeys. The women followed with babes in arms. The children did not complain except when it was cold in the high mountains at night. But it was not a pathetic sight unless you were sentimental or guilt-stricken and conditioned to regard refugees as a particular category of unhappiness. The old clichés could be made to fit the boat people of Indo-China or the Chinese escaping to Hong Kong. But not the Afghans. They never lost their dignity. It was as if in all that great migration of humanity they were party to knowledge that nobody else knew.

'There are three and a half million refugees in Pakistan and another half million in Iran, maybe more. The figures are indistinct.'

The Pakistani official sat with his hands on his lap reciting the statistics as the car bounced along the road to Khyber. He was an earnest young man and had obviously done this before. Journalists and politicians regularly made the pilgrimage to the refugee camps. Each was received like an honoured guest in the camps, which ring Peshawar and stretch for hundreds of miles north and south. After four years many of the camps had a semi-permanent air about them. The tents supplied by the United Nations High Commission for Refugees had been replaced with sun-baked mud homes.

Children surrounded the car as it stopped in a cloud of dust. They all carried large pale balloons which they waved at us and exploded behind our backs. The balloons were in fact condoms. Bang goes another United Nations population control programme. The camp elders were concerned about a water tanker which was bogged down. The camp was the same as the others. At that time – nearly noon – there seemed to be no life to speak of. The sun was high and the haze seemed to make all the structures move to and fro. In all directions you could see the mud houses and tents march to the horizon which was where the haze made them vanish. Nothing stirred.

Huts and tents were cordoned off by mud walls for privacy. Each courtyard thus created contained a shady area in one corner and cooking facilities, partitioned off to spare the modesty of the women. The men took me to one of the shady areas and ordered tea to be brought. Black or green, without milk and very sweet. Some of the men in the camp had found work in the cities of Pakistan; others hoped to find work. I was always struck by their lack of bitterness. That they would be avenged they left you in no doubt, but they spoke of the day of reckoning in a matter-of-fact way.

There is an absence of cynicism among the Afghans which leaves them vulnerable. But you abuse them at your peril. The unyielding nature of the Code of the Pathans frees them to accept things at their face value, to speak freely and honestly as children do. If the other's motives are bad then retribution is at hand. Because of this and because of the high esteem the Afghans have for oratory, talking to them is a true pleasure. Atrocities committed by the invader were recounted in a straightforward way, almost with a sense of wonder that people could commit such acts. That they could be so stupid.

Said Ahmed was still limping from the bullet wound he got in an attack on a communist post in the northern province of Balkh. He was charmingly naive despite the four years which had transformed him from a student to a guerrilla warrior. His home was near the city of Mazar-i-Sharif and he had been studying in the USSR to be an engineer when the Russians invaded. He believed the stories that the troops had been invited into the country as peacekeepers. The staff at Rostov University told him that it was the Americans and Chinese who were stirring up trouble in Afghanistan. Said Ahmed believed them until he had had no news from his family for months and contradictions began to appear in the propaganda. He made his way back to Afghanistan to find his village destroyed and his family dead.

'I was very happy to be a student. It was a good life and they did not try to stop me being a Muslim even though they said it was wrong. The Russians were teaching me to be engineer and then they showed themselves to be usurpers. Newspapers said the Russians were making peace in Afghanistan so when I came to know they were actually fighting my country I was very upset,' he said mildly as the local doctor changed the dressing on his wound. When he spoke of the Russians it was in an exasperated tone which suggested he was dealing with a child who fails to see the elementary logic of a lesson. 'What the Godless Russians do not understand is that we fight in the name of Allah. We started this Jehad with only some old rifles and our faith. Now we have modern weapons and we are better organised and we still have Allah. There is no Afghan who would not die for Allah.'

The little car would not start and the Afghans were delighted to be able to push us along the track until the engine coughed into life. They laughed off the trials of a hard, indifferent life; always welcomed the challenge. The official, hands on lap, sighed and pronounced the water tanker unserviceable. You sympathised with him as he wrestled with great figures which dwarfed him and threatened to crush him. I said I wanted to visit the camps far from Peshawar to the north in the tribal areas. He sighed deeply and said I would have to apply for special permits. I did not press the issue as I did not intend to travel in these areas under official escort. My only interest had been in his reaction to the mention of areas where there had been some trouble. Exhaustion had rendered him incapable of bureaucratic procrastination.

Growing resistance to communist rule and arbitrary persecution meant that there were 400,000 Afghan refugees in Pakistan before the Russians invaded. That figure doubled within four months of the invasion and doubled again within a year. By 1983 a quarter of Afghanistan's estimated population of sixteen million were refugees in Pakistan and Iran. It was remarkable that Pakistan had been able to accept such a burden without widespread dissent. There were hardships after the original influx of refugees but by 1983 the Afghans had shelter, food and a small monthly cash allowance. Roughly half of the cost of the refugee programme was met by Pakistan and the balance came from international aid. Cynics said that General Zia was using the refugee crisis to deflect internal dissent but it is hard to see how anyone could use such a potentially huge liability. The inhabitants of the North West Frontier Province found additional pressure on grazing lands from the flocks of the refugees, and greater competition for jobs. The essential homogeneity of the tribes on both sides of the Durand Line undoubtedly helped the absorption of such large numbers. There was a remarkable lack of trouble between the host population and the refugees. Just as important as the racial similarities between hosts and incomers was the tradition of Islam. The borders of most Islamic countries were drawn in the days of European empires and probably mean more to outsiders than to those who live within them. Muslims regard themselves as belonging to a single nation or Umma. It is the duty of every Muslim to render assistance to a fellow Muslim when he is in need. The Prophet Mohammed was forced to migrate from Mecca to Medina where he and his companions were accorded the warmest welcome. Thus the tradition of extending hospitality to refugees is as old as Islam itself. The tradition is maintained in the Muslim world even when the exile is a political liability (the Shah of Iran taken in by Egypt; Idi Amin taken in by Saudi Arabia).

The condition of the refugees in Pakistan compared very favourably with that of the Indo-Chinese boat people in the camps of South-East Asia in the 1970s. There, governments made it clear that the refugees were not welcome. There, descriptions like 'pathetic' were applicable. In the hundreds of camps in Pakistan you did not get that feeling of hopelessness; rather you left them with your spirits elevated.

'Yes they are brave but they are still refugees. I will never be refugee.' The Tadjik businessman with the mild disposition and enormous moon face had introduced himself on the roof of the hotel. His great face was like one of those lanterns cut from pumpkins at Hallowe'en and it seemed to hover above his shoulders. He was gentle, almost serene, like all the Tadjiks I met. His family fled from Tadjikistan in the Soviet Union, over the border into Afghanistan after the 1917 revolution. The Bolsheviks did not want to be troubled by Muslims so they killed them or drove them over the Amu Darya. Such is the barbaric logic of overmighty men driven by ideology which has characterised so much of the unhappiness of our century. The family had entered the Lapis Lazuli trade in Afghanistan and my friend had inherited the business. Now he concentrated on imports and exports and lived most of the time in Bangkok. 'Now some of my family are in refugee camps in Pakistan but I get them out whenever I have the money. My business has made me free of the camps. It is all the freedom I want.'

I wanted to travel to the remote refugee camps in the north not because I believed they would be inferior to the showpiece camps around Peshawar but because they were remote and rarely visited. Abdul Ghafoor said simply, 'It is possible', and looked at me wryly when I raised the subject of permits.

We rattled along in a car heading north with all the windows open as the air-conditioning had failed. Abdul Ghafoor sat poised between officiousness and contemplation. He had brought along a young Afghan whose family lived in the camp we were going to in Buner district. Like many Afghans he was initially shy but soon blossomed and was chatting happily when we stopped for lunch in the dusty, featureless village. The food, kebabs, rice and a fatty stew, was as anonymous as the environment, with its sense of departed hope. All over the world there are such places and you do not need to know their names or speak the language of the inhabitants to recognise them. No amount of urban planning or social engineering can salvage hope in such places. Neither Abdulwahed, the young Afghan, nor myself finished the meal. But Abdul Ghafoor seemed impervious to the dull ambience and finished the food in a fastidious way. The journey resumed and the fields of sugar beet gave way to a mixture of crops. Abdul Ghafoor, an agricultural graduate, recited them in a half-bored way while the driver glared at us in the mirror and Abdulwahed slept in the waves of hot air.

The driver insisted he was being underpaid for a journey which entailed risk and he raised the matter of the fare again. I told him to go to hell. He bounced the car off a rock and punctured a tyre and I told him I might deduct money for his incompetence. He muttered something in Urdu. It was probably 'Go to hell'. Abdulwahed and Abdul Ghafoor wandered up the road talking intimately and I felt a rough tug on my sleeve. A little boy in ragged clothes led me by the hand to a shelter. A fat man was supervising a motor repair shop adjacent to the shelter and he beckoned me to sit in the shade. A beaker of cold water was brought to me and I drank it gratefully.

50

We set off again in the exhausted daylight, along smaller roads but the discomfort was offset by the beauty of the valley through which we passed. It had a tropical feel to it and was full of banana groves and palms. You glimpsed large homes enfolded in the rampant green. They were the homes of the wealthy, made rich from fruit and tobacco. And then the verdure became exhausted until the valley was a hazy smudge of green in the rear view mirror and all that lay ahead were the barren mountains. We climbed slowly through the loops to the Ambela Pass. I pulled my turban over my face and pretended to be asleep, but the police officer at the checkpoint just waved the car through and we began the slow descent into the Kogar valley.

We walked the last couple of miles over a rutted track through wheatfields to Kogar camp. There were mountains on all sides of the broad flat valley and the camp was located in the eastern corner near the streams that ran off the peaks. The camp was new and it had been established to take some of the pressure off Peshawar district. There were about 10,000 people living there. It was a tented camp but some mud huts were being being built and mosques had been constructed from timber and woven brushwood. The tents were surrounded by mud walls topped with fencing of wood from the trees they called Walaskar and Nashtal.

We were taken to a large orange tent and cushions were brought for us to sit on. Tea appeared. Children were shooed away by a well-built man with a ramrod back who stood at the entrance of the tent with his hands clasped behind him. An old man sat at the head of the gathering, one knee drawn up under his chin as he talked. Old Sakidot had that bright-eyed, kind-hearted and ultimately vulnerable quality of old men everywhere. He was listened to with respect but authority in the family had passed to the eldest son, the man who stood to attention at the entrance to the tent with the iron-plated features of a British sergeant-major. There was a wall-eyed man who lay smoking hashish and who spoke rarely. A Mujahiddin commander spoke of his exploits against the Russians. I asked him when he was going to return to Afghanistan and the wall-eyed man replied for him: 'Never'. He had become afraid. He did not conceal his contempt.

The family came from a village near the town of Charikar in Parwan. Old Sakidot said that they had left after an air raid in 1981 in which one of his sons had been killed and himself wounded. The village had been concerned with agriculture but some of the men had gone to work in a cement factory. When the resistance began the workers had gone on strike and the factory had been idle since. Between two and three hundred villagers had been killed in air raids and shelling.

'If you see my village you would think it was Balkh after Genghis had destroyed it.' Genghis. There it was again. The idea of what we call history as though it were yesterday. The legends of the past bandied about and the stories retold – Timur, Mahmud, Sikander – as though they were talking about warriors in the next valley. Themes of unity, which Muslims seem to delight in and spend much time contradicting, extended through time as well

Youngsters from Kogar camp.

as space. These misty legends were as real as the mountains. This is how it must have been among the ancient Greeks before the legends of the *Iliad* were set down in writing, or among the Germanic tribes before *Beowulf* was committed to paper.

Old Sakidot waved a gnarled hand. 'Genghis was a very bad man but Andropov is worse. Genghis did not say he was good man. Andropov says that communism is good for all people, that it is for poor people, and then Russians come and kill poor people.' The mindless ugliness of the Mongol holocaust came home more vividly than any written account. Our storage of history in books so distances us from the past that we are able to fool ourselves into thinking almost that it has nothing to do with us or our time. The oral culture of the Afghans compresses time so that it becomes unimportant and, in the stories of the orators, the figures of history come alive. In the West we use linear time to escape from the ideas or wrongs of the past. We see that in phrases like 'water under the bridge' and 'it's all in the past'. Here there was no such escape.

There was a peaceful rhythm to life in the camp. I slept with the men of Sakidot's family on chapakats (frame beds) in the courtyard beneath the stars. The brightest lingered in the sky above the mountains after sunrise. First light was breaking when the old muezzin would ascend the mud platform in the mosque next door and begin the cry 'Allah O Akbar' (God is great). The call to morning prayers sounded faintly down the slopes of the camp, through the lines of tents to the stream where the men were carrying out their ablutions, obligatory before each prayers. The call would reverberate faintly through the valley and mingle with the distant sound of other muezzin crying from the rude mosques in other parts of the camp. In most Muslim countries the figure of the muezzin has been superseded by technology. Tape recordings of the call are fed through speakers perched high on minarets.

In those earliest daylight hours – it was 4.30 am – the world was a mixture of pink light and purple shadows through which the men moved in silence. You rarely saw the women, other than as silhouettes, crouched over the fires behind screens of wood.

I would doze and wake later to see Abdul Ghafoor sitting cross-legged on a chapakat under the arbour rocking gently to and fro and reciting verses from the *Qoran*. Abdulwahed was still asleep under his partouk, the multi-purpose Afghan sheet of embroidered material which serves as everything from prayer-mat to cloak. I wondered if he had actually poked his wispy beard into the mosque. The sergeant-major, his brother, would not have let him escape his religious duties even if he had wanted to. By 6 am it was not possible to sleep any longer: the sun was too hot and the generator in the little flour mill under canvas would erupt into life. As soon as the first flour was spilled into little heaps the men would gather to feel the texture and discuss it for the pleasure of shared expertise. As of wine or pipe tobacco.

The women came to wash and collect water from the stream in a deep gulley beneath the mountain. The men had to climb the foothills out of sight of the women to wash in the steep tumbling tributaries so cold that they paralysed your face. The eyes of the women followed you and sometimes you would catch a glimpse of them before they turned away in their modesty. False modesty. They had the most expressive eyes of any women I had ever seen. Women are so distant in Afghan society, so remote. One glance said so much: all the resources of imagination, allure and suggestion would smoulder for a moment, new and sensual worlds flare and fade. A moment was all you could bear.

Breakfast of nan and black tea was taken under the arbour with the mountains on the west side of the valley regaining their colour. People would tell their stories. Sitting in the circle in their loose garments with grave bearded and Biblical faces, the men would recount the grim repetitive unhappiness of war without self-pity. They were philosophical. It was the will of Allah. Homes could be rebuilt, the dead honoured. Islam was their salvation and remained with them by their hearths or in exile. Ein-a-Dinn was from Laghman, a man of middle years with bright red hair and beard. Was he descended from the Greeks of Alexander as he claimed? He had been a clerk in a merchant's company in Kabul and had enjoyed money and an urban life. He had become a Mujahid when the communists took power.

'We know the purpose of the Russians. They come to destroy Islam. We will win back our freedom or we will die.' He said it without bravado. His was not a stoic acceptance of death or an indifference to it: he – and many like him – welcomed it as the ultimate affirmation of their faith.

The men would ascend the foothills to a shady spot overlooking the camp where they would sit and talk. There was Abdul Ghafoor, Abdulwahed, the sergeant-major and old Sakidot. The adults would be followed at a respectful distance by a crowd of boys. The sergeant-major had selected the tallest to bear my rucksack. He was Samahand Mujahid, about 14, with great dark eyes like a woman, whose features wavered between shyness, vacancy and adoration as he walked in my footsteps. We would walk a couple of miles into the hills until the camp was far below us and smudged with little spirals of smoke. Then the men would spread their partouks in the shade of great boulders to sit on. Here I discovered how the Afghans love to be photographed. Some time ago a photographer had discovered that the technical magic of the Polaroid camera won him friends and was a useful tool for social diplomacy. The legacy was that those of us without the capacity to deliver instant pictures delivered much disappointment.

We set off in bathing parties in the heat of the day to enjoy the icy water in pools off the high paths. Abdulwahed, whose tendency to stroke your hand led me to speculate on his sexual proclivities, was hanging about outside the rock wall while I bathed naked inside. Every so often he peered over the wall, for all I knew to check whether the feringhi came equipped with the same tackle as the faithful. At length he could contain himself no longer and exclaimed something in Persian while gesturing at my body in such a way as to confirm my fears that we feringhi had indeed been sold short. As I was speculating on the dimensions of the Afghan member, he leaned over and tugged the hair under my armpit. 'Mista you shave. This hair bad.' Though I never found out why, it seems that the Afghans found such hair impolite.

At dinner I was accorded a place of honour with the elders who gathered in Sakidot's courtyard. The old ties of family and village were carried over the border to the camps in Pakistan. I discovered that feuding came too: the family I was staying with were at war with another family in the camp. The details were never revealed as it was considered impolite to burden a guest with such matters. My inquiries on the subject were met with polite smiles and prevarication. My presence in the camp was going to be used as a pretext to raise the dispute again.

Around 7 pm as the mountains turned a deep purple and the mosquitoes began to whine like dentists' drills, the hurricane lamps were brought. A boy with a pitcher of water would wash the hand of the diners, each in turn. Then great flatbreads, wrapped in brightly patterned cloth, were spread out. The dishes would arrive: mounds of rice, bowls of mutton and salads. We ate with our right hands only, the other being reserved for the toilet and regarded as unclean. The talk was of life at the camp. The Afghans claimed that some of the camp officials were corrupt and that supplies of food were being spirited away and sold in the villages. The elders had written to the refugee commission in Peshawar. I was told to avoid the officials as I had no permit to be in the tribal agency.

As we lounged in the lamplight the muezzin called the faithful to prayer. The young men vaulted the wall while the older men walked around the compound to the mosque. I asked if anyone would mind if I took some pictures of the mosque the following day. My hosts readily agreed. It would lead to some tricky moments. The only person left in the courtyard was a Mujahid who sat sullen and menacing. Even the sergeant-major was more formal than fierce, more upright than uprising. Among the Afghans I observed two expressions that I did not care for. The first was that of my scowling companion who was plainly harbouring some sense of injustice. It was sullenness mingled with contempt, even hatred, set on a low and steady burn. The other expression was a kind of vacancy in which the eyes seemed to see nothing. Then the jaw would drop and a terrible light would grow in the eyes, as though before some devilish vision. It was something utterly other-worldly. The children who gathered about me, a pleasant distraction from the cheerless Mujahid, scattered as the adults returned. I lit a cigarette and offered them around. Everyone politely declined and I wondered why among the members of Hezb I had met not one had been a smoker. The sergeant-major explained that Hekmatyar had delivered an edict banning smoking among party members. I offered to desist and so concerned was the sergeant-major that I should feel such an obligation that he promptly took a cigarette and lit it. Judging from the expression on his face I do not think he had ever smoked before.

I was returning from my ablutions one morning, from the mountain the face of which was pervaded by a faint smell of shit, and ruminating on the gloomy possibility that it is possible to pollute an entire mountain. It was to be my last day at the camp though in the cool of the dawn nobody, least of all me, was aware of that. I was joined by Abarg Marjan who came from the province of Baglan and who was regarded as a prominent chief in the camp. He had a grave and compassionate face and a proud bearing. He told me a story of Russian atrocities which he said he had witnessed. At the village of Pouza-i-Shak, the inhabitants had been rounded up by troops who shot and clubbed them into pits which had then been filled in. He said a similar incident had happened at the village of Sakelweg. It was impossible to prove this story though I heard similar indirect accounts from others of that region. The Afghans are aware of the value of propaganda and some invent the most ludicrous tales to impress journalists. But you learn to distinguish between imaginative types and those telling the truth. Abarg Marjan did not seem the type to deal in lies.

I had noticed a change in attitudes in the three years since my first visits to the camps. In 1983 I detected a marked resentment among some Pakistanis at the burden the refugees placed on the economy. The Afghans had virtually taken over the trucking industry in the north-west. There were outbreaks of trouble: about thirty people had recently been killed in the Kurram agency. Still, the impressive thing remained the lack of more widespread friction between the host communities and the refugees. A political commitment by Pakistan, the teachings of Islam and the innate dignity of the Afghans all helped.

'We want only to return to Afghanistan. If you see my beautiful country then you will understand that we wait only for the day when we can go home,' said Sakidot.

My hosts escorted me along a dusty track to the central mosque in the camp to take pictures. The mosque was a large wooden structure, open along one end like a stable and facing onto a large courtyard. Being Friday, the Muslim holy day, many of the men came to pray at this mosque and to listen to the wild oratory of the imam. We arrived in the middle of the imam's fiery speech. Hundreds of pairs of sandals and shoes were lined up outside the courtyard and we shed ours before joining the throng. My hosts were worried that my presence in such a public place might lead to trouble and so it turned out. The imam's voice rose as he quoted from the *Qoran* and harangued the Russians and the non-believers. I felt vaguely uncomfortable. The crowd was hypnotised and you felt they might obey any instruction the imam cared to give. All over the region on Fridays imams passionately addressed their flocks in Nuremberg rally tones, drawing on that bottomless

The central mosque on Friday: discomfort and wild oratory.

well of religious sentiment. This was not a place for reason but of faith and absolutes. There were no doubts on the faces of the men and no questions that could be asked of the man holding them spellbound.

Events moved swiftly. No sooner had we returned to the compound than a thin, officious-looking man accompanied by two venal acolytes appeared. The camp administration officials demanded to see my documents authorising a visit to the tribal areas. Abdul Ghafoor said haughtily that I was a BBC journalist. I was not but had long given up trying to convince people of the fact. Any journalist in the area is automatically assumed to work for the BBC World Service. It is futile to deny it because nobody will believe you anyway. As one Peshawar-based reporter put it: the Afghans think the BBC is a place.

The officials left with expressions which suggested they would be back and we settled down to a lunch of kofta (balls of meat) and rice. Afterwards Sakidot began to sing traditional tribal songs about honours won in battle. Abarg Marjan appeared to press a packet of cigarettes on me as a gift. A man asked if it was true that the big hand of Big Ben weighed exactly 3,320 kilograms. Somebody else asked if I was aware that American astronaut Neil Armstrong had converted to Islam as a result of sounds he heard while on the moon? He did not, but I was intrigued how such stories moved about in this wild territory. I recalled travelling in the desert region of Morocco among the Berber tribesmen and nobody believed that Armstrong had actually been to the moon. They explained patiently how the Americans had faked the whole exercise on a film set.

Now Sakidot called on me to sing an English song. There seems to be a tradition among travellers to remote places when called upon to sing to render the *Eton Boating Song*. I did not know the words and it seemed singularly inappropriate for a people from a landlocked country. My repertoire extends to rugby club tap-room melodies. A rendition of *The One-eyed Trouser Snake* left the gathering ruminating on the theological implications of serpents in both Islamic and Christian teachings.

Suddenly a messenger appeared and spoke with the sergeant-major. The cheerful mood changed. You could read it in their faces. A unity of thought, part of the extraordinary symbiotic world which seems chaotic yet on closer inspection is all but a single organism. This telepathic aptitude was an extension of the oral culture in which everything is carried out on a communal basis. Abdul Ghafoor said we would have to leave immediately and he set off to try to hire a vehicle. The sergeant-major said that they could no longer guarantee my safety.

'There are bad peoples in the camp.'

It was related to the feud that Sakidot's family were engaged in. I had been seen by hostile elements in the mosque. I discovered that during the last night the men had broken out their guns and mounted a guard about the courtyard. Children gathered outside the courtyard and threw stones over the fence. The sergeant-major scattered them.

It was three hours before Abdul Ghafoor returned with a lorry whose driver was prepared to journey to Peshawar. At a price. At the outskirts of the camp a group of men blocked the road. They crowded around the cab as Abdul Ghafoor went off to talk. There was an air of insolence about the crowd and I told the driver to keep the engine running. Hands reached into the cab and prodded me. I glared at them and they smiled back before prodding me again. I wound the window up and a large character opened the door and climbed into the cab.

'My friend,' he began in a supercilious manner which drained the blood into places it should not be and rearranged the nerve ends, 'Where you come from? Why you come to Kogar?' I told him I had come to enjoy the charm of the residents and sample their legendary hospitality. 'You are Muslim?' he asked, patting my knee.

It was twenty minutes before Abdul Ghafoor reappeared, a span which seemed a deal longer. We set off with a shared sense of relief. 'We have lucky day today. Allah protects us,' he said.

We crossed the Ambela Pass and began the long winding descent as the stars began to fill the sky. Along the way we picked up a group of Afghan refugees hawking a lift to Peshawar. One of them, a middle-aged and voluble Pathan, showed me his battle wounds. As we careered along, headlamps picking out thousands of frogs hopping across the road, I asked him what it was that made him fight when the odds were stacked so heavily against the resistance. He would think for a while and then articulate each reason.

'Because the Russians come to destroy Islam . . . because they bomb my village . . . because they kill my family . . . because they kill my sheep . . .'.

He lapsed into contemplative silence and then, with a smile bursting free of his dark features, 'and because my friend I like to fight,' and he roared with laughter as he repeated it all the way to Peshawar.

6

The Long March

The Mujahid walked into the little restaurant on the first floor of the hotel in Parachinar. He wore the loose dress of the Pathans, a turban and a luxuriant beard that jutted out sharply. The angle never changed as he never lowered his head. He carried a Kalashnikov which he placed on the counter. Then he swung himself up onto the counter and sat cross-legged. He placed the little leather satchel containing a copy of the *Qoran* wrapped in silk next to the gun. He ordered food and the hissing gas lamps threw his huge shadow into relief on the wall behind. It had the quality of a cartoon or a symbol: the prayer book and the gun, Ayatollah Khomeini and the theocratic state in Iran; the Islamic renaissance. The shadow commanded the room.

It was the end of the day's fast and Abdul Ghafoor and his friend Bismallah were eating mutton and rice enthusiastically. We had been together for forty-eight hours, since the knock on my hotel door. I had changed into my Pathan costume – tombon (baggy pantaloons), pirahan (long loose shirt) and partouk (shawl). Abdul Ghafoor took me to Bismallah's home in the Afghan quarter of Peshawar. At first light we set off across the hard-baked ground, past a group of men who were slaughtering a sheep. They recited verses from the *Qoran* before cutting its throat in the way of Islam. The sheep barely struggled.

The battered old government bus roared out of Peshawar on the long journey south to the Kurram agency. At police posts I pulled my turban tight about my face but the checks were desultory: it was too hot to bother and checking the passes of those at the back of the bus meant negotiating belongings piled up in the aisle. Beyond the fertile Peshawar plain with its orchards and nut groves were the baking hills. The passengers were going to Thal or Parachinar on the cheap government bus. The government buses run on time somehow and against the odds but they are spartan and uncomfortable. The tribesmen chattered in shrill tones until the heat became too intense and everyone dozed.

The bus ground over the Kohat Pass and you could see that far below you had left one world behind and were entering a new and mysterious one. Bismallah pulled maps from his bag and gave them to me. They were of his home province of Bamian – my destination – and showed the areas held by

the resistance and safe roads and trails. Bismallah was lively and articulate with devil-may-care eyes which flashed at you. He loved to make a joke of everything he encountered and I wished that he was travelling further than the border camp.

We followed the narrow gauge railway built by the British to supply their forward posts, past the hill forts with their medieval gun slats. This land was part of modern Pakistan and yet the forts were still manned and the little trains still wound through the barren hills. There were still tribal areas where the Pakistan military feared to tread. Abdul Ghafoor awoke and spent the rest of the journey trying to unravel the mystery of the straps on the rucksack he had bought in the bazaar at Peshawar.

Now in the little restaurant he and Bismallah bought two water melons and we retired to our room. Abdul Ghafoor's feet were already blistered and Bismallah was making fun of him.

'Abdul Ghafoor is great Mujahid,' he said and chuckled.

I checked my equipment: mostly cameras but some spare clothing, first aid equipment, compass and what crude maps I had been able to acquire. I had a dozen pink washing tackle bags to keep cameras and films dry and Abdul Ghafoor helped himself to two which he pulled over his blistered feet.

'A great Mujahid,' Bismallah repeated.

'Which camera you give to me?' asked Abdul Ghafoor examining them in a covetous, almost sensual way. The greedy streak is the worst side of the Afghan character. I had chosen Shakespeare plays for the journey. Yet I felt I had deprived myself of many useful items and somehow the rucksack still managed to weigh 15kg. I read, then switched off the light. By moonlight I could see the two pink washing bags protruding from Abdul Ghafoor's partouk.

Another day's bus ride brought us to the forward camp close to the Afghan border. The mountains of the Safed Koh dominated the skyline and snow still capped the high peaks. The camp was based on a small town, swollen by thousands of Mujahiddin and refugees. The place was in a state of perpetual excitement as camel and donkey trains arrived and departed. There is an animation – almost intoxication – peculiar to border towns; the anticipation of worlds about to change and possibly our lives too. We walked past the money changers, tea shops and arms dealers where you could buy any weapon up to a medium-size anti-aircraft gun. In one chai khana a young Afghan boy was singing a love song without self-consciousness. Sweet cool air drifted down from the towering peaks. It had an alpine quality in the smell of the air and the sound of bells tinkling about the necks of animals. Beyond the huddle of houses and tents were the hills in which automatic rifles chattered as Mujahiddin tested new weapons. Camels, horses and donkeys grazed or were led through the narrow streets. Had they come from Afghanistan or were they about to set off? The land of legend was less than a mile away. Beyond the peaceful grandeur of the mountains was the war, though it seemed unlikely.

Minaret in Parachinar.

The men carried AK 47s designed by Kalashnikov over their shoulders. We were escorted to a row of wooden two-storey buildings which formed one side of a small square. It had a sense of the wild west: guns, horses and wooden buildings with balconies overlooking the dusty square. Swagger. One Mujahid gave me his rifle to hold. After the *Qoran* in the little leather satchel about his neck, his gun was his most cherished possession. The AKs and the AKMs were nearly all captured from the Russians but intelligence sources had told me that the West was buying some on the international market and shipping them through Pakistan. Kalashnikovs are readily available on the arms markets, used as they are in at least thirty-five countries. It is the most successful post World War 2 rifle and can be easily used by soldiers of any standard of education. It is light and extremely reliable in all conditions. Another Mujahid had an old bolt-action British Indian army 303 of 1930s vintage. It was heavy but powerful and such weapons are still produced in the gun factories of the North West Frontier Province.

'Which gun is better?' demanded one of the men.

'Each has its virtues,' I replied diplomatically.

The ground floor of each building was piled high with ammunition: thousands of brown plastic mines in one room, hundreds of cases of bullets in another. Mortars, rifles, machine guns and cases of grenades. All afternoon tons of arms were hauled out of the armoury and slung in nets over the backs of camels and donkeys. Mujahiddin sat with rifles across their laps, ticking off lists on clipboards. To my horror I found that the living quarters were above the armoury and I reflected gloomily on the chapter of accidents at the party HQs in Peshawar. As the Afghans at the camp were now officially Mujahiddin the fast of Ramadan no longer applied to them and biscuits and dried fruit were passed around as they cleaned their weapons. There were many young men, no more than teenagers, yet they handled their weapons skilfully. Personal gear consisted of a bundle containing some dried fruit and nuts for the march which would take at least a week. These belongings were wrapped in partouks which were slung across neck and shoulder and tied firmly about the chest. Then there were the little satchels containing the *Qoran* and their rifles. On top of that, each had to bear some of the heavier arms such as a sack full of rocket-propelled grenades (RPGs).

Initially shy, the young men slowly introduced themselves. For two hours they helped me with my Persian and then at dusk we watched the loading of the animals from the balcony. About seventy animals would set out with a hundred Mujahiddin who were destined for resistance strongholds in three provinces. There was no expedition commander. The Mujahiddin belonged to different districts with different loyalties and, on the march, tended to go their own way.

After a final meal of mutton, salad and rice in a smoky room made so by a crude iron samovar, where the walls were covered with gaudy Islamic posters and a hyperactive quail sang in a cage, I returned to the living quarters. As I wrote my diary the window facing on to the balcony was filled with young Afghan faces. One by one they introduced themselves. Khan Mohammed . . . Abdul Qadir.

'Ah Abdul Qadir,' I said. 'Any relation to the great Pakistan spin bowler?'

I knew instantly that it was a mistake to mention cricket, a game which remains a mystery to the Afghans. That the high water mark of the British Empire was in what is now Pakistan is evidenced by the fact that whereas in India and Pakistan cricket is high passion, west of the Durand Line the other 'great game' is unheard of. Later I came to dwell on the idea that the reason the British never actually colonised Afghanistan was because once they got there they discovered that nowhere is there enough flat ground to make a decent cricket pitch. Abdul Qadir the Mujahid looked blank so I made batting gestures. The message did not get home. Bowling movements followed. 'You know, Abdul Qadir,' I cried pitching an imaginary ball. Enlightenment spread across his young face, he chirped 'Ah, Abdul Qadir,' and disappeared. I sat down and resumed writing. Five minutes later a hand grenade landed on my lap. Then another on the mattress next to me. RGD-5s were dropping all around me, bowled with determination by Abdul Qadir the Mujahid from out on the balcony.

'This good Abdul Qadir?' he cried. I decided to go and find a money changer.

At 3 am I was shaken from my sleep and in the cool starlit square I watched the final preparations for the march. Venus beat like a chunk of gold and the countless millions of stars were beautiful and the world felt wild and free. The camp commander shook the hand of every Mujahid who was leaving and Bismallah said goodbye to Abdul Ghafoor and me. And then at last we were on the road. The road out of Pakistan was lined with turds and the air was high thanks to the hundreds of animals which daily use the ancient route. Nearly two hundred animal and human shadows moved through the darkness like ghosts in silence.

We climbed the first mountain in a series of sharp loops and it was dawn as we crossed the border. The frontier post had long before been destroyed by the Mujahiddin and the communists forced to flee. Here the Mujahiddin prayed and I was able to linger and admire the countryside. The burning plains of Pakistan were now behind us and all around conifer-clad mountains marched into the distance. Signs of the lumber industry run by the Mujahiddin were found on most mountains. Abdul Ghafoor said that there was some replanting of trees but it was not being done on a large enough scale to ensure long-term supplies. By the road was the hulk of an armoured personnel carrier (APC). The eastern provinces were extensively liberated in the early days of the war. Even the sight of old battles did nothing to convince you that the war was not still a long way off. As I stood looking at the wreck a mule kicked out and I felt the wind from its hoofs close to my face. My journey had nearly ended a few hundred yards over the border. The Mujahiddin thought this great sport and were still smirking an hour later.

We marched in single file along the sandy mountain trails, scouts pressing ahead to check for anti-personnel mines which the Russians scattered from the air. The mines are peculiarly nasty devices, shaped like commonplace objects such as pens, which can blow off a limb. The only people injured by the things were children who could not resist their attraction. The scouts also went ahead because there were rival resistance groups in the area, said one of the men.

After a few miles of that labyrinth of paths your thoughts were drawn to the repeated Russian demand that the Pakistan government seal the border and the wholly understandable Pakistani response that if the Russians wanted the border closed they should do it themselves. It is a demand doomed in the face of reality. The British empire was never able to close the border which runs through 1,500 kilometres of tortuous terrain. Divisions of troops could be lost among those mountains.

We descended into a broad and fertile valley. By the time we had reached the other side the sun was high and the air was warm and filled with the smell of flowers and pine. The men had broken up into small groups, each taking a different path. The camel-train could be seen crossing the valley a mile away, strings of rubber-bellied beasts with their arch expressions, led by fighters. That was the last we would see of them. Later I learned that of the seventy camels and donkeys, two were lost crossing the Kabul River and another died from exhaustion. The rest got through. We passed through a village. At a tiny window the plain face of an unveiled woman was perfectly framed as she watched the procession. We climbed a long subsidiary valley strewn with huge boulders where a noisy stream meandered from one side to the other. It seemed lost in the great valley. It was hard to think that melting snows filled the valley with a raging torrent powerful enough to roll the boulders like pebbles. We rested at a chai khana perched on the slopes of the valley. The air was sweet and bulbuls sang in the trees.

'Welcome to Afghanistan,' said one man with a radiant smile and shook my hand.

Mujahiddin spontaneously embraced each other and began firing their rifles into the air. The man who had welcomed me was called Abdul Rahim, the younger brother of one of the party's top commanders in Parwan. Abdul Rahim was painfully shy yet handsome and possessed of many virtues so that in a crisis you automatically turned to him for guidance. Yet he was slow in asserting himself. This lack of self-confidence was apparent only in dealing with others: within himself he was composed and self-reliant. He pressed some biscuits on me. With his beautiful brown eyes and well-groomed hair he had the appearance of having just stepped out of a Hollywood studio.

Then for hours it was uphill and the pain began. Pain and joy would alternate in extreme degree throughout my travels in Afghanistan. There was

64

'Welcome to Afghanistan': a Mujahid rests on top of the first mountain to take in the view.

the pain of climbing the mountains followed by the abandon of the descent. An order to halt the march and rest would banish the pain which had seemed eternal. The plenty of the streams was followed by thirst.

We were travelling through Paktia *en route* to Logar and Ningrahar. The political and tribal allegiances in the eastern provinces are as tangled as the terrain. We met many Mangal tribesmen who just after the invasion were reported to have accepted payments from the Russians to cease hostilities. That had been forgotten and all the men I met were enthusiastic for the fight. 'You must understand that all his life the Pathan is fighting against other tribes, governments, invaders, communism. Sometimes he needs a rest. It is good when the enemy pays you to rest,' said Mohammed Ali with a laugh when I asked him about it. 'But they are our brothers.' The Mangal were at the heart of an uprising in 1959 over the lumber industry and central government plans to build roads in Paktia. The killing of an Afghan army officer (he rode into a battle zone with a *Qoran* tied to his head – the traditional sign of a neutral) by a Mangal led to thousands of tribesmen fleeing across the border to Pakistan. The Pakistan government initially welcomed the tribesmen as something of a propaganda coup – Pushtunistan was an issue again – though there was discernible relief when the thousands of armed and potentially dangerous Mangal left the country under an amnesty granted by the Kabul government.

The fertile wooded valleys and mountains of Paktia.

It was in the eastern provinces that a formal declaration of the Jehad was made by Said Ahmed Gailani, one of the leaders of the resistance, in April 1979. The call was endorsed by other leaders. In subsequent months there was fierce fighting between Mujahiddin and government troops in the area and the resistance claimed control of many of the provinces. In Paktia in October there was a major battle in which the resistance destroyed an armoured column. A sign of the strength of the resistance in the east was that Amin threw his best forces against them at the end of 1979 in a last desperate attempt to save himself. Villages in Paktia and Kunar were systematically destroyed. After the invasion the Russians established a strong garrison at Jalalabad. But holding the wooded and mountainous countryside was another matter. In the Logar Valley a new copper mine – developed with Russian assistance – was blown up by the Mujahiddin.

I made slow progress on one mountain and Abdul Rahim called from above: 'Paktia bad province for Russians and bad province for you.' Then he strode down the path, took my hand and led me upwards. So it was that I made that summit hand in hand with a Pathan warrior.

We passed many people. Shepherds moving flocks of fat-tailed sheep to new pastures; a man on a horse with an ancient gun across the saddle like a dignified and self-possessed cowboy. Mujahiddin on their way in and out of Afghanistan. We passed through the Mangal Valley and shook the hands of everyone we met while the Mujahiddin gathered news of the route ahead. In this way news travels remarkably swiftly in a land without high-speed communications like newspapers and telephones. What media there is is controlled by the communists so if you want to know what is happening you ask a traveller. Abdul Ghafoor appeared with a delicate creature called Uztod who giggled a lot and whose sole purpose in life was to please the party official. Uztod was carrying Abdul Ghafoor's bundle and regarded it as an honour. I called him Minikin. There was one thing worse than a party hack and that was someone who toadied to the species.

'You tired Mista Mike. You buy three horses for us,' said Abdul Ghafoor gesturing at several skeletal nags grazing on the hillside. I was tired but not that tired and had no intention of buying horses for someone who boasted of himself as a Mujahid.

We walked 48 kilometres that first day. In one chai khana a grave old man sat in his robes on the straw-covered floor addressing all who would listen on the *Qoran*. The scene had not changed in a thousand years. At another chai khana we stopped for the night after marching for eighteen hours. Our group had become further fragmented so that there were only eight of us now. Abdul Rahim fell to quarrelling with Abdul Ghafoor and accused him of leading us along a wrong trail. Minikin giggled like an idiot in the shadows of the room. The puzzled expression of the man who was priming an RPG prompted me to go outside and smoke a cigarette. The men spent an hour executing brutal massages on each other's aching limbs. Several cried out in their sleep with pain.

There was a remorselessness to the marching and you quickly felt there were no limits to what the Mujahiddin could endure. We were up at 3 am and marching after tea and nan. The young fighters who had cried out in their sleep now showed no signs of pain. We had crossed the Safed Koh and now moved through interminable boulder-strewn valleys. We rested as the sun came up over the mountains. A group of men held a partouk like a fireman's blanket while another shook mulberries out of a tree. Slowly my companions came into focus. Old Mohammed Nassim who never complained despite the suppurating wound in his stomach which he endured by binding a cloth about him. Jassim striding along in his pride and joy, a brand new jacket which held a dozen ammunition clips in special pockets. The young Mujahiddin tried to emulate this dashing man. Yves St. Laurent goes to war. Mohammed Ali was large and taciturn with a black curly beard. He seemed to have acknowledged long ago that the way of the world tended to defy our most cherished dreams. He bore a sad and thoughtful expression as though the turmoil of the world about him was somehow rather unnecessary. He was a smoker and did not care for edicts issued by remote leaders. Unlike many Mujahiddin he was not enthusiastic about martyrdom and I liked him for that. He was merely prepared to die and did not see why he should give up smoking along the way.

The English, he ventured, were a rum lot. Was it true that when a dog walked into a room all the adults stood?

Mohammed Ali was good company and we walked together through interminable demoralised hills where drifts of fine grey dust made walking uncomfortable. We stopped at a chai khana, no more than a shack, and an old toothless cross-eyed man sang in dolorous tones for half an hour, accompanying himself on a two-stringed instrument with a sound box made from a one-gallon oil tin.

'He sings of the brave Mujahiddin, ' said Adbul Ghafoor grandly.

'He sings bad,' said Mohammed Ali, closing his eyes against the sound.

Jassim shouldered his RPG launcher and led the way through a narrow gulley in the heat of the day. He was always cheerful and his taste for battle merely an extension of his enjoyment of life. He cared less for the party under whose banner he fought than for a smart suit of clothes to march through the mountains in. The style was the thing. He gestured to the colossal Surkh Rud Valley and the countless peaks beyond.

'Ah Afghanistan,' he said. It was an expression that contained all the contradictions and delights of a land which to its inhabitants was still pristine and enchanted.

Progress was slow as Abdul Ghafoor and Minikin had decided to try to hire a donkey and could not negotiate a satisfactory price. We waited in the shade of a mulberry tree while an old man brought a huge kettle of tea from a house half a mile away. Two horsemen thundered up the trail. A Japanese journalist called Bong and his escort. He had come from the town of Jagdalak where nobody spoke English. 'Issa problem.' The Japanese are a

68

Through the Safed Koh range.

deeply insular race who at heart would rather stay at home and tend their economic garden. But their extraordinary economic success has obliged them to play a prominent role in global affairs. As a result Japanese journalists are now found in all corners of the globe. Bong had wound up in the wrong part of the globe: he had asked to be taken to Jalalabad where there was plenty of action but something had been lost in the translation and he had been taken to Jagdalak where there was not. 'Issa big problem.' Meanwhile Abdul Ghafoor had negotiated a price for a donkey with the old man who brought us tea. The donkey was loaded with bags when there was an argument and the old man unloaded the beast and threw all the bags in a heap on the ground before stalking off with his kettle and donkey.

'Issa problem,' murmured Jassim and lay back under the tree.

Bong rode away and we set off down the valley, stopping regularly while Abdul Ghafoor made his pitch for another donkey. The others were becoming irritated but said nothing. It was evening prayer time and Minikin approached in his obsequious way and offered to show me the correct Islamic way to conduct one's ablutions. He led me to a stream and explained that the important number was three. All parts of the body are washed three times beginning with the face and ending with the private parts, execution of the latter succeeding only in drenching my clothes. The others were facing Mecca and praying. Now, said Minikin, emboldened by my compliance and his role as acolyte to Abdul Ghafoor, I must pray too. I declined politely but Minikin persisted. I had performed vazoo (washing) so I was ready to submit to Islam. He grabbed my neck and playfully tried to force me to face Mecca. I was angry and grabbed him by the lapels, offering to pray with him when he was prepared to pray in the Christian fashion. Contempt crossed his wheedling features and he giggled in a slightly hysterical way. The others were watching. They were not on my side even if they did hold Minikin in contempt. Islam was the absolute against which everything was measured.

By nightfall we had still not found a place to sleep. Abdul Ghafoor's quest for a donkey had wasted hours and now we found ourselves stumbling about the boulder-strewn valley in darkness. Mujahiddin were falling over their weapons and I trapped my foot under a rock and damaged the big toe. For an hour we crossed and re-crossed the valley like blind men following Abdul Ghafoor. Finally we settled for sleeping in the open to avoid more hazards. I was angry with Abdul Ghafoor for getting us into such a mess and railed at him while Minikin sat giggling under his partouk. In the absence of a commander the Mujahiddin tended to defer to the party hack which was illogical and dangerous when they knew the country and he clearly did not. I told him that if he wanted to act the commander he should bear the responsibility that went with the job. Later Mohammed Ali whispered that most agreed with me. It was some compensation for a bad day.

From the little mud homes perched on the side of the valley, a girl ran down to greet us. She carried a pile of nan in her pinafore and handed one to each Mujahid as he passed. We filled water bottles at a stream before

Abdul Ghafoor tries out a more comfortable mode of transport while Minikin poses with AK 47.

Desert.

crossing miles of semi-desert. The trek was through low barren hills where nothing grew and no water ever ran. The temperature was well over 40°C. It was a terrible place to be and worse when the water ran out.

'This bad way to come,' said Mohammed Ali as we took refuge in the tiny shadow cast by a great boulder at noon. Nobody demurred. It was too hot to argue. It was certainly a tortuous route as the compass showed. First west then north and then west again in a great zig-zag movement which brought us to Ningrahar province. The Mujahiddin insisted it was the safest route. As we stumbled in silence over the hills we heard the first jets. It is remarkable the energy to be found in a crisis, and we scattered behind rocks or into hollows. The jets bombed villages over the mountains. I was glad of a rest and pulled off my rucksack. It was sodden with sweat and I wished I had packed less. Mohammed Ali crawled over to my hollow and told of the television combat crew who had burdened several donkeys with their equipment which included several volumes of the *Encyclopaedia Britannica*. Nobody ever discovered why but they had established the legend of the learned men who went to war.

Beyond the desert we walked into a parched village barely clinging to life. Amidst arid sun-blasted homes of clay, boys bathed in a fetid pond and men dozed under straw awnings. It was a place at the end of the world but a

Beyond the desert (background) a village barely clinging to life.

blessing after the desert. I drank a lot of water. I knew it would do me no good but even the men, who gravely counselled against water while on the march, could not resist it. Minikin redeemed himself when he found two chickens and produced an excellent meal, the only hot food on the eight-day march. Villagers gathered in their curiosity and Abdul Ghafoor presented me as the representative of an Islamic party from the Philippines. There were suspicious glances when I did not join the others for prayers. Beyond the desert lay a fearsome range of mountains which we began to climb in the heat of the day. The foothills were enough to exhaust me and I had gone no more than a few miles when dizziness and nausea overwhelmed me and I collapsed. I came to and found Abdul Rahim mixing a glucose solution for me to drink. I drank it but each time I tried to stand I fell down again. Slowly the feeling returned to my legs and we began the ascent which was harrowing.

The night in the mountains was bitterly cold even in summer yet the Mujahiddin slept in the open with only their partouks to cover them. Mohammed Ali managed to acquire an enormous quilt which we shared. 'The skies are painted with unnumber'd sparks.' The line from Julius Caesar fitted well. The sky was like the one I had looked up at three years before in Zabul province when I decided that I would return. It had been the fullest sky I had ever seen and now here was another just like it.

73

Mohammed Ali said that his father, an imam, had managed to send him to college to study engineering. At first his lecturers had been American. They had plenty of money but they were good lecturers. The advent of the communists saw the Americans replaced with Russian lecturers. They were not so wealthy but they were lazy and did not seem to care about the students.

'I understand why Russian tanks always break down,' he said.

The camp of Senna Gul was located at the heart of the great mountain range in Laghman. Some Mujahiddin thought we might stay there overnight and the prospect appealed to me as the foot was causing me pain. We passed through the first bombed-out villages. 'Maybe we stay one week,' said Minikin. I had learned to take all such pronouncements lightly. With nobody in command of the group, decisions tended to be made by concensus and at the last moment. We carefully descended a 200-metre cliff face composed of bald and hazardous rock, into a ravine which took us north. Mohammed Ali stood contemplating a donkey with the strange ability to bray and fart simultaneously. 'This donkey no good,' he said, as I wondered at the effect this strange habit had on its diaphragm.

Dozens of Mujahiddin appeared from behind trees and began to embrace members of our party. I recognised some of the men who had left Pakistan with us. The camp was perfectly concealed among trees in the deep ravine. It was on a series of tree-covered plateaux. It was a cool and beautiful place and anti-aircraft nests on the peaks guarded it from air attack. It would be an ambitious general who decided to penetrate the mountains. The camp was the Hezb HQ in the mountains. From here raids were carried out on the main Kabul-Jalalabad road a few miles to the north but its main role was to guard the supply lines to the central provinces. We relaxed among huge boulders which dominated the camp by a babbling stream which ran down through the levels and was used for washing and cooking. We dealt with cuts, blisters and chapped lips and bathed our stinking feet in the cool water. Slowly the world was restored in that shady grove. Mohammed Ali tossed me a cigarette and we lay in the sunshine with our eyes closed, smoking. Abdul Ghafoor chose this moment to lecture me on what was good for 'the people' of Afghanistan. I have an innate suspicion of those who invoke the name of 'the people' in justifying their cause, whether communist or Muslim. I was developing a dislike for this party hack whose ideal was to fight the war from an office in Peshawar.

Helicopter gunships scudded by to the north, well clear of the mountains. They came from the airbase at Jalalabad and patrolled the main road which was in the hands of the Russians by day. We had to cross the road but Arcadian contentment made it seem a distant prospect. In 1982 Senna Gul had attacked a convoy on the road and used captured vehicles to block it for thirteen days. Gunships had finally dislodged the Mujahiddin. They did not have the weapons to take on the gunships and feared them more than anything else.

The camp of Senna Gul concealed amidst trees high in the mountains.

The commander sat alone on one of the higher levels reading the *Qoran*. He was about 30 with a big frame and a luxuriant beard. When not planning raids he would read from the *Qoran*. He was a most holy man, said the Mujahiddin. He was a dramatic figure as he descended the levels to the main plateau where the men gathered for prayers. Here he delivered an impassioned speech in which he savaged the Russians and extolled the virtues of the fighters. He seemed possessed and his voice carried far down the ravine. When he had finished he came and introduced himself to me, his manner now rather shy. He took me by the hand to a shady corner where we talked.

'When the Russians have been driven from Afghanistan only the Islamic revolution would be acceptable', he said softly. This meant the unqualified acceptance of *Qoranic* law. 'Any party which is against the law of the *Qoran* . . .', he paused and smiled engagingly, 'well my friend we cannot accept that.' Would he fight rival parties? 'We say only that we do not accept any party which will not follow the law of the *Qoran*. Neither will we accept social law from the *Qoran* and economic law from socialism or imperialism.' How long was he prepared to fight? He said: 'Forever,' and then muttered something in Persian to his men sitting nearby. Later I found out that he had said: 'We fought the British Empire for 100 years, why not the Russians?'

After our interview I happily returned to dozing in the heat. Mujahiddin sat in groups cleaning their weapons and talking. The talk of the older men always had the quality of mature eloquence and each was a master of his words. The younger fighters were not far behind and they held their own in the endless conversations. The very young teenagers could be very silly. When I was not in the company of the older men they would pester me with questions, each repeating the same inquiry and happy with the same answer. They would interrupt whatever you were doing or cheerfully wake you to ask the time of day. You were a plaything. They became overbearing at times and I called them the tomtits. But you always remembered that these youths were prepared to die.

The Mujahiddin wore the tombon and pirahan tunic usually with an embroidered waistcoat. Each wore a hat. Embroidered skull caps, turbans or the expensive karakuls made from lamb's wool. Many wore Chitrali caps which may well be a sartorial inheritance from Alexander the Great. Their boots were captured from the Russians though many wore plastic or canvas shoes or sandals which seemed designed to cut the feet to pieces. Yet they covered hundreds of kilometres through savage terrain without complaint. I saw men walk barefoot through the mountains.

The Mujahiddin welcomed fresh challenges at times I felt to the point of masochism. To be an Afghan means to pit yourself constantly against the environment and thus the people renew their respect and love for the land. It is an intimate relationship, the heightened intimacy of the poet and his environment. The Mujahiddin are an élite, in a land where physical endurance and the warrior ethos are a commonplace. They are the warriors of Islam. There is no shortage of candidates for the job. Availability of weapons and the support of the population in terms of food supplies determine numbers. If a million rifles had suddenly become available in Afghanistan I had no doubt that there would be a million men to pick them up. Hezb had stringent criteria for choosing its men. Candidates had to be Muslims and the piety of applicants was closely examined. Mujahiddin had to be prepared to accept any order from their commander at any time without demur. They had to be prepared to die.

The order to march came suddenly that day but it was futile to protest. It was hard to leave that peaceful spot high in the mountains with its sweet air and sound of falling water. I followed the trail through the ravine in the company of a fighter called Murcha. He was very young but composed and full of curiosity for the world and a sense of fun to temper its harsher side. His handsome features always expressed his inquisitiveness and he walked with the purposeful gait of an athlete. He had travelled extensively through Iran, less out of interest for the Islamic revolution of Khomeini than out of a broad curiosity. You would say of Murcha that he was as keen as mustard and was always getting into scrapes which he met with a sense of infectious fun.

We came to the northern limits of the mountains: in the vale below was the

The view north from the Laghman mountains: across the valley lay the Kabul-Jalalabad road, the Kabul River and then more arid mountains.

east-west road between Kabul and Jalalabad. The latter city, just 65 kilometres from the Pakistan border, has a history of standing on the great trade routes and of going its own way. In the Saur Revolution the garrison at Jalalabad alone resisted the military coup. In the early centuries after Christ Jalalabad stood on the secondary trade route between the Roman Empire and China. Trade moved on to Taxila, the Indian Ocean and the sea routes. In 1979 the resistance tried one of its first mass attacks against the communist troops stationed there. It failed due to poor organisation. After the invasion the Russians made good use of the airport which had been built by the Americans. Back in the era of King Habibullah a Scottish engineer commissioned to build a bridge near the city introduced the first golf courses into Afghanistan. In the early 1950s a plan to build a mosque to exhibit a hair of the Prophet Mohammed started a political row. As if they did not have enough shrines in the city. One has a reputation for curing lunacy.

Beyond the road was the torrent of the Kabul River and then the arid corrugated mountains that filled up the horizon and shimmered in the late afternoon heat. The road was defended by a series of Russian and government posts. The hundred or so Mujahiddin hid in a narrow gulley resting until dusk would permit the descent. It was too hazardous in daylight as the faces of the mountains were under surveillance and large-scale movement attracted gunships. Again, in the absence of a commander, decisions concerning the descent were taken by concensus. A murmured debate went on in the gulley like the susurration of wind among beeches. At dusk we would go in twos down the mountainside and when we reached the valley it would be night and safe to cross the road. Such a committee approach would no doubt make a British soldier gnash his teeth but it suited the fiercely independent Afghans. Yet at times their bravado and exuberance led to anarchy: concensus was lost and an individual's actions swept all along. As I contemplated the shining ribbon of the distant river and the moonscape beyond, Jassim and Abdul Rahim strode by on a path above us waving their guns and roaring with laughter. 'Don't be afraid,' they cried, 'it is time to go down the mountain.' They disappeared down the trail. It was far too early but everyone thought this a splendid ruse and we all followed, infused with a sense almost of immortality. The march was a microcosm of a culture. Only afterwards did it seem reckless.

I descended the mountain with Murcha, taking cover every time the gunships moved down the valley, above the killing ground like primeval birds of prey. Slow, watchful and deadly. It took two hours to climb down the mountain and we rested in the courtyard of a farmhouse while the Mujahiddin regrouped and waited for dark. Murcha had an enormous bag of concentrated protein and vitamin tablets and he sat feeding them to a couple of stray ants. He speculated whether such a diet would transform them into giant ants and I replied they seemed big enough already. He managed to infest the entire courtyard with ants so that the earth was dark with them and the air filled with reproaches as the Mujahiddin evacuated the place. But it was impossible not to like Murcha: you felt that he would succeed at anything he turned his hand to. Enthusiasm alone would carry him through. Provided he lived. His finest moment came when I found myself being pestered by a hornet. I waved it away but it persisted until Murcha took up the cause and tried to catch it between his hands. He chased it beneath a fruit tree still clapping his hands to kill the insect. What Murcha did not realise was that the hornets' nest was in the tree. Suddenly Murcha and half a dozen Mujahiddin who had been sitting beneath the tree, fled pursued by a swarm of hornets. It was a rout.

And then the road. It loomed suddenly like a river of ink in the dark night after we had walked for kilometres across the foothills in silence. We crouched in the dark, waiting for a signal and then we were running in silence and the feel of the road's level symmetry was strange after days walking over uneven ground. It was as though we were treading on forbidden territory and the smell of the warm, muggy tarmac added to the sense of sin. I followed dozens of running figures down the bank and for hundreds of metres to safety. Adrenalin drove out the fatigue and, as we entered the shadowy labyrinth of the village, I guessed we would spend the night there. Time to relax and smoke a cigarette and seek out Mohammed Ali. We moved silently in single file through the narrow clay streets, overshadowed by the anonymous walls of the houses. There were no lights and nothing stirred yet it seemed inconceivable that the whole village was not aware of our presence. The Russian post was a kilometre away. The parade of silent shadows that disappeared into the dark ahead left you with a sense of Ali Baba and the Forty Thieves. Suddenly one of the great carved wooden doors opened and a hand beckoned us inside. The image was complete. We trooped inside and each was met with a warm handshake from an old man and his sons. I found myself in a courtyard and in the light of a single hurricane lamp I saw two hundred Mujahiddin beneath the spreading branches of a huge walnut tree.

We stayed long enough for a violent quarrel to break out among the Mujahiddin. I found a corner to squat and smoke. I was exhausted and did not care what the row was over. I had just fallen asleep when I was rudely awakened. 'Burrow, burrow. Harakat Mista.' Walk, walk, march. The words would come to haunt me. I never found out the purpose of the visit to the house and did not care as we filed through the streets once more. Now there were hundreds of armed men moving silently about the village and forming up for a new march north. We had been on the move for eighteen hours with a break of three hours at the camp of Senna Gul. There were no complaints but that carefree joy which accompanied the march was displaced by a dogged determination. Only willpower kept me going. Something else, deeper and more enduring, sustained the Mujahiddin and I wondered if there was any limit to it. An old man pressed a piece of nan into my hand and uttered a blessing in the darkness.

We queued along the bank of a river while the leaders negotiated a slippery log across it. Suddenly the shuffling silence was broken by an old villager who shouted something sarcastic in Persian and leapt into the stream. There was laughter which seemed to fill the night and travel for kilometres as the old man splashed through a couple of centimetres of water. We crossed ploughed fields until the roar of the great Kabul River filled the air. Here it ran in three broad and fast channels. The first two we waded, half a dozen men at a time, arms linked and boots around our neck. The raging water came up to the chest and I felt sure we would be swept away. The river bed was a mass of slippery boulders but the chains of men, muscles straining against the current, prevailed. I looked with dismay at the third channel which was 100 metres across, deeper and the fastest of them all. Here the river ploughed into the luminous white cliffs on the other bank. I asked the man next to me how we were supposed to cross it.

'On sheep,' he hissed.

I had to bury my face in my hands to suppress the laughter. It was a fit of the giggles you get in outlandish places at strange times of the day when the world has an alarming habit of drifting off into the surreal. There was a story from the Falklands war in which a sergeant-major was detailed to brief a group of city-bred journalists on the rudiments of survival. He waved a picture of a sheep and declared that its meat could be used for eating, its skin for keeping warm in an emergency and invited suggestions for further uses. Most of the journalists shared the soldier's attitude that this was a chore and were prepared only to listen. However, one enthusiastic sort piped up: 'A pack animal?'

'Arsehole', declared the sergeant-major.

Now, as I waited for the flock to appear I felt that my colleague had been vindicated. The Afghans were a resourceful lot. The mirth that such odd associations brought in the midst of tiredness was a blessing. As we crouched in silence by the river looking across the boiling water to the ghostly luminescent cliffs, there appeared old men selling biscuits from baskets slung about their necks. Then Minikin demanded that I carry a sack of RPGs for him. I was heartily sick of the wretch who now felt he was invested with power derived from his obsequious attitude to the party hack. Abdul Ghafoor sat scowling in the darkness.

'Arseholes,' I snorted.

The 'sheep' turned out to be a ship, or rather an inflatable dinghy. It was designed to take ten men but on each crossing it took at least fifteen with their gear. The odds seemed against getting to the other side. The technique employed was for three men to paddle furiously across and then hurl a rope to others on a ledge below the cliffs. The latter would then haul the craft into still water. It was no easy task in the dark. The dinghy was swept 200 metres downstream and there was only one chance to hurl the rope and the aim had to be perfect. Beyond that point the cliffs were sheer and there was no landing spot. To ferry all the Mujahiddin across took several hours. A kilometre away the Russians lay asleep dreaming of home. We scrambled onto the narrow ledge beneath the cliffs and began to climb the smooth, steep rock. It was hard going and we all ended up with lacerated hands and legs. Again I thought that here we would rest for what was left of the night. But as soon as our group had been accounted for we set off through the darkness, stopping every few metres while scouts checked the coast was clear. We were close to another post and delicate bird imitations filled the night.

I found the night walking arduous and seemed to trip over every boulder. As Afghanistan seemed to be largely covered in boulders that meant a lot of time spent picking myself off the ground. Slowly you developed the technique used by the Afghans. They have a slightly ungainly walk in which the legs are relaxed enough to ride out undulations and obstacles. It is different from walking by day when your feet are boldly planted in the direction you want to go. Then you subconsciously direct the muscles to form the movement you wish to make and then forget it. By night you have to remain aware of each part of the footstep and be prepared to adjust at any moment of its execution depending how your foot falls. The automatic reaction to walking blind is to tense up. The technique requires the opposite. You must relax until you develop the necessary confidence.

From then the march was relentless and, in the end, you neither knew nor cared whether it was night or day. By day you roasted and by night you fell over. When the call to halt came you snatched what sleep you could in your boots and still wearing your rucksack. You no longer thought about an end

The march becomes a gruelling slog.

to the march because you did not believe there would be an end. Horizons shrank and hope was reduced to a vague belief that there had to be water beyond the arid hills. A terrible weariness sacked the heart and suggested that you would never be the same again. The Mujahiddin chewed aspirins to quell the pain but soon the tablets were finished. You stank and did not care any longer. You did not take your boots off because you were afraid that the pain would make it impossible to put them on again. The bleached landscape, scorched and infertile, seemed incapable of supporting life, yet people would appear and thrust a little bread into your hand. I ran out of cigarettes and accepted it as you had to accept every hardship and keep going. Willpower became an instrument of torture. The Mujahiddin were driven by something better than will. There was a sense of grace about their determination.

It was Eid, the Muslim festival to mark the end of Ramadan. It was a time of feasting and I remembered the grand round of celebrations in The Gulf. Roasted sheep and merry-making late into the night; little children parading the streets in their bright new clothes. Somebody joked that we should buy a sheep to roast but it was a bad joke as we stumbled through the bald hills. We came to a village where they were celebrating Eid, though the war had robbed them of the means to do it in style. The embraces were warm even for the *feringhi*. The affection and respect that the people felt for the Mujahiddin was evident. The resistance was a true expression of the Afghan people. This was a true popular movement; not the semantic deception practised by seedy plotters of the left whose 'popular movements' are usually as popular as bubonic plague. Such deliberate abuse of the language was all part of the big lie upon which the communist edifice rests. An old crone in veils thrust two boiled eggs into my hand and somebody brought some nan. It was Eid and for a delirious moment I felt a deep and abiding peace.

'Burrow. Harakat.'

I no longer believed anything I was told about how long we would march or rest. Afghans have little concept of time yet they would always tell you that we would rest for two hours. Ten minutes later came the shout to move. Distance and walking times were always underestimated dramatically so that in the end you did not bother to ask. It increased the psychological strain because any physical task is half accomplished in the imagination. The very art of civilisation is when people individually and collectively imagine their futures. Anything can be done if you set your mind to it: to conceive first a difficult task is to prepare your body to accomplish it. The body is then paced to a known end. For me there did not seem to be an end and I never knew whether I would be marching for two or twenty-two hours. The imagination was unable to cleave to anything in a void of uncertainty. At the limits of your physical powers, only the will kept you going and you felt your humanity being stripped away. It was not like that for the Afghans.

We crossed another mountain and now, at 2 am, we sat on boulders in another valley while scouts went in different directions to establish where we were. I did not care that we were lost, just happy at the respite from walking. Pull up a rock and I will tell you a story. Everything had taken on the doubtful lustre of fantasy and illusion. I did not realise then that I was sick. I dimly remembered the titanic struggle on the mountains as the Mujahiddin coaxed the horses over the pass. On one precipice a huge load shifted so that the horse nearly toppled over the edge. Half a dozen men clung to the beast while others heaved cases of ammunition from its back. The horse was rigid with fear. One move would have taken it and the men to their deaths. Yet no sense of drama registered. This was a commonplace. Lower down the mountain I found Mohammed Ali sitting astride a donkey trying to beat it into life.

'This donkey don't go,' he said in disgust and climbed off its back. The donkey trotted down the track.

We slept in the valley and woke in the early morning mists which shrouded the world you no longer cared about. We resumed the march and the valley disgorged into a much broader one, several kilometres across. As the sun rose and burned off the mist you could make out the fertile green which filled the far side of the valley and ran for kilometres from north to south beyond the reach of the eye. We had come at last to Tagob.

It was an oasis but I had become so demoralised that it might as well have been a mirage. Abdul Ghafoor and Minikin had acquired donkeys and the party hack rode past on a big beast followed by his acolyte on a tiny one. We crossed the flat open land and disappeared into the trees. We passed through kilometres of shady lanes with baked mud walls overhung with fruit trees. It was all a gorgeous green. Mujahiddin appeared in the lanes, Kalashnikovs slung over their shoulders, and shook our hands. They led us to a spot beneath a spreading walnut tree by a stream. Beyond a mumbled 'salaam alaikum' I was incapable of speech. I took off my boots and bathed my bloody feet in the stream. Mohammed Ali found some cigarettes and we smoked in silence until we were pleasantly giddy from the poisons. Then we giggled in a stupid happy way. I found a comfortable spot in the shade and fell into a deep and unyielding sleep.

7

Flat Earth and Fertile Ground

I awoke to the steady gaze of Commander Ahmedi. He was a man of middle years yet he had the gravity of somebody older. He was a superb orator, as I would discover, yet he spent much of his time listening to others and surveying the world with his strong and patient eyes. Behind the solemn gaze was a man who liked to joke in private. He governed his territory with strength and paternalism and his fighters and the civilians alike had much affection for him. I felt that I had arisen from a bad dream. Food arrived: scrambled eggs in oil, nan fried in oil and sprinkled with precious sugar, followed by water melon. After eight days of austerity it was a feast. Afterwards I smoked cigarettes and drank green tea. Abdul Ghafoor announced that he and Minikin would travel on to Jebel Seraj which was three days away. His family lived there and he wanted to be with them just after Eid. Our parting was a mutual relief and we spent several minutes apologising to each other over our misunderstandings. Perhaps a separation would enable us both to see things with greater sympathy. The Mujahiddin left too, for their villages in the provinces of Kapisa and Parwan. Some I would meet again, others never.

The commander explained that we had come to this remote spot because they were expecting an air raid and it was safe away from the villages. But the danger had passed and now he suggested a walk. He had seen my feet and gave me his sandals to wear while he pulled on my boots, several sizes too large. He had trained as an electrical engineer and worked for a company in Kabul before joining Hezb when the communists took power in 1978. He commanded hundreds of men in fifty sub-groups deployed in the great fertile valleys of Tagob and Nijrob. There was one small post on the west side of Tagob but the road had long been in the hands of the Mujahiddin and the troops had to be supplied by air. Mujahiddin were everywhere. The valley enjoyed comparative wealth from fruit and could afford to support many fighters. We walked through dusty lanes between orchards full of plums, apples and pomegranates. Then cherries, mulberries and grapes. In the fields the wheat was being harvested. Commander Ahmedi explained that because of the harvest farmers had come to him and requested that raids be curtailed. They meant reprisals and much suffering had been caused in the first two years after the invasion by the burning of crops. The commander would resume raids after the harvest. The post in Tagob was only a symbol anyway. The soldiers never left camp and were quite cut off from the population.

We entered a covered platform like a large rectangular bandstand with open sides and supported by pillars. Embroidered cushions and mattresses lined the floor and here we reclined drinking tea and eating almond-flavoured sweets called nockle. There were sub-commanders, imams and elders present. Engineer Zulmay had a dark squat face like a troll but he was a friendly sort and began the discussion. A toothless man, like a debauched caliph of old, sat next to me with a permanent smile. It was as though he had heard it all before. A long discussion took place about Islam, politics, Iran and the war. Each orator spoke at length, with grave gestures, while the others listened intently. None listened more closely than Ahmedi and it was he who spoke last and longest. The old man was asleep, through heat not boredom. Then we had a great lunch of stewed chicken, nan and salad.

Answering nature's call – now a rather frequent business – meant finding a spot behind a rock. Those scrambled adjournments were in the company of an escort of Mujahiddin sent for my protection. From what I never discovered. It was something else to get used to. I slept for several hours beneath a tree and then the commander led the way to another village. He showed me the artillery piece his men had captured during the Russian spring offensive. It was a 122 mm D-30 field howitzer with a range of 15 km. There were several captured shells and his men had already learned how to fire the gun. The commander planned to barter some hashish for shells from the communists at the post. There was nothing they would not sell for hashish or food. This kind of trading between communists and the resistance was widespread and an indication of how desperate the government troops were for basic supplies. Ahmedi acquired his additional shells, I later discovered, and turned the gun on the post with devastating results. The retaliation by the Russians was savage: they bombed the villages for two weeks as a punishment.

After prayers we sat around another platform, with no roof, and talked more politics beneath the stars. The sense of well-being engendered by the delightful environment of Tagob disguised the illness which was about to strike me. I put the discomfort down to exhaustion and took little notice, but the next morning I was feverish and sick and expended what energy I had sprinting behind rocks. For the best part of a week I lay in a fever, unaware of events about me and not caring. I had dysentery and, even when the fever cleared and I was up and about, I suffered the unremitting indignity of 'rock sprinting' for a month. I would suffer from sporadic attacks throughout my travels.

When I came out of the fever the first person I noticed was an old man who spoke a little English and who constantly and sagely stroked his beard.

'Eeena,' he said shrilly and pointed at my cut feet which had not healed. I nodded and he dispatched a boy who returned with a bowl of red mud. They caked this cool mud onto my feet so that all the cuts, infected blisters and assorted irruptions were covered and then bound my feet in rags. In the morning I washed the mud off to discover my feet coloured bright red. Eeena was in fact henna, the red dye made from an Asiatic shrub and used by women to colour their hands and feet for cosmetic purposes. The old man insisted it had medicinal qualities and that its application would strengthen my feet. The results were mixed: most of the cuts healed into little hard chips of mud but one became infected.

The young lad who had brought the henna now sat at my feet gazing at me in affection and wonder. Abdulahad was ten years old when he was pulled in by the communists and ordered to say 'zindebad communism' – 'victory to communism'. He refused and was jailed for three months and frequently beaten. He never said what they wanted him to say and in the end they let him go. A boy of ten is no longer regarded as a child by either side. Abdulahad was rewarded with a job as bearer of Ahmedi's briefcase in his daily walks about the villages. Most of the time the lad was speechless with pride as he trotted along behind the grave figure of Ahmedi, his little chest puffed out like a sparrow.

There were many such stories in the villages of Tagob and, as my strength returned, I began to tour them and talk to farmers and Mujahiddin. My companion and interpreter was Mohammed Akbar with a long, sad face like Alexander Solzhenitsyn, and a former captain in the Afghan army called Amanullah. On the west of the valley dotted on the slopes which rose to the mountains were 35 burned out military vehicles. Trucks, infantry combat vehicles and a few tanks, with an air of prehistoric irrelevance, decorated the arid slopes. In the spring offensive hundreds of Russian tanks and support vehicles had fought to regain control of the road which ran across the naked hills but failed despite battles for three weeks in which both sides lost many men. I asked Mohammed Akbar why the vehicles had been moved so far from the road to spots high on the hills, and he replied for inspection. I did not believe him. They had been arrayed as trophies. They were the badges of war set out on the hillside for all the people of the Tagob to see. They articulated the brave and uneven struggle of the people to free their country. They could be seen from the communist post. But the civilians had suffered badly for the successes of the Mujahiddin. For days the jets flew low over the valley bombing the houses to dust. The worst destruction left you with a feeling that there had been no life there anyway: just mounds of rubble the same colour as the earth from which the buildings were fashioned. Villagers spent half of their lives in the mountains where valuables from each household were buried in metal trunks. Each family had a mountain refuge to which they fled in hurried and anxious flocks at dawn bearing a little food for the day. All along the mountains bordering the valley thousands of pairs of eyes would follow the jets, like flashing darts below them, and wonder if the bombs would fall on their village, their home. In the evening they would descend from the mountains. On the edges of the valley were the graveyards

Remnant of a Russian attack arrayed on the slopes above Tagob.

where the Shaheed (martyrs) were buried. Mujahiddin and civilian alike were considered Shaheed if killed in this war. Many commanders made no distinction between the fighters and the civilians: they were all Mujahiddin. A large stone marked each grave and little flags of white and Islamic green hung limply above. Standing in the fields of stones you sensed the awesome odds confronting the Afghans. But any sense of hopelessness was your own and not theirs.

'Islam can defeat anything,' said the farmer while his sons brought dishes of plums and mulberries to the spot in the orchard where we sat. It was not the voice of bravado, but of faith.

Islam means submission (to God) and it was the last of the three great monotheistic faiths. Muslims insist that the appearance of the Prophet Mohammed and the writings of the *Qoran* resolve all paradoxes and uncertainties in Judaism and Christianity. Mohammed was the last – and greatest – prophet after Abraham, Moses and Jesus. The writings of the *Qoran* are the literal word of God and provide a blueprint for all aspects of a man's life. This fact is crucial to the understanding of the rise of fundamentalist Islam in the latter part of the twentieth century. In the West we are accustomed to the separation of Church and State in our polity. We may recognise the Ten Commandments as the basis of our laws but government is secular. The Reformation of the sixteenth century which emancipated many countries from the power of the Roman Catholic Church and led to the separation of Church and State, has no strict parallel in the Muslim world. That there was a drift in some Muslim countries towards secularism in government as first steps towards development there can be no doubt, but even in the most 'liberated' countries the faith still occupied a central role in government. At the philosophical level doubts were being expressed by Muslim intellectuals about this drift towards secularism in the early part of the twentieth century, but it was the explosion of wealth resulting from raised oil prices by the Arab states and Iran which threw the arguments into dramatic relief. There were fears that the rush to development would demand too great a price of Islam. Islamic fundamentalism – a return to the basic tenets of the faith without compromise with alien ideas – was a key factor in the destruction of the Shah of Iran, though not the only one. In the aftermath of the King of Kings' flight into exile, it was the fundamentalist Muslims who filled the power vacuum and then set about creating the theocratic state in which Islam occupies the central role of all aspects of life, whether in the legal system or the way a person dresses. The Islamic revolution – in truth only partly Islamic in its origins – has inspired fundamentalist Muslims seeking to overthrow governments in a dozen countries.

Mohammed was born into one of the leading families of Mecca around 570. He was raised as an orphan and became engaged in the caravan trade. Mecca was a great trading entrepôt which dominated commerce between the Indian Ocean and the Mediterranean. Mohammed married Khadija who bore him four daughters. His monotheistic preachings posed a threat to the Oligarchs of Mecca who saw in his teachings a challenge to their authority. The veneration of pagan gods and the annual pilgrimages to the Ka'ba (later adapted by the Muslim faith) were being undermined by these new ideas and Mohammed and his followers met with hostility. He moved to Medina to the north. There the people accepted his Divine message. Even then this religious association of men was developed along political lines. Not only did it appeal to the spiritual side of people but it proclaimed a quite pragmatic political dimension with an implicit threat to the established order of the day. It was not merely theory and belief that were being preached. The Arab tribes of the Arabian Peninsula were subdued but Mohammed realised that the key to the future of Islam lay in the acquiescence of Mecca and thus devoted himself to wooing that all-important city.

The pillars of Islam are faith in one God, giving of alms, prayer, fasting and the pilgrimage (Hajj). No Muslim, mighty or lowly, is exempt from these universal obligations and they point to them as evidence of an equality which puts socialism to shame. Communist notions of equality are a sham next to the true equality of men before God. The daily profession of the faith reaffirms the Muslim's belief and the pious Muslim sees all actions as an extension of that immutable conviction. The giving of alms in Muslim countries covers everything from taxes raised according to rules laid down in the *Qoran* to individual acts of benevolence. The awkwardness of 'charity' in the West does not afflict Muslim countries: the beggar knows it is his or her right and the donor that he has the blessing of God. I recall a story my paper had carried years before in Bahrain, of a woman forced to sleep in the open when her home burned down. The Prime Minister ordered that a large tent be given the woman and money to build a new home. We reported this, yet our Muslim readers, including the Prime Minister, were baffled why such an act should warrant a news story.

The most obvious manifestation of the faith and the pattern which dominates life in Muslim countries is the prayers said five times a day; at dawn, noon, late afternoon, early evening and before going to bed. The ritual involves the Muslim cupping his hands about his ears and reciting Allah O Akbar, the recitation of the opening verses of the *Qoran,* then a series of bows while standing, before sinking to the knees and the prostration of the body, face to the ground. The process is executed while facing Mecca. Prayers are rarely missed. On my first journey with the Mujahiddin three years before we were crossing a wide plain and the men were constantly scanning the skies, fearful of attack. Yet they halted for afternoon prayers and when I observed that we were sitting targets they replied that God would never allow Muslims to die while at prayer. I felt rather vulnerable.

Tagob farmer in his orchard.

Each year at Ramadan the Muslim renews and strengthens his faith by fasting during daylight for a lunar month. Once in the life of each Muslim they should try to make the pilgrimage to the holy shrines of Mecca. This pilgrimage is called the Hajj and those who have made it add the word Hajji to their name. The most poverty-stricken peasants in remote villages scattered throughout the world will spend a lifetime saving for the Hajj.

'La ilaha illa'llah Mohammedan rasulu'llah,' intoned the young man. There is but one God and Mohammed is the apostle of God. Then he began to softly chant in slow melodic phrases verses from the *Qoran,* gently rocking back and forth. He had pulled the *Qoran* from its little leather satchel, carefully unwrapping the bright silk cloth which covered it and kissed the holy book before opening it. The gentle sounds had a pacifying effect on the men who reclined on cushions beneath the fruit trees. All the beauty and glory of the faith was illuminated for them in the soothing and persistent tones of the young man.

More fruit appeared as if by wizardry. I asked why the men dipped the plums into salt before eating them. The old farmer replied that it was to make the plums, which were not fully ripe, taste sweet. I tested the paradox and discovered they were right.

Often on these long walks from village to village you ceased to think of Afghanistan as a country at war. People would far sooner engage you in a

Goatherd in a Tagob lane.

discussion about theology. Did I believe that Christ was the son of God? Everyone asked that question. To the Muslim Isa (Christ) is a prophet to be revered but he was not the son of God. The Afghans always went to the heart of where Islam and Christianity diverged and yet disconcertingly they would ask the question and then leave matters dangling. They were content to hear my misguided view and would nod sagely among themselves but not dispute the matter. I was never really sure if this was out of politeness to a guest or because they felt I was beyond redemption. It was difficult to draw them and you felt patronised.

At this time of the year the main river was no more than a large and rancorous stream which grumbled through a maze of huge grey boulders which you had to negotiate to cross from one fertile side of the valley to the other. One day we had crossed the river bed to visit a village on the west side. Mohammed Akbar stood motionless like a bearded bloodhound amidst the destruction of the village. 'Eight people die in this house. A man, one wife and six children. He was Islamic scientist.' Everything bore the prefix Islamic and I was faintly irritated by it. I suggested that science did not alter a jot according to whether the scientist was a Muslim or a communist or a pigeon fancier. Mohammed Akbar fixed me with one of his doleful gazes. The scientists of the West had made it their business to celebrate atheism and disprove the existence of God. I objected and said they merely pursued objective truth which at times had brought them into conflict with the Bible's teachings. As we clambered over the ruins, Mohammed Akbar said that the only truth was God and that any science which tried to disprove that was evil. The man was an Islamic scientist!

I was thinking that God was not against knowledge, when we came to another village where the ruins were being rebuilt by a gang of cheerful men. Two jets appeared low and shattered the peace as they flew directly over us. We dived for cover but the workmen perched on the scaffolding did not move. They raised their fists and cried Allah O Akbar. The old man in charge greeted us by stroking Mohammed Akbar's beard and then kissing his hand. It was the second time he had had to rebuild his home and he seemed to revel in the task. It was his act of defiance.

'The communists must never be allowed to believe they can change Afghanistan even by destroying it,' he said.

Throughout the valley the rubble of the bombed-out homes was being turned into bricks, moulded in wooden frames and baked in the sun. They were for the new homes. You saw no remorse or bitterness, only the shared pride of a common task in hand and the satisfaction of applied craftsmanship.

The old man walked with us to the house where we were to have lunch. He said that Lenin, on his deathbed, had said to the Russian people: 'If you want the West then you must invade Afghanistan. From there you can have a warm water port and then the West will be yours.' The sprightly old man recited the tale as if he had been present to hear Lenin's words. We walked within half a kilometre of the communist post but none of the Mujahiddin took any notice of it. It was a cuckoo in the nest.

Hezb raised taxes based on the Zakat laid down in the *Qoran*. This was usually about ten per cent of what a farmer produced but many gave more. The money was used to feed the Mujahiddin who received no pay. Many of the fighters were part time, working on the land and breaking off to form patrols or, best of all, go raiding. This amorphous quality of the organisation was a reflection of male Afghan society where a man will suddenly abandon his work when a friend happens by and take off with him for some distant village. Local government in the valley was run on traditional lines with a jirga which debated policy and made arrangements for communal undertakings such as irrigation. The jirgas comprised village elders, imams and senior members of the party and, while debate was vigorous, there was something in the Afghan character which strived for concensus above simple victory by a majority. Perhaps it was the knowledge that grievances left to fester could become the heart of violence. Paradoxically, the Afghans who at times appeared to revel in conflict would exert themselves to the limit to avoid it. It was a sure knowledge of themselves that made such gatherings vital.

I asked about a story that I had heard that there had been large-scale defections from Hezb the year before because the party had been too demanding of the population. Not surprisingly they denied this and in my travels I found no evidence to support it. The party organised primary education almost exclusively along *Qoranic* lines although in a few areas other subjects were taught. The party guaranteed law and order although the Pushtunwali tends to exert a self-regulating order on the people. Again one sensed that it was the Afghans' own understanding of their own inner anarchy which made the code so binding. It safeguarded them from themselves. The party also provided courts and judges trained in *Qoranic* law. Punishments such as amputation of a limb for theft or stoning to death for adultery were stern deterrents and the impression was that there was very little crime.

We had just finished lunch when the door of the garden burst open and a man clutching his belly collapsed among us. While several Mujahiddin examined the gaping wound, others were dispatched by the village sub-commander to apprehend the assailant. They slipped the safety catches off their rifles and set off. The wounded man was tended by the Mujahiddin, most of whom of necessity had a working knowledge of first aid. Our host was mainly concerned that I, as his guest, should have been upset by such a vulgar display and came and sat next to me and engaged me in cheerful conversation. I told him that I was not offended and he explained that it was a long-standing dispute over farmland. He said that the dispute could hopefully be resolved before a jirga without the judges. Provided the wounded man lived, he said, nodding at the man groaning among the empty rice platters. He, like many Afghans I met, was deeply shocked at such individual acts of violence. The conventions designed to avoid it had failed and it was as though a mirror had been lifted to their faces.

My inflamed toe and the repetitive miseries of dysentery had left me feeling weak, but I felt it was time to move north to Nijrob. Ahmedi sought to persuade me to stay and looked sad when I insisted on leaving. I had grown to like this grave man. He had a wistful side and a curiosity about the world beyond Afghanistan. Like many Afghans his primary delight was in the world about him; each day meant joys renewed. He approached everything with freshness and simplicity. He took me by the hand one day and led me to a spot high in the hills where an icy spring rose in a fissure in the rocks to form a translucent pool of pure mountain water. He had ordered great baskets of mulberries to be borne up the slopes after us. Now they were washed in the pool and tipped out into little purple and white heaps on partouks. You could feel the warmth of his pleasure at this simple treat for a guest. Then he suddenly announced that he would personally escort me for the two days it would take to walk to the northern boundaries of Tagob. I was happy at the prospect of his company and he radiated delight at my pleasure. He abandoned his business to his sub-commanders and after many warm handshakes, we set off with a small armed escort. We passed from village to village and slept on the platforms called sufas beneath the stars.

In the clearings throughout the valley wheat was being winnowed by methods unchanged for centuries: bullocks yoked together were driven round and round in circles with the wheat beneath their hoofs and a pall of wheaten dust through which the knots of farm boys who watched were transformed into impressionistic smudges. Occasionally a sound like a distant and persistent throb of a great ship's engines would herald the approach of gunships but they rarely passed low or close.

One night as we lay beneath a spreading tree whose leaves ran down against the starlit sky like green streams, we were joined by a villager who presented Ahmedi with a letter in Persian. The commander sat and read it and said a few words to the villager who was invited to stay for dinner. He had arrived with the air of a supplicant but slowly relaxed. Ahmedi said the man had run the village shop and had lost everything in an air raid. His petition had asked for money to start his business again. His request would be raised before a jirga and Ahmedi expected some money could be found. As we relaxed in the warm night air, Ahmedi turned and asked:

'Tell me, the West has now seen what a poor nation whose people are driven by Islam can do against a super power. Why don't all the people in the West become Muslims when they see that power?'

He was perfectly serious and puzzled by the absence of mass conversion. To the Afghans, their country was the centre of a titanic struggle between Islam and atheistic communism. It was the central and abiding issue of the world. I did not have the heart to tell him how remote his country was in the minds of people in the West, illuminated only by Kiplingesque mythology and, briefly, by the Russian invasion. I asked if it was not possible for

Muslims and Christians to respect one another's faiths instead of dreaming conversion and universalism? He remained politely and eloquently silent. Anyway, I knew the answer. The Jews and the Christians, according to the Prophet Mohammed, were people 'of the book', believers in one God, and to be respected and certainly tolerated. Yet Islam remains a faith utterly sure of itself and its universal destiny. As the last and greatest revelation of God's word, it was the inexorable fate of all men to submit. No matter how close you felt you had become to an Afghan, in the final analysis you always suffered from this distance. Islam was the common denominator and the template from which all things were made. Inherent in every relationship in my travels was this central pathos.

Tagob narrows at its northernmost boundary and ends abruptly with a steep and barren escarpment which led to the network of fertile valleys that composed Nijrob. At the limits of Tagob the streams gushed through every available gulley in noisy profusion. We climbed the sweltering escarpment with its surface of flaked rock and took one last look at the vastness of Tagob, so cool and green and vanishing into the heat haze. Then we set off across the rice fields of Nijrob. Farmers waved or dropped their tools and came to talk or offer tea. In Afghanistan, arriving was as pleasurable as parting was poignant.

My escort left me in the company of Mujahiddin we met sitting in the shade of a large tree. The new group bade me sit while tea and an interpreter were fetched. A letter of passage from Ahmedi to the commander of Nijrob, Hashmatullah Khan, was passed on. 'France?' they asked. Loyalties were always established first. 'Nay, Inglestan,' I replied. 'Doctor?' French doctors had a noble record of volunteering their services to help the Mujahiddin who were desperately short of medical expertise. 'Nay, journalist.' A look of comprehension spread. 'Ah BBC. BBC London,' they cried in imitation of the announcer on the World Service Persian Service. 'Nay BBC,' I ventured but it was useless. The truth had been established. Henceforth when I was not referred to as Mista or Inglestan I was known as BBC.

Afghans tend to appear rather like mushrooms do – suddenly and without warning. They excite the same delight and fascination, as if their appearance had something to do with the fairies. Abdul Ghanim, my new interpreter and companion, joined us under the tree. He was not a commander but he was literate and educated, qualities held in high regard in a country where the great majority cannot read or write. He was small and businesslike and a bit of a fusspot. I must see everything in Nijrob, he announced. 'Now we go.' He clamped a leather briefcase under his arm and set off briskly, pausing only for a moment to commandeer a Kalashnikov which he slung over his shoulder before disappearing into the trees.

Nijrob is composed of seven long valleys radiating from a fertile plain. It is like a splayed hand with two extra digits. In the centre of the 'palm' is the large village of Badakshi where the only communist post of the district is

Communist post, Nijrob.

located. Like Tagob everything else is under the control of the Mujahiddin. The post is a token blemish on the landscape. Though it is only a few hundred metres higher than Tagob it is cooler and in the summer the climate is perfect. The reason is the snow-capped mountains towering over the valleys to the north-east. Beyond this formidable barrier is Panjshir, for long the focus of the war, though no longer.

If anybody in the West had heard of any of the Mujahiddin leaders it was Masood in the Panjshir. The closer I came to Panjshir, a huge valley which runs for 90 kilometres to the north-east in the shadow of the Hindu Kush, the more it dominated the conversation. Yet diplomacy ruled: Masood was a commander with Jamiat-i-Islami, one of the other major resistance groups, and principal rivals of Hezb. Beyond the purple and white peaks began Jamiat territory.

The subject dominated the talk in the simple and comfortable guest room at the home of a farmer. But the men spoke only in Persian, and if I ventured a thought on the subject the conversation tended to die among polite smiles and evasion. Though Masood was an obsession among the Mujahiddin, officially he was an unperson.

The room was a model for guest rooms in all Afghan homes. It was lined with mattresses and bright cushions and lit with a single hurricane lamp which shed just enough light to render everything indistinct. In one corner was a great pile of colourful quilts and blankets, the sort which were fashionable in smart London shops. The single window sometimes had glass in it and sometimes plastic sheeting and sometimes nothing. In the front line villages glass was too dangerous. The ceiling was made of wooden rafters, often with a bees nest in one corner. There might be cotton curtains and sometimes a cotton print sheet hung on a wall to add colour. Decoration was rare. More usually there was a party poster: Gulbuddin Hekmatyar shaking hands with an Iranian Mullah, a calligraphic maze of Persian characters rendering a verse of the *Qoran,* or photographs of the Shaheed as the heads of poppies in a field of flowers. Gaudy propaganda, no more subtle than anybody else's. War is the one time when political leaders genuinely want to communicate in a language they think will be understood. The crudity of propaganda is eloquent testimony to contempt on high. By the door a dozen pairs of sandals. On the floor a spitoon shaped like a chalice. Its nickname is a 'Babrak' after the communist leader.

The Mujahiddin asked me the by now familiar questions about Christianity: was Isa the son of God; how many wives could a Christian take? The divorce laws of the West. Muslim men can divorce a wife if for instance she fails to bear him a son. He does it by merely repeating three times 'I divorce thee'. My companions simply did not believe me when I said that Western women had a greater say in marriage and divorce. If they believed any of it, it only confirmed their doubts about the sanity of the West.

'Mista, listen to me,' began Abdul Ghanim with the formality of the classroom of old, 'this man asks who do you think were the good rulers of Afghanistan.'

All eyes turned to me as I said the two nineteenth-century leaders Dost Mohammed and Abdur Rahman. A tall, thin man squinted at me through spectacles and shook his head. These men were traitors to Afghanistan, he declared. Agents of the British. I protested that skill in diplomacy when dealing with a mighty power on the border did not make them agents, but I found no sympathy for the argument. To treat with the foreigner was enough. There is a powerful streak of xenophobia which runs through the Afghan character which may be because most peoples of the world have invaded them at some time. I asked him who the Afghans celebrate as great leaders and he replied Mahmud of Ghazni and Babur. It was an insight into the ambitions and dreams of the Afghans and how they see themselves. I found a fascinating uniformity about the esteem that the old empire builders were held in. They were the masters of great empires and each had conquered north India. Dost Mohammed and Abdur Rahman had merely succeeded in consolidating power over what is now Afghanistan but Babur and Mahmud had a questing urge which took them far beyond the boundaries of the country. I found that the hearts of many Afghans remain with these visionaries. More than that: many Afghans simply do not recognise the borders of their country. And not just because they were drawn by British and Russian boundary commissioners. The reality of history to the Afghans is the glory of ancient empires and the business of the present is how to re-establish the ancient boundaries. This ambition lingers not just among a few dreamers. It is as though Englishmen still harboured designs on America.

'We do not accept borders made by imperialists,' said the thin man. 'Muslims will decide their own borders.'

But it does not end there. To the north in what is now the central Asian 'republics' of the Russian empire lie the ancient cities of Bokhara and Samarkand, once renowned centres of Islamic civilisation. To the Afghans it is self-evident that once they have driven the Russians out of their country they must seek to liberate these Muslim cities. By the time that intelligent men are talking about an eventual march on Moscow, you are convinced that ambition and reality have parted company. Later you see a man of 80 whose son has been killed come to offer his services to the party, see men take on gunships armed only with automatic rifles and Mujahiddin laughing casually as the bullets whizz by, and all in a country where such acts are commonplace. It is a land of fabulous half-crazed dreams yet suddenly you begin to doubt the iron precepts of global politics.

'Eeena,' said the young Mujahid after careful examination of my bad toe. 'No thank you. I'll limp.'

I rejected the herbal solution to my bad feet which had made the toe worse. My feet were still bright orange. It was painful to walk for the first ten minutes but then the pain eased and you could enjoy the ever-blue sky and the pure cool air which drifted off the peaks. Like Tagob, the valleys of Nijrob had an abundance of fruit trees fed by countless bubbling streams which were brought progressively under control by simple and ingenious irrigation schemes as you passed down the valleys. Also like Tagob, Nijrob had been briefly overrun by the Russian spring offensive in which an armoured column had pushed to the heads of several valleys. Unlike Tagob, here I did not believe the casualty figures I was given nor the claims about vehicles destroyed. I did not blame Abdul Ghanim for lying to distort a picture perceived as unfavourable to the Mujahiddin but neither did I respect the lack of subtlety in the fabrications. Truth may be the first casualty in war but Afghanistan was setting new standards in creative propaganda. The wild and inspired imagination of the Afghans ran riot with statistics but you were able to build a reasonably accurate picture by a tedious process of continuous cross-checking. The broad truth was that the Afghans had taken a beating in the spring and when I suggested this to Abdul Ghanim he sulked and then announced we must set off for Dera Ghous, the central valley.

After two days' walking he and the Mujahiddin proudly displayed the remains of a gunship shot down the year before. It was also a part of that broad truth that no matter how many Mujahiddin were lost in the fighting, it was only a matter of weeks before the local commanders were back up to strength. Further, the Russians did not stay but pulled back to their bases

The remains of a helicopter gunship.

and, as they withdrew, the Mujahiddin resumed control of the territory.

We dozed under trees on a grassy plateau above the valley after cake and tea. The cake had been a special treat as I had noticed for the first time that I had developed a sweet tooth. Perhaps it was the body signalling a need for sugar to convert to energy during the long walks through the valleys. Then several Mujahiddin appeared with baskets full of mulberries and plums. It was a peaceful interlude when the sun was at its highest and I read *A Midsummer Night's Dream* in a world momentarily as enchanting as that splendid fiction.

> Be kind and courteous to this gentleman.
> Hop in his walks and gambol in his eyes;
> Feed him with apricocks and dewberries,
> With purple grapes, green figs and mulberries.

War is an ultimate refinement of reality and yet it was hard to perceive anything but the remotest suggestion of conflict: talk, a distant gunship, a pink scar proudly displayed. The communists stayed hidden in their posts. Theirs was a military position as absurd as their ideology had become in intellectual terms. The self-fulfilling fallacy: the totem for little gods, their ideas mangled by cant and tyranny.

Time drifted by pleasantly as we walked from village to village gathering stories about the war, and always the host more concerned about the simple comfort of his guest. A dour old householder produced an enormous jar with just a trace of honey at the bottom and sat patiently for twenty minutes while the viscous liquid drifted down the glass so that I might have something sweet to dip my bread into. In the midst of this hospitality you knew that countless tens of thousands of Afghans had died for their faith and their country. A reverie in the Arcadian charm of the valleys, where youths would burst into song or recite Persian poetry, was troubled by thoughts of how the Russians had systematically destroyed whole villages.

A great figure of a man was climbing the slopes, like a great ramshackle galleon before shifting winds. He was followed by thirty Mujahiddin. He might be Little John with all the gentleness and simplicity and strength of romantic legend. You knew he was Hashmatullah Khan who commanded the valleys you had been walking. You knew it was him by the *frisson* of anticipation which electrified the men and there was no doubt when he seized your hand and embraced you like a friendly bear. He laughed all of the time, too much in a land burdened with misery. He loved to lounge beneath the trees in the sun where he would read the petitions brought to him by the villagers, and he tended to nod off when the elders waxed tedious, his great black beard resting on a barrel chest. He was not a great orator as Ahmedi had been. He merely woke up, stretched his enormous boyish features into a look of boredom and mumbled his decision before leaving the elders who set about reading into his words far more than he had intended. He did not care for that side of the job but he rumbled around the villages all the same and attended to the needs of the community, most of which seemed to fill him with a mixture of alarm and despondency. Written work was mostly left in the hands of an aide to whom he would dictate the first line or two before throwing up his hands and telling him to get on with it. But there was no doubt that Hash Khan was adored by his men and the people just as the patrician Ahmedi was venerated. Besides, no man became a senior commander unless he had the absolute respect of his men as a fearless warrior. That was an old truth in Afghanistan.

I had resolved to move on to Kohistan – I was already behind on my schedule for Bamian – but Hash Khan would have none of it. Ahmedi had given me a length of fine cloth to be made into a suit of clothes as a farewell present. Hash Khan gave an order for a tailor to be summoned. The obsequious tailor duly appeared, I was measured up and he was dispatched with the cloth.

'Now you will stay for two days. Then you go wearing new clothes,' boomed Hash Khan and led me through a doorway barely wide enough to take his huge frame. 'Business,' he added sullenly and sat down at the head of a great gathering inside the mosque.

He presided over the meeting called to decide a dispute in which a love-match had been ended by the bride-to-be's father. He had withdrawn his consent to the marriage after a sudden change of mind over the suitability of the bridegroom. First the old one-eyed father spoke in passionate terms about the young man's lack of virtue, even casting doubts on his qualities as a good Muslim. You sensed that it was a pack of lies and at the heart of the matter was pride and the ownership of women. Hash Khan grunted a few times and smiled lamely through the gap in his teeth before succumbing to the stifling heat of the mosque. The young man was simple and direct. He said the bride price had been agreed, the wedding arrangements fixed and he had the means to keep the woman. Hash Khan woke up on cue to listen to deliberations of the elders and the imams. When they had reached their decision, Hash Khan bluntly told the old man he had lost the case and to accept the decision philosophically. As he did so he could not resist making a joke about the case and roaring with laughter. The old man flew into a screaming rage and then burst into tears and spent ten minutes by turns oathing and weeping, before falling to the ground in a catatonic trance. Throughout this performance the commander sat looking faintly bemused and apprehensive.

Hash Khan waved goodbye and set off down the dusty path surrounded by his men. He had business to attend to in another valley and would return in a couple of days Inshallah. Earlier he had been reading a letter from the communist commander at the post.

'This man writes to me and offers money if I make peace. Communists spend all their time writing letters. I am not a Masood.' Masood in the Panjshir had signed a temporary truce with the Russians, but the motives of the man the French newspapers called the Afghan Tito remained unclear. 'When communists write to me and say "join us" we attack their post that night. It is better than writing to them.' Hash Khan careered out of sight through the trees.

My toe ached like hell and I realised that the nail would have to come off to ease the pressure. That unwelcome truth had come to me while watching a group of Mujahiddin in the valley. One had dislocated his shoulder and two of his companions were working it back into place. The hurt man made no sound though rivulets of sweat poured from his brow. The others sat about comparing guns and drinking tea and took no notice of the unfolding drama. The man was in great pain but he showed only a slight grimace as his shoulder was worked back into place and a minute later he was engrossed in conversation as if nothing had happened. Medical help was largely a matter of do-it-yourself and improvisation, I realised as I limped along behind Abdul Ghanim.

As soon as we arrived at the house where we were to stay for the night I took myself off to the stream and found a secluded spot in the shadow of a vine-covered bluff. Inevitably word travelled faster than I could secrete myself and a dozen young boys materialised on the other bank to watch 'Inglestan' pull his toenail off. They squatted in silence as I eased my boots and socks off and their silent nods suggested that the wound was worthy of their attention. Their gaze flickered between my expression and the job at hand as I gingerly prized the blackened nail from its bed of mangled flesh before numbing the foot in the icy water. I had managed to remain expressionless more from shock than stiff upper lip and the gang of little boys seemed to approve. It was the Afghan way.

Then they disappeared and I decided to strip off and treat myself to a comprehensive wash. Only when I was standing naked and examining the protruding bones where the ravages of dysentery and poor diet told most, did it occur to me why the boys had scattered. It was the time of day for the women to come to the stream and collect water. They wandered down the path in a long line, bearing brown clay pitchers, buckets and giant blackened kettles. In their billowing tent-like chadors and veils, some brightly coloured and others black, they seemed like an odd assortment of voluble ghosts. I applied all the resourcefulness of a man in a desperate situation, which is to say that panic prompted me to plunge headlong into the deepest part of the icy stream and begin singing in the unrestrained tones of one who believes he is alone. To my horror the women set to work filling their containers just 20 metres away, their incessant chatter punctuated by giggles. After all it was their time of the day to be at the stream. There was nothing for me to do but to go on singing in louder and more desperate tones and to contemplate my shrinking manhood in the icy drift.

Abdul Ghanim contemplated the scene with horror and shooed the women away like a flock of chickens. Then he scolded me but the effect was lost as his eyes kept straying to where chaps are normally identified as such but which in my case had taken on the appearance of neutral ground. At best a button mushroom. It was then that the shelling began. First tracer flashed by very low towards the other side of the valley. If you looked in the direction it came from the angle of observation gave a slow, almost lazy and aesthetic appearance. Then the shells began to explode on the other side of the valley. Machine gun fire could be heard nearby and it dawned on me how close the communist post was. Hash Khan was delivering letters.

'Mista. Come now. We must run.' The disembodied and urgent voice emanated from behind a tree. It was Abdul Ghanim.

'Go to hell. I can't get my clothes on and I'm not running around bollock naked for anyone.' My hands were so frozen from the water that I could not dress myself, so I wrapped them in the thermal underwear I carried and sheltered in a recess in the bluff. As the shells thumped into the far side of Dera Ghous, Abdul Ghanim's pleading became more insistent.

'Mista, mista, come now. You will be killed.'

I reckoned it highly unlikely. Abdul Ghanim dispatched a Mujahid who appeared around the bluff, apparently under orders to march me off at gunpoint if necessary. He was a large middle-aged man with a shaved head and bucolic features who, judging from his expression, was not sure what to expect from the recalcitrant Inglestan. All the unflappability of a man of the land showed in his face: a brief hoisting of the eyebrows. He lowered his ancient 303 and crouched down in a recess next to mine, his back to the rock face, knees up under his chin. The strangled sounds coming from behind the tree suggested that Abdul Ghanim was in pain. My new-found companion calmly shouted in Persian that we were staying put. He too put dignity first and tossed his partouk over for me to wrap myself in. There was a groan of despair from behind the tree and Abdul Ghanim disappeared into the night. Sufficient life returned to my hands to enable me to offer my companion a cigarette. He accepted and we sat out the bombardment smoking in silence.

The man introduced himself as Juma Gul and, when I had dressed, he led the way to the house where we were to stay for the night. Abdul Ghanim did not appear – terrified I might further shame him – but a cheerful old imam did. He had studied the *Qoran* for twenty years and, in his late 30s, the village had invited him to be their imam. His duties were to teach young boys the verses of the *Qoran* and their meaning. He was the spiritual guide for the village. My host was proud that he had come to dinner. The interpreter was a young maths teacher who had joined the Mujahiddin when the communists came to power. One of the most substantial buildings in Nijrob had been the school, built by the government but now a ruin of stone and burned furniture. The teacher said that hundreds of schools had been attacked and destroyed when the government tried to introduce Marxist education. Outside of the towns and cities, education had virtually ceased to exist. The imam was curious about air travel and asked me questions about my journey to Pakistan: flight times, the height of the plane and aerodynamics. He asked me how long it took to fly from Europe to America and then west across America.

Then, through the teacher, he asked: 'Where does a plane go if it flies west from San Francisco?'

'Japan,' I ventured, but he did not believe it. Then it dawned on me that the imam was arguing that the earth was flat. It did not seem possible but nothing could shake his view. I suggested to the teacher that it was fruitless me arguing the point and that he should try. But he was reluctant, not because he was afraid of offending the imam but, he confessed, because in his heart he too believed the earth was flat. His scientific education was a matter of the mind. That same sense of despondency which had gripped me in the company of Engineer Imran in Peshawar returned, and for a moment I understood the frustrations which had driven people into the arms of the communists. Neither, I discovered, was the imam's medieval outlook an isolated case. Beneath the dreams and visions of these brave people there was a very flat earth.

The next day I set off at 5 am with Juma Gul and several Mujahiddin. At the lower end of the valley there was a patch of open ground less than a kilometre from the post which had a clear view across it. Farmers worked in the fields, oblivious to the danger from across the valley, but the Mujahiddin concealed their weapons under their partouks. We walked across in twos. The mountains on our side of the valley were scarred with artillery fire which was aimed at the trails. It was one of those days when the dysentery was unrelenting; a sharp signal in the bowels followed by a desperate rush to shelter. As I crossed the open ground I felt the urgency of the moment and, as I dipped behind a mound of earth, the first shells crashed into the mountain above us. The Mujahiddin scattered and Juma Gul waved frantically from behind a tree. But nothing could move me and I squatted in resignation as the shells whispered overhead. Afterwards, when I had sprinted across the rest of the open ground, the Mujahiddin congratulated me on my nerve.

'Inglestan a Mujahid,' exclaimed one.

'Inglestan taken short.'

It was my last night in Nijrob. I felt a pressing need to move on in spite of the pleasant days I had spent in the orchards and villages. But the illness refused to abate and had become a little demoralising. I think I concluded that to go on would make the possibility of turning back that much more impractical. Juma Gul said very little but took his duties as escort very seriously. He managed to find some toilet paper.

We stopped at a home and the village dignitaries turned out: the imam, the sub-commander and the professional classes. The imam liked his food and ate the meal of meat and soup heartily. He had a soft bushy white beard and spent the evening telling me how successive governments had jailed him without trial. It was already a familiar story. The knock on the door in the middle of the night; picked up off the streets by men in an unmarked car. The stories were told without embellishment and almost without reproach. It was almost as though these were the accepted rules in a bitter game and the implication was that it worked both ways. That was the way of the Iranian Revolution: the destruction of one apparatus of terror which is replaced by another. The French Revolution. Besides martyrdom was an honour. The imams did not go into hiding in the cities when the communists came to power and their faith was a direct challenge. In the early days the communists had tolerated them, believing that their textbook reforms would circumscribe the power of the clergy: a benevolent secularism would show the way forward. It was a misjudgement by the communists and the early persecution of a few activist imams became a widespread terror against the clergy and the population as a whole. I always asked survivors of the political prisons if they had ever been charged with a crime or put on trial. Many regarded it as an odd question. They were Muslims and that was enough. They fully understood the terrible logic of the fight to the death and always they told the same story of brutality in a matter of fact, even casual, way.

I asked this imam, with his clear brown eyes and shy gaze, why he thought he had been jailed for seven months in the times of Daoud.

'I was in Mazar-i-Sharif in the bazaar. I was with 200 imams at a meeting. Into the bazaar came some communists. They were giving propaganda to the people which said that Islam was bad. So we stoned them to death.'

'Oh.'

8

Tomtits and Emus

The bull-headed Mujahid youth held up the lizard skin and a look of contempt creased his ugly features. His head had been shaved but a shadow of stubble had returned so that he looked like an English skinhead. His light blue clothes, like denim, and huge Russian army boots heightened the effect.

'Mista,' he grunted, 'Russians eat this.' The other half dozen youths laughed in an unpleasant way, as though they had found a form of life lower than themselves.

They were all in their middle and late teens and once away from the discipline of the commanders they let their hooligan instincts rule. They were my escort on the day's march to Kohistan and I could find no saving grace between them. At first I had been like a plaything to them; someone to ply with endless questions about trivia. But they grew bored and preferred to try to trip me over or throw stones at me. That was when they were not shooting off their guns into the endless loneliness of the barren hills through which we passed. Bull-head threw the lizard skin into my face and thought it a grand joke. Tomtits!

The switchback hills were criss-crossed with tank tracks and littered with cartridges from some old battle. It seemed incredible that the Mujahiddin should choose such ground to fight on. There was no cover and the terrain was ideal for fast-moving tanks and APCs. Here the Russian BMP carrier with its 73mm gun, missile launchers and troops able to fire on the move, was lethal. It can reach speeds of 40 kph. The vehicle proved a disaster in the 1973 Middle East war but that was against strong defences. In Afghanistan the only weapon against the BMP were RPGs and the Mujahiddin needed cover to ambush them. In the hills there was none. It was a dismal place after the green of Nijrob. Nothing grew there and there was no shade from the relentless sun. We passed many sites where the Russians had camped. By the fires were blackened ration cans and many skins of the large lizards. The idea of eating the lizards appalled the Afghans and they pointed to the habit as evidence of the inherent barbarism of the invader.

The only thing that broke the monotony of the landscape were great donkey trains carrying fertiliser to Nijrob and Tagob whose gardens were modelled on Kashmir. As Bull-head burst into the droning racket he called song, I wished that I was back in Nijrob even though the women did not like men with beards. This odd piece of intelligence had come from Juma Gul. It was odd because 90 per cent of Afghan men wear beards – it is 'the way' of Mohammed. (They seemed bemused that an Englishman should wear one for decoration.) I had hoped that Juma Gul was going to be my escort, but this group of unruly youngsters who hailed from Kohistan had offered to guide me. I had grown to like Juma Gul for his pragmatism and simple uncluttered dignity. I had wanted to get close to the government post in Nijrob and that last morning he offered to take me despite warnings that it was hazardous. The first view had been from a ruined house but we left hurriedly after I dislodged a wooden door and came face to face with three twisted skeletons. So we wormed across fields on our bellies and hid behind a screen of saplings by an irrigation channel. Between us and the perimeter fence was 300 metres of open ground. Inside the camp were lines of neat huts and paths which radiated out to camouflaged gun emplacements and tanks dug up to their turrets. The guns appeared to be D-30s, similar to the one captured by Ahmedi. The tanks appeared to be T-55s. Juma Gul's normally placid countenance gave way to some excitement as we crouched by the stream and watched distant figures running between the huts and the guns. They always ran, said Juma Gul. Fear. He had been on many attacks against

The road to Kohistan: a flag marking the graves of the Shaheed (martyrs) and a village flattened by Russian bombers.

the post. They did not expect to be able to overrun the camp unless they had help from inside, but they were content to pick off a couple of communists at a time. The rest would always live with fear. Communists were frightened people, he said. It was no way for a man to live.

His favourite memory was of an attack shortly after the troops had cleared the ground around the camp which for months had provided cover for attacks. Mujahiddin brought shrubs and, concealed behind them, moved on to the open ground under cover of darkness. As dawn broke the troops found themselves under fire from a motley collection of moving bushes. Juma Gul sat with his back against a tree, his rifle propped up between his knees and chuckling softly.

'Until Great Birnam wood to high Dunsinane hill shall come . . .'. I explained the lines from *Macbeth* to Juma Gul, who said that Shakespeare must have been a great English Mujahid.

Juma Gul did not think much of the rabble from Kohistan. He found Bull-head poking his nose into my rucksack and scolded him. Bull-head gave me a surly and insolent stare and demanded I give him a present. I had found that the best way to deal with such youths was to read them the riot act from the start. If they thought you were angry they would usually behave themselves and go to great lengths to win back your favour. They would offer to carry your rucksack or press a piece of biscuit in your hand, but it was best to remain aloof. If you gave in too quickly it was a signal for them to begin the pestering and pranks again. Most were merely high-spirited and in need of constant discipline. They were really just good-natured and I always made a point of parting friends. Bull-head and his friends were of a different order. Juma Gul offered to come with us to Kohistan but I knew that his duties with me had already kept him from the harvest and I reluctantly declined.

We shared some rice and though I normally struggled to feed myself with my fingers like the Afghans, on this occasion I accepted the luxury of a spoon. Bull-head and the others jeered. Juma Gul came and sat next to me and produced a spoon with which he pointedly ate his meal. Outside a large gathering of Mujahiddin from the valleys of Nijrob had gathered to say farewell. There was Hash Khan, like Falstaff, and to my delight Mohammed Ali whose home was nearby. He insisted I stay with him for a week 'or a month or come and live for all times'. I promised that when I returned I would call on him and he looked sadder than ever.

I never did return that way, but now, as we sat where once the Russian troops had sat, I wished I had stayed or Juma Gul had journeyed with us. The dysentery forced me to stop every few kilometres which Bull-head thought a huge joke. The constant draining of the body left me exhausted and the heat was oppressive. I noticed during the march that instead of ignoring the tomtits I was actually provoking the constant arguments. It was a subconsciously deliberate attempt to generate the adrenalin to keep me going. Bull-head kicked the little blue and blackened ration tins down the hillside. I thought of the Russian troops and imagined them by the fires

Camel train passing through Kohistan village.

dreaming of home, Arcadian or real, in a cold and hostile night.

It was sunset when we came to the end of the hills and, ahead of us, hundreds of metres below in a great valley ran the Panjshir River in great glittering loops and bands like a geography lesson. We descended to the valley and plodded north. Behind us the river disappeared into a deep and narrow gorge on its journey to join the Kabul River at Sarobi.

We came to a seedy little village where the children ran about in ragged clothes. Afghanistan is a poor country but that is not a word the visitor thinks of to describe it. Poverty is a state of mind as well as a condition and in few places did you sense that emptiness of spirit. This village between the bare and dismal hills was an exception. An effeminate and unprepossessing character sat on a low wall and stared at me with that faraway expression that made the blood run cold. He was the village commander and he led us to a house. He struck me as a psychopath.

The tomtits were products of this rundown place with its air of brooding malevolence. Kohistan of legend has produced some of the tribesmen most given to warring. A raucous gathering pressed into the small and airless room. In all my travels I had never happened on a finer collection of cutthroats and pirates. It was far from the manners and peace of Nijrob or Tagob. The commander said nothing but sat next to me all evening, inches from my face staring until the nerves began to jangle. The rest degenerated into argument after eating greedily: they wrangled, wrestled and staggered from the room for air. Bull-head sat scowling at me from a far corner. An old dumb and wild-looking man sat before me waving his arms madly in a sign language even he did not understand. It was a sink of incomprehension and malice. Another Mujahid asked about religion and sneered at my answers. There was not the slightest interest; they merely wanted confirmation that I was a non-believer. A *kafir.* I succeeded in striking up conversation with a Mujahid who sat caressing his Kalashnikov. I asked him about the Unity.

'What Unity?' There is no inity in Afghanistan.' He gestured at random. 'I kill him or him or they kill me. Today we kill Russians together. Tomorrow . . . What unity?' His chilling reply ended the conversation.

The old man grabbed my arm and thrust a crude drawing into my hand. It was of a cow. These is little tradition of representational art in Islam and that was something else I missed. There is the ingenuity and complexity of calligraphic art but I missed drawings and paintings. The cave-man work of the old man – more a way of communicating than art – was all I ever saw. He wanted to know if we ate cow in Inglestan. I nodded and the drawing was passed around and studied by the light of the hurricane lamp. The old man set to work feverishly and each time he had finished a drawing he would thrust it at me and make frantic eating motions.

'Yes, we eat sheep . . . no we do not eat snake.'

Then he carefully drew a picture of a pig – taboo meat in Islam – and presented it to me. Everyone pressed forward to await the reply but I would not be lured into this trap and pretended I thought it another sheep. Yes, we eat sheep, I said, as they added more and more porcine features to the beast. It was still a sheep, I insisted. Bull-head cleared his throat loudly and spat out of the door.

The commander came out of his trance and ordered a Persian-English dictionary be brought to him. The little book had its origins in New Zealand and he now absorbed himself in it for the next hour. At length he spoke.

'Mista in Inglestan you eat emu?'

Then his eyes glazed over again and he resumed staring at me. It was one of the few times in the country that I feared for my safety among the Afghans. The Pushtunwali was thin ice here. They did not seem to care for anyone or anything. When at length the room finally cleared I lay down on a mattress. Only Bull-head and the commander remained and the latter stretched out, again his face only inches away from mine like some demented lover. He came up with his second gem: 'Mista, you know that 60 years ago Afghans fight the British. We kill many British.' I said rather lamely that that was all in the past and he smiled distantly. 'Many, many British.' I was convinced that the very least I could expect from the commander were homosexual advances in the night. I was so unnerved that when I went out to attend to my ablutions I found a bottle, broke it to the neck and concealed it beneath my pillow. That night I only pretended to be asleep. Each time I glanced at the commander by the light of the moon, he was still awake staring into space. Bull-head slept deeply, in some dim recess of humanity out of which the species escaped long ago.

I could not get away from that desperate place quick enough and, despite feeling ghastly, insisted on leaving at first light. The commander announced that when I returned he would join me on the journey to Pakistan and from there I must take him to Inglestan. I smiled. I would surrender to the Russians before I returned that way.

My escorts changed at each village as we moved through the valley. After the company of such desperate characters, any companions had to be an improvement and they were. Ahmed the shopkeeper who explained why killing Russians was preferable to selling vegetables; Samaludin whose degree course in agriculture had been ended by the war; Nazir whose leg had been blown off in an air raid yet who still managed to outpace me with his artificial limb. The dusty road rose above the valley which now broadened out and became more fertile. There were tanks and APCs burned out by the road and in each case nothing but the shell was left. The Afghans strip everything out of vehicles and find some use for it. Nasir clambered up the rocky cliff above the road and showed me favourite ambush points where the convoys had been attacked. Nasir was disappointed because the Russians had long given up the area. The Russians had been so stupid they had fallen for the same ambush every time; boulders rolled down the mountain to block the road followed by RPG attacks.

'The Russians are donkey people. Allah O Akbar,' he cried and his voice carried across the valley where farmers looked up from their work and waved.

I heard about how, when the Russians were active in the area, the gunships would suddenly appear over the mountains, land and the troops rob people of money and clothes. Dear God, low tobies from the air. It seemed inconceivable in this death struggle that such curiously petty acts could take place, yet the stories were common.

'Keep travelling north my friend,' said the old farmer who had shared his lunch of bread and fruit with us as we sheltered from the sun behind great boulders. 'There you will find the fighting. Then you will know what we do with these robbers.'

To travel north was fully my intention but each day the march became more arduous. The sickness was costing me hours of lost sleep. I was being drained of energy and I reckoned I had lost two stone. Mosquitoes plagued you at night and bit through the thickest cloth. The bites turned bad and became open sores which refused to heal. By day, flies swarmed over you and under your clothing to feed on the sores. As someone who had always enjoyed perfect health it was especially hard. The keep-fit programme I had worked at in England seemed a mockery. Progress slowed. Each time we rested I fell into a desperate sleep and at times the Mujahiddin found it difficult to wake me. The valley broadened so that the mountains became distant and hazy. I tried to resist water from the streams but my body had become so drained of fluid that I had a permanent unquenchable thirst and fell to drinking greedily.

We moved from little grey village to village, each time my escort changing and the commander writing out a fresh letter of passage. Helicopters and jets were often overhead and the villagers would speculate where they were bound. North. Sometimes I would stay for a day to try to recover strength but I could sense a crisis was at hand. Somewhere in the valley I collected hepatitis, perhaps in one of the houses of the wounded.

'We must fight the US imperialism as well as the Russians. In Iran they fight the imperialism, here we fight the communism. Iranian Muslims are true brothers.' The solemn party ideologue was an ex-student of Kabul University. Hezb seemed to hold powerful sway over the intellectuals and middle classes. Among its followers were an abundance of students, teachers, engineers and other professional people. Among them, Afghan xenophobia was elevated to a crude delineation of the world into Western imperialists, Godless communists and corrupt Muslim countries which seemed to cover every Islamic nation bar Afghanistan and Iran. There were not many good guys. References to 'Western imperialism' were universal though few seemed able to define what they meant when I challenged them. I found myself at odds with the Mujahiddin when they talked blithely of the imperialists and of the 'Islamic revolution' they were fighting. To the world this was a war of resistance but not to members of Hezb. It was the Islamic revolution and they would go to great lengths to prove that this pure struggle had begun long before the Russian invasion. It added legitimacy to their claims to power. To me they had merely hijacked a war of resistance through semantic corruption. Argument was futile. They viewed the world from the impregnable fortress of Islam and the world had little to commend it. They were impervious to contradiction and their sanctity became irritating. There was too much self-righteous cant for you to feel sympathy for their cause beyond ridding their country of the Russians. You clung to admiration for their bravery and sacrifice. The sympathy came when you talked of ordinary things to peasants and farmers. The hacks and the ideologues were ruthlessly uncompromising in their view of a world without subtlety. If I regarded their cant as no better than the polemic of the third form then I had to admit that perhaps only such fanatical dogma could successfully take on the pitiless ideology of Russian communism.

In this oral culture, where communication was almost exclusively by word of mouth, human contact was constant and unremitting. Food and sleep were communal affairs and this, and a world in which original thought was regarded as heresy, led to a feeling of claustrophobia. It was compounded by illness, so that the quality of a day could be altered by the slightest thing: a chance meeting or some gesture of kindness.

We halted in a village and I was taken to a shady garden where I fell into a feverish sleep. I woke to find my escorts had gone and a gathering of new faces gazing at me inquisitively. The commander was a dashing and handsome type and his men cheerful and friendly.

'Now we go to the river and wash our bodies. Then we have the games,' announced the commander. And off we went through the woods and fields to the River Panjshir. There were about fifty Mujahiddin and they hung their rifles and RPG launchers in the trees before stripping off. The water was a blessed relief in the blazing heat and the men allowed themselves to be swept downstream by the current, whooping and laughing. It was a scene from a golden age: Robin Hood and his Merry Men, fighting a just cause in which they would never die. We dried off in the sun and then in a little grove the 'games' began.

'Worsay,' announced the commander as we lay in our underpants on the grass. The men began to hop about on one foot and to charge each other to the ground. The one who remained standing was the winner. It was an eruption of fun and chaos and the air was filled with shouts and cheers. The war, now quite close, receded in the imagination further than ever and you were filled with an unabashed happiness of the sort which seems to have been lost to our Western culture. It was innocence.

I stayed the night at the home of one of the Mujahiddin and his old, deaf father. The house was enormous and built like a fort and everywhere was the four-leaf clover motif. Glazed ashtrays were shaped like it, and it provided the pattern for curtains and even the carvings on the window shutters. The Mujahid tenderly fed his father and kept him apace of our conversation by bellowing into his ear at which the old man would nod and gurgle in his dotage. Once he had been a renowned exporter of grapes but the trade had suffered with the war and the family now had to make-do with cut-price dealings with Pakistani merchants who were eager to exploit a buyers' market.

For days I had heard contradictory stories about fighting between Hezb and Jamiat Mujahiddin. The young man said there was fighting. Others, conscious of the adverse propaganda of fratricide among the Afghans, denied it. The fighting was justified by Masood's truce with the Russians, said the young man. Quite. But it was also fired by a deep envy that the Jamiat commander was the only name celebrated beyond Afghanistan. The Panjshir had been the heart of the war before the truce. Journalists had flocked to the court of Masood and French doctors to tend the wounded. The insolent egalitarianism of the Afghans contains at its heart a paradox. In a land where 'any man can be king' the very aspiration to greatness spawns a thousand rivals: where heroism is a commonplace, the idea that one commander should rise to such eminence bred not respect but violent jealousy and hatred.

Rebellion in the Panjshir predates the invasion by several years. There was an uprising in 1976 and by the time of Amin, just before the Russians swept in, an Islamic government had been proclaimed with its own judiciary and

In Afghanistan the young boys learn to handle weapons at an early age.

tax collectors. The Russians were initially preoccupied with sealing off the eastern provinces to stop the infiltration from Pakistan but they turned in late summer of 1980 to the Panjshir with the intention of clearing it out. That offensive was repelled and the Russians only got as far as Rokha about 30 kilometres up the valley. More than 150 villages were bombed but the Russians lost many troops (some put the figure at 1,500), at least thirty-five tanks and one gunship. They tried and failed to take the valley before the winter. The following spring they launched a new offensive but that too was repulsed, despite the deployment of crack mountain units. Again in 1982 they threw their might against Panjshir in an all-out attempt to overrun the valley which had become the focus of the war of resistance. Aerial bombardment was followed by gunship strikes against Masood's positions. Artillery fire was kept up throughout the nights to bludgeon the villagers into submission. There was strong evidence to show that the Russians were flying the jet strikes from their air base across the Amu Darya at Termez. There was extensive hand-to-hand fighting before the Russians finally withdrew in June. Panjshir was still in the hands of Masood and his Mujahiddin.

Then suddenly, in December, 1982, Masood signed a temporary truce with the Russians. Nobody was sure why although Masood claimed the Russians had asked for it. It was certainly useful to both sides: it gave Masood a

Cycle of violence: pedal power enables the Mujahiddin to move between villages near the front but crude roads mean frequent repairs.

chance to replenish food and ammunition stocks which were known to be short; and for the Russians it was a chance to deploy troops elsewhere. They had bought themselves temporary respite in the great tradition of Danegeld diplomacy with the tribes. Three years before I had been trying to cross the border independent of the major parties. With a single guide I had travelled north of Khyber through Mohmand territory. Though the Mohmands were initially friendly, one morning they suddenly forced us to return to Pakistan without giving us any reason. Later I discovered that at that time Radio Kabul had announced that the Mohmands were now loyal to the communists. That was a euphemism for the fact they had been temporarily bought off.

The Mujahiddin of Hezb and the other rivals of Jamiat said in public that it was disgraceful that Masood had signed the truce. In truth they were mostly delighted. Now they could accuse him of collusion, even of secretly being a communist. The only way the legend of Masood would be destroyed was at his own hand. He seemed to have obliged.

The truce between Masood and the Russians broke down in Spring, 1984 when the Russians launched yet another major offensive against Panjshir. For the first time in the war they used high level bombing raids to soften up Masood's positions before attacking the Jamiat chief with armoured columns which penetrated the Panjshir Valley at several points. Masood was forced into another tactical retreat.

The further north I travelled the more the venomous slander gave way to half-whispered stories that Hezb were fighting Jamiat. As we plodded along the straight and dusty road through fields of wheat and rice, my companions talked about Masood. The Mujahiddin listened to the BBC, about the only source of information they trusted outside of themselves. The only accusation of bias I heard against the BBC was over Masood. They were jealous over the many stories broadcast about Panjshir. I told them there was no bias; it was merely that the Panjshir had been the heart of the war. I said the BBC was independent but nobody believed it. Everyone and every organisation had its loyalties. There was no such thing as objectivity. You pledged yourself to some cause or some individual. The rest was conflict. But there was a further dimension to their hostility and I think that it was that the Mujahiddin recognised in the growth of Masood's power the history of their country. Could it be that Masood might grow so powerful that after the communists the mantle of power might fall on him? The assumption was that any post-communist government would be based on the political leadership of the resistance. But Afghanistan has a history of pre-eminent warriors welding the nation by force. Dost Mohammed, Abdur Rahman. The warrior statesman is a tradition as old as history.

Farid with his men: a legendary band.

'When Masood was fighting he fight only for himself. We fight for Islam and to make an Islamic republic,' insisted the Mujahid. 'Now you have met Ustoz Farid, a great commander. He hates Masood and goes to Bolerain to fight with Jamiat.'

It had been a curious encounter with one of the area's top commanders. His black hair and brown eyes were illuminated by a shy smile. He denied that he was Ustoz Farid yet I recognised him from his photographs. Perhaps it was the Afghan passion for mystery and intrigue or a reflection of the commander's dislike or distrust of the West. It was useless to challenge his deception. He was making preparations to lead another assault on Jamiat positions between Panjshir and Kohistan. He was feared by the Russians and at one time had conducted a feud with a fellow Hezb commander. He was a formidable fighter but that day he had chosen to deny his identity.

So where did this fratricide leave the Unity? The Unity had been imposed by Arab supporters who wanted to deal with a single coherent group in Peshawar. Translating it into reality inside Afghanistan was beyond the powers or ambition of the party leaders. Loyalty was not to Sayyaf, the leader of the Unity, but to the party chiefs. Real power remained with Hekmatyar, Younis Khalis and Rabbani. Lip service was paid to the Unity while war between some of the parties went on inside Afghanistan unabated.

My life swung like a pendulum from the fear and depression of an evening in the company of a psychopath to the innocent delight of an afternoon bathing. I was behind schedule in reaching Jebel Seraj and Abdul Ghafoor would be wondering where I had got to. But anticipation extended no further than waking up and hope was merely that you would not feel too ill. Days had the quality of a dream.

I met a mercenary who told a lot of lies not least of which was his name 'Dave'. He supplied arms to the resistance and had taken up an offer of a short tour 'to keep my hand in'. He spoke of the 'joy' of battle. He was just another character on the outskirts of life. He might have impressed in the bars of Hong Kong or Bangkok, but sitting by that dusty road he seemed tired and diminished. Now he was travelling back to Pakistan and his companions were anxious to move.

'I decided to get the hell out of this mess when half way up some goddam mountain the commander calmly tells me we're going to kill other Afghans. I told him he was out of his mind and to get me out of here. I tell you, these guys are in a league all of their own'.

There was something vaguely reassuring about a man with no allegiances taking exception to the contradictions of somebody else's war. The pendulum swung again and I found myself in the village of Jamalara in a cool garden eating grapes and waiting for Doctor Akhram. He was the village commander and appeared not with a Kalashnikov but with a little black bag. A deep and gentle river flowed through the village and wooden platforms with railings and public benches protruded from the banks. Here old men sat and talked and seemed to define the tranquil nature of the

village. The doctor was the commander for such a place. People would call him into their homes and he would stop and write prescriptions in the street. He was tall, handsome and shy and he had an air of fatalism in the face of impossible odds, yet it was tempered with dogged resilience. As long as he dwelt on the case in hand and not the hundreds waiting, he could cope.

What had been the little bazaar in the heart of the village was now rubble where gangs of men worked, rebuilding homes and shops. The very heart of Jamalara had been torn out: all of its little alleys led to this devastation, in which fifty people had been killed in spring. First the jets pounded it and then the gunships machine-gunned anything that moved.

Doctor Akhram led me to his large and unkempt house by the river. He lived alone and there was an air of solitude about the man and his house. He apologised for the untidy guest room. He was friendly and absent-minded. The house had an atmosphere as though once it had been a lively centre of social activity, cut short by personal unhappiness, and now the man did not seem to have the heart to try to restore it. While he treated the sores on my hands and legs with red tincture and iodine that burned, food was brought to eat. Over the meal of rice, potato and fruit, he said that he was one of twelve brothers: seven were Mujahiddin but the others were communists in Kabul. That was why the house had fallen on bitter times. I asked him the impossible question. Would he fight his brothers if he had to? He smiled sadly: he hoped

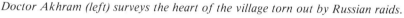

Doctor Akhram (left) surveys the heart of the village torn out by Russian raids.

117

Destruction at Jamalara.

it would not happen but, yes, he would. After dinner he gave me some tablets for the dysentery and a prescription to buy some more when I came across a pharmacy. He excused himself to go and make some calls in the evening. I was left with several Mujahiddin and an old man who spoke good German. He had worked in Switzerland and he leaned over like a conspirator.

'In Zurich I drink beer and wine. The Islamic revolution is a good thing but there will be no beer or wine,' he said.

The others were preparing to make a night march to one of the villages near the front and were hoping to see some action before dawn. They had already been marching for sixteen hours a day for four days but they showed no signs of fatigue. As they left I wished them luck and remarked on their stamina. There was nothing remarkable about what they were doing, said one.

'We are the fighters of Mohammed.'

The Prophet Mohammed succeeded in consolidating the power of Islam in the Arabian Peninsula but it was left to his followers to spread the word beyond the frontiers. Abu Bakr succeeded to the leadership of the Muslim community upon Mohammed's death and his armies irrupted forth. Damascus fell in 634 and two years later the Byzantine armies were defeated. Iraq, Syria and Palestine all fell to the east. Then Persia crumbled. To the west, Egypt fell in 640. The victorious armies of the caliphs who succeeded Abu Bakr spread the word of Islam from India in the east to the Atlantic coast. Much of the civilised world fell to Islam. The respect that Mohammed felt for Judaism and Christianity was reflected in the treatment of Jews and Christians by the conquering armies. Under the Ummayad caliphs (661 – 750) Jews and Christians tended to be merely taxed for their faith in the Islamic Empire and conversion was voluntary. But the accession of the Abbasid caliphs marked a shift of power away from the Arabs to non-Arab Muslims. Mutual respect and tolerance between the religions gave way to forcible conversions. With most of the known world under the sway of Islam, it was a golden age. Perhaps the yearning for unity among Muslims is a dim inherited memory of this period when learning, science and the arts flourished. The political, social and schismatic rifts so evident in the Muslim world today, and so dishonestly blamed on the later colonial period, belies a genuine yearning among Muslims for the Umma. But the genesis of those rifts is to be found in the tenth century when the caliph's powers were circumscribed and the empire split into separate dynasties.

The heirs to those Islamic warriors of old disappeared into the night.

In the morning the doctor gave me some more tablets and wrote out a letter of passage. Then he commandeered a pony and trap to take me and an escort a few miles further along the road. I was feeling worse than ever and felt a sense of bitter disappointment when we were decanted into the heat. I managed to walk a few miles but then even the willpower disappeared. The last I remember was a feeling of overpowering nausea and legs buckling before a world of trees, slowly turning.

Old and young sit by the tranquil river which drifts through Jamalara.

9

A Hawk Winged

I dreamed of a hospital and when I came to in the bright room I realised it had been less a dream and more the mind trying to bring some coherence to bear on the fever. I would then slip back into that deep and impenetrable sleep. When I finally emerged nobody bothered me with their insatiable curiosity. Perhaps I was no longer in Afghanistan. Anyway it was a relief. There was silence too; the universal chatter of the Mujahiddin was absent. I found the strength to prop myself up on cushions and looked about the room before saying my salaams. Most of the men were wounded and the sunny room had been designated a recovery centre. Two characters dominated even the almost studious silence: a young man called Jamakhar who had been badly wounded in the arm and leg and lay flat on his back by the window; and a man known as 'The Hawk'. He was sharp-featured and sat hunched in one corner, staring at me in an intense and friendly way. Jamakhar chain-smoked and said little as he lay with a cynical expression which suggested he had seen the folly of the world and survived it. The Hawk's penetrating gaze was a quest for understanding. Jamakhar threw me a cigarette and The Hawk leapt forward to light it.

'I am Allah Kador,' said the bustling bearded commander as he strode in and proceeded to inquire after everyone's health. He carried a carton of cigarettes and tossed packets to his men. There was no cant and nobody gave a damn about rules dreamed up hundreds of kilometres away in Peshawar by politicians. This was the front line. 'Here you will stay until you are better. This is Doctor Yacoub.'

The doctor drained wounds and dispensed tablets from an old school satchel. 'You must drink only water that has been boiled and eat only boiled eggs and nan. No meat, no rice, no soup. Then you will be healthy and go to Jebel Seraj.' He pushed his hands through his thick black hair and smiled.

Allah Kador cared passionately about his men and they looked upon him as a father. They were an easy-going crew and the fanaticism which so often left you feeling despondent was absent. They had been fighting constantly for months and Allah Kador admitted that recently the action had been exclusively against Jamiat. He insisted they had fired the first shots. I might have been sceptical but for a feeling they were too busy staying alive to

Mujahiddin in one of the houses near the front converted to cater for the wounded.

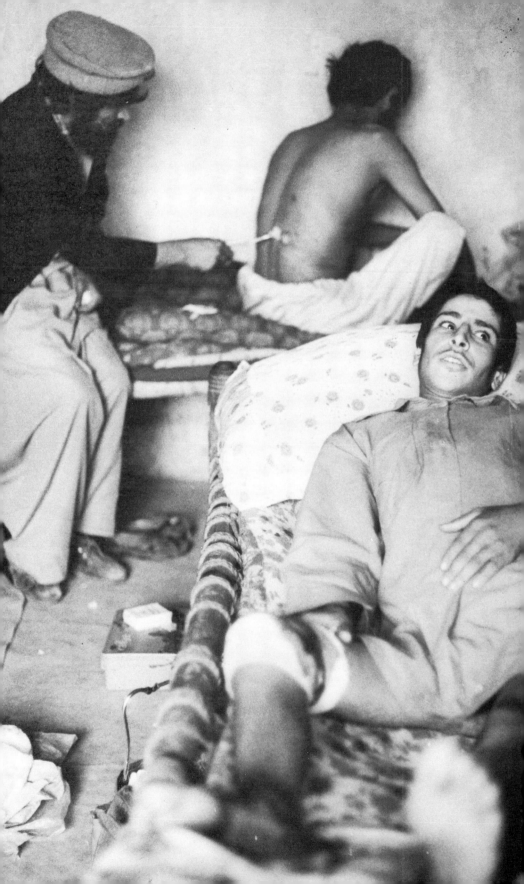

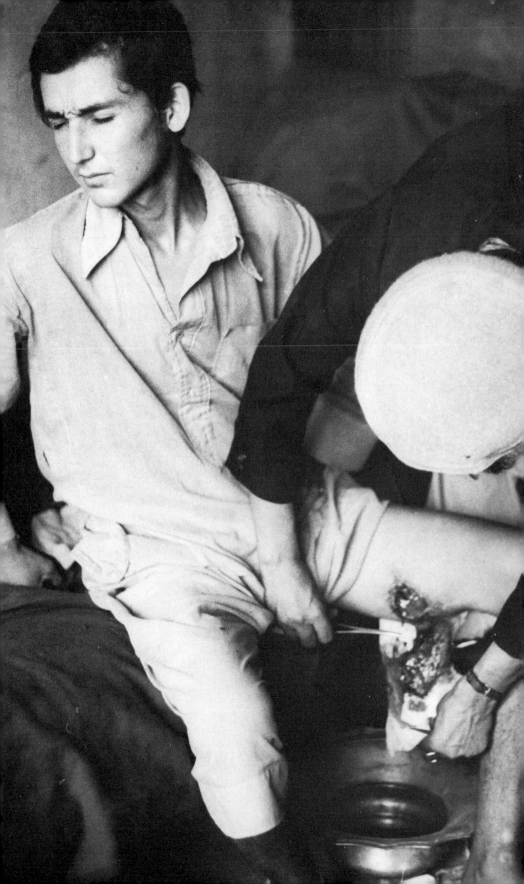

bother about propaganda. Allah Kador himself had an aristocratic disregard for lies which were a part of stupidity. He had been a governor of Badakshan and his father a general in the time of Zahir Shah. The family had been influential. Babrak Karmal himself had written to Allah Kador exhorting him to give up the fight, accept money for his men and a powerful position for himself. The commander waved his hand in a gesture of contempt and roared with laughter. Karmal was a seedy little man who lacked style. Allah Kador had exchanged a comfortable life for an austere one with the Mujahiddin.

'Why does Karmal think I do this? Because I like? I do it because I hate the communists and Karmal.'

It was a happy few days in the house of The Hawk. The men would wake at 4.30 am to say prayers but then they slept until the sun was high over the courtyard. Shortly after 9 am the shelling began. It came from the posts to the north west. Nobody took much notice unless it came close but I noticed in The Hawk a faraway look as he sat with his chin and arms on his knees. Jamakhar's smile broadened when the jets passed, as though he felt the true measure of the enemy and that they had been found wanting. He seemed quite happy in his horizontal life on the mattress by the window. At 7 am each morning I was woken by the sound of him lighting his first cigarette of the day. After he had taken his first long drag he would toss me one. All day

Time to relax and a game of hide and seek.

Draining a wound.

he lay smoking with that same insolent smirk on his face even when Doctor Yacoub came to drain the huge blisters on his legs. The others often went for walks at least as far as the big walnut tree where they smoked hashish in large quantities. Sometimes vicious rows broke out always involving The Hawk. He would sit for hours, Kalashnikov between his knees, with an unchanging and intense expression. With his high cheekbones, mane of black hair and eyes sunk without trace he seemed fierce yet he was always solicitous towards me. But he would suddenly turn on one of the others and taunt them. At first they ignored him or humoured him but pride inevitably dragged them into the arguments which ended in screaming matches. Jamakhar was never drawn and one day he looked at me and tapped the side of his head. The Hawk was a little crazy.

Despite these outbursts, the peaceful environment and the diet enabled me to regain my strength and a feeling of wellbeing was only disturbed by visitors. One such was a rancorous old man who rested his long grey beard on the palm of his hand as if he was about to fire it at me. The crotchety old xenophobe accused the West of decadence and the Muslim countries bar Afghanistan and Iran of corruption. I said he was jealous of the wealth of the oil states. He invented fantastic stories to prove his point: the Saudi Royal Family was under the sway of Jews: drunken orgies in Kuwait. The corrupt ones would be swept away by the Islamic Revolution. I told him he was a fool.

The Arabs and the West wanted the Russians out of Afghanistan and had given support to the resistance groups. The purity of the revolution in Iran was stained with the extermination of the mullahs' enemies, who were as ruthless as the Shah and Savak. The old man did not challenge this. Naturally the Godless ones must be put to death, he said, triumphant that I had argued myself into this self-evident truth. The old zealot saw no distinction between politics and religion. It was the old wretched story of ends justifying means. Europe before the Reformation. Anything permissible in the name of God. In Afghanistan there was nothing rare about him or his arguments. Freedom was only possible when all men were Muslims: democracy was meaningless: only Islam could purify the world.

Nothing could shift that man from his twisted and implacable views. Faith you respected but this fanaticism became a psychological strain.

The truth was that Islam had not made a significant contribution to scientific thought in hundreds of years. Only recently had the will to change that and restore Islam to its rightful role in world affairs become manifest. The Islamic Renaissance was to be found in the land that yielded up the faith: Saudi Arabia and the Gulf states were using the oil wealth to establish a powerful place on the world's stage. It would be wrong to see it merely as a rush to materialism. The popular images of Cadillacs and gold bath taps are superficial. The intellectual driving force in states such as Kuwait, Bahrain, Qatar and the United Arab Emirates is nothing less than the restoration of Islam to its former glory. Its architects understand that education, industry

124

Proud solitary figures stride through daunting landscapes.

and health care are the keys to this renaissance. The zealotry which marked the Iranian theocratic regime manifests itself in some resistance to the changes in the Gulf but on the whole is absent.

I am most closely attached by sentiment and experience to Bahrain. It is a good example as it does not command the oil wealth of its neighbours yet it is a symbol of hope and achievement for those who believe in progress. It is a powerful commercial centre which has capitalised on the Arab genius for business and, as an offshore banking centre, has repeated the success of Singapore. Great strides have been made in education – the island state is home to the Gulf University – and its health care network is a model for other developing nations. Such are the nuts and bolts of development, yet Islam remains the abiding spiritual force. The dramatic changes are being carried out in the *name* of Islam. The vision of the future is of Islam restored to its rightful place in the affairs of a world ordered by mutual respect and tolerance. The unyielding nature of Islamic fundamentalism is inherently hostile not only to the world at large but also to those Muslim nations whose vision has brought them abruptly into the twentieth century. Its odour of self-righteousness renders the diplomacy of the real world impossible.

'The question is,' I said to the old man, 'does Afghanistan want to take part in the twentieth century?' He pushed his beard out with the palm of his hand. He was courteous in his contempt. The true followers of Islam, that is the Iranians and the Afghans, were guided by God. Western imperialism, the Godless communists and the corrupt ones in Arabia would all be defeated. He and the flat earthers seemed to make God a small thought.

But his was a view apparently shared by many in Afghanistan. Oddly, they reminded me of the dogmatic Marxists of my acquaintance. It was not fair to compare Islam to the ideology the Muslims were fighting but the way that human minds were held hostage left me with an uncomfortable feeling of *déjà vu*. Communism is a Christian aberration – the belief of a heaven in this world – but its adherents pursue it with all the passion of a religion. The more its innate failures lead to greater brutality, the more the 'faithful' are reduced to fanaticism and repression. None could admit that communism was the great self-fulfilling fallacy when it was possible to blame the capitalists. Yes, it was wrong to compare the two and yet that same self-righteousness and appalling certainty coloured the speech of the communists and the Islamic fundamentalists. That same retreat into fanaticism. What cruelties would be committed in the name of each. They were blueprints for human life; they were inevitable and deviants would not be tolerated.

The nature of Russian communism left it incapable of facing its own contradictions. The commonplace of lies was the product of the central lie which is communism itself. The Russian Empire will probably drift into the hands of a military dictatorship which will merely authenticate the tyranny which has existed since Lenin hijacked a popular revolution and cursed the world with a promise of unending agitation and even war until every country had succumbed to communism. Karl Marx's vision that societies follow an inevitable pattern into communism has tended under Soviet interpretation not only to diminish men and women but to be at odds with the reality of the twentieth century. Yet, despite the evidence, intelligent men and women cling to the big Russian lie while the power brokers of the Kremlin cling to power. Like all tyrants they seek to deflect the attention of their subjects from domestic inadequacies to some real or invented external threat. With poker faces the old men invoke the spectre of Western imperialism long after the European empires went home, while they continue their own programme of expansion. The lie is used to disguise the reality of the world's last empire which is not only trying to consolidate previous territorial gains but is still expanding.

The Czarist dream of a warm water port has been largely replaced by Russian designs on the oil fields of the Gulf. The balance of global power rests there. Control of the Arabian Gulf by Russia would not only guarantee oil for itself well into the next century but by denying oil to the West and Japan could cripple their economies. The Russians are cautious and believe that time is on their side. They know that a frontal assault on the Gulf would trigger World War 3. So they move by stealth and subversion. They constantly probe for weaknesses in the Western alliance and in their vision – nothing to do with the communist ideal any more and everything to do with the realities of power – any sign of a weakening of resolve is to be exploited. Subversion, invasion and détente are merely pawns in the game of Russian foreign policy which is still underpinned by the idea of the 'historic destiny' of communism.

President James Carter was considered by the Russians as a weak opponent: the unprecedented expansion of Russian influence in Africa was a result of that perception. Only after the invasion of Afghanistan did President Carter turn on the Russians and accuse them of betrayal. In fact the Russian leadership had remained consistently true to the idea of communist expansion. President Carter went on to draw the line at the Arabian Gulf, stating that any direct attack on the oil fields would be considered a direct assault on the interests of the United States. It was a question of closing the door after the horse had bolted. The Russians must have been most satisfied with geo-strategic advances made during Mr Carter's presidency. They would not make a dash to the Gulf (the Russians do not want war any more than anyone else) but the truth was that they now had the region virtually encircled. This policy of encirclement had taken them into Ethiopia and South Yemen where they had an enormous military commitment. More significant is the way these forward bases were used to spread subversion and terrorism throughout the region. To the north of the Arabian Peninsula were Russia's client states Syria and Iraq (although Iraq had showed signs in the early 1980s of wanting to put distance between itself and the Russians) not to mention its own long border with Iran. The invasion of Afghanistan effectively increased that border by hundreds of miles. The West and Japan receives its oil through the Strait of Hormuz, the narrow channel between Iran and Oman, and if it was closed – an easy thing to do – supplies would virtually cease. After the Russian invasion of Afghanistan, the empire was in a position to mount a great pincer movement against the Strait, using armour based in western Afghanistan and in South Yemen. This was just one opportunity that became available after the invasion.

There is both naïveté and a sense of the heroic in the inability or refusal of many Afghans to countenance the realities of global power. The old man refused to acknowledge the common cause the West had with the resistance. The debate was polite but futile and anyway it was cut short by the sound of automatic fire nearby. A few bullets hit the house and even Jamakhar grabbed his rifle and limped from the room. There was an exchange of fire and then it ceased abruptly. Two Jamiatis were seen running away. Nobody had been hurt.

Allah Kador would appear at least once a day and dispense cigarettes or joke with his men while inquiring after their health. I dozed or smoked or went for walks in the fields and my health improved. Henceforward the bug remained in my system but lay dormant most of the time. I observed the Mujahiddin and their idiosyncracies: they would never accept the third light from a match, insisting it was an old Afghan superstition and nothing to do with World War 1; they fastidiously peeled everything from apples to tomatoes before eating it.

A tough life even for an old man.

The bitter rows continued to erupt without warning but I noticed the lengths to which the Mujahiddin would go to avoid arousing The Hawk. This was his home and he proved a classic host, attending to my every need. When I said I needed cigarettes Allah Kador reached into his bag for a pack, but The Hawk refused them on my behalf and went to the shop two kilometres away to buy me cigarettes. It seemed to be carrying the rituals of hospitality to absurd lengths but I did not realise then how desperately he needed to cling to the familiar forms of life.

One morning The Hawk arranged for me to wash in a little cubicle in the house. I was dirty and delighted at the prospect and his hollow cheeks inflated into a smile at my response. The water would be warm, he promised, and there would be shampoo, soap and even toothpaste. He led me to the cubicle where he had lined up the articles. 'Look, soap,' he said, slipping the scented bar from its packet. 'Shampoo,' he said searching my face for a favourable response. 'And toothpaste,' he added, squeezing some onto my toothbrush. He waited until I had tested the water and seemed in an agony of suspense until I said it was fine. He brought towels and only when I had felt their texture and nodded my approval did he seem happy. Something in that distant look of his made me realise that this attention to the details of my comfort was for his own sake and not mine. For his sanity. He was a man clinging to the forms of a world which had receded in the face of war. The Hawk was shell-shocked. It was a bad case – one of the very few I came across – and Allah Kador hoped he would go to Pakistan for help. The unpredictable rows affected everyone. The Hawk only felt alive in the adrenalin and instinct worlds of battle. And for a few random moments in attending to his sick English guest. From then on I felt very strongly about The Hawk who seemed perfectly human in a world of supermen.

I took some photographs of Jamakhar lying smoking. One of the others removed the cigarette from his lips. It would look bad in Peshawar. I protested and Jamakhar laughed and lit another, smoking it with exaggerated gestures. Allah Kador appeared and said he would take me to a nearby village which had been destroyed by the Russians.

We set off in the late afternoon when great flocks of birds were making their last flight of the day. There were about thirty Mujahiddin who had brought RPGs and several machine guns as well as automatics and 303s. Allah Kador explained it was a precaution as we would be fairly close to one of the Russian posts.

The village of Bokoham straddled the dusty road which I had followed with varying degrees of misery for days. We reached it at dusk and the village was the more desolate for it. Bokoham was a place of ghosts and only a few of the poorest people who had nowhere else to go remained. You would glimpse them for a moment as they turned with fearful eyes at your approach, before hurrying into the tangle of grey mud ruins. Here and there a room had survived the bombardment and within the survivors slept and ate. On twelve consecutive days in 1982 the artillery and jets had struck.

More than 200 people had died out of a population of 800. The rest had fled, some to become refugees in Pakistan. Allah Kador wandered thoughtfully among the mounds of rubble.

'They were brave people. You know the civilians are Mujahiddin too. All Afghans who are not communists are Mujahiddin. But it is very hard for them here. There are many government and Russian posts.' He gestured to the north and west. 'You will go this way and the further you go the more danger there is. There is our front line.'

Though we did not realise it, the front line was a shade closer. We milled about on the road until one of the men suddenly shouted to take cover. About 300 metres away on the road were several figures. In the failing light they were indistinct but their khaki was enough to give them away as government troops. There began one of those surreal sequences of events which were to mark my travels. The soldiers lingered, perhaps confident that they were out of range or that the light was too poor to aim properly. Allah Kador ordered everyone back into the ruins. The Hawk did not seem to hear. I watched his face which was suffused with a look of joy, almost radiant peace, as he rested his shoulder against a tree and took aim. There was no return fire as The Hawk loosed off a whole magazine. We heard the clank and squeak of the tank and then we were all running through the ruins as the first shells plundered the darkening sky and exploded a long way off. We could still hear the lone gun of The Hawk as we scattered across the fields. The Mujahiddin were still laughing and whooping at the unexpected encounter as we reached Allah Kador's large fortress-like home 5 kilometres away.

'Now we drink tea, my friend,' he declared and disappeared through the carved wooden doors and waved for us to follow.

Back at The Hawk's home that night Allah Kador stared for a time at our host who had returned safely. The commander had been concerned that The Hawk's inspired action might have endangered them all and particularly his guest. He was torn between a mild reproach which risked triggering the Mujahid's uncontrollable fury, and silence. The Hawk sat hunched in the corner. He seemed to have retreated into another world. Then he suddenly began a bitter tirade against one of the others. Everyone hoped that his fury would abate and nobody answered back. Allah Kador tried to placate him but The Hawk goaded the commander and accused him of leading Mujahiddin against the Jamiatis instead of fighting the invader. Allah Kador grew angry and upbraided him for endangering us all on the road. Some of the others could no longer restrain themselves and began to argue. Jamakhar remained aloof but for once his smile was missing. Now The Hawk had lost control. His hysterical rage provoked the full fury of the commander. Some of the others joined in but more out of frustration at the irrational and unjustified nature of The Hawk's attacks. Their tolerance was strained to breaking point and I watched fearfully as two men slipped the safety catches off their Kalashnikovs.

130

Bokoham, where 200 people died.

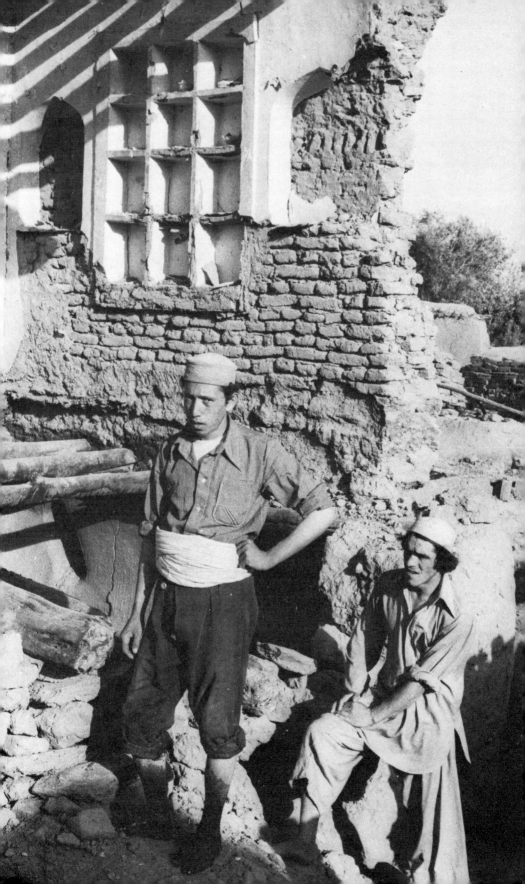

Suddenly Allah Kador got up and stormed out. It was a grave insult to the host. Most of the men followed the commander and below in the courtyard new arguments broke out as some tried to persuade their chief to return. The Hawk sat staring at the floor, his body coursing with fury. Suddenly he got up, seized his rifle and ran from the room. Simultaneously Jamakhar leapt up and shouted something in Persian from the window. The Hawk was jumped and disarmed as he entered the courtyard and struggled against half a dozen men who held him. I looked from the window. Allah Kador had his pistol in his hand. He ordered The Hawk to be released and recriminations filled the air once again. Then The Hawk rushed from the courtyard and I never saw him again.

The local party hack duly arrived. I recognised the type as he stood in the doorway. It was his weasel eyes and look of contempt and the self-important way he stood there. I feigned sleep but he came forward. 'Mista, mista.' The sound grated on the nerves. Though my stomach problems had subsided I still suffered from gross flatulence and let slip a great billowing product of my bowels. He was undeterred and began to lecture me on the needs and aspirations of 'the people' and suggested I record his words. I was sick of hearing about 'the people' from characters who had only contempt for individuals. The smirk on Jamakhar's face suggested he held similar views about the party intelligentsia. The hack sensed I was not in the mood for doctrinaire pep talks and began to retreat. He paused in the doorway.

'Mista, you stay here and get better. Why you not walk in the fields with the wounded Mujahiddin? They find it therapeutic. They are inspired by the beautiful Afghan homeland. The flowers and the beautiful mountains of their beloved homeland make everything very peaceful.'

Peaceful they were indeed. I knelt with Jamakhar by the window and we roared with laughter as a little plume of hashish smoke drifted up through the branches of the walnut tree. I felt much better now. For the first time in weeks I had been allowed just to be alone, to read and not to talk if I did not want to. These men understood 'alone'. I would miss them very much.

10

Sour Grapes

The shells drifted overhead in an almost lazy way. The bearded figure flattened himself in the earth corrugations of the vineyard. After the whispering of the crystal air in motion there was the crack of the explosion and a plume of smoke would rise slowly among the trees. Sometimes white, sometimes grey. The man resumed his dash towards us until the report of the distant guns heralded more shells. It was a cycle of sounds to which the ear became acutely attuned: the flat pop of the artillery pieces, long seconds of silence, then the hissing of the invisible shell when you always tried to guess the trajectory and then more silence until the projectile crashed into the village. From the tiny underground bunker the horizon was low and very close and was filled with smoke which slowly mingled into one dense cloud. Against this hazy screen the figure resumed his run and suddenly loomed at the entrance like a laughing giant before jumping feet first through the little hole. He landed on top of us scattering bunches of grapes.

There were six of us crammed into the tiny sweltering bunker. Abdul Ghafoor seemed quite untouched by the sweat and dust in the earth burrow. He was explaining that Afghanistan boasted the sweetest varieties of grapes in the world while we stripped the huge green and purple bunches. Whenever I made a run to collect grapes I ended up with sour ones. The Mujahiddin instinctively homed in on the few vines with sweet fruit. It would be a few weeks before they had fully ripened and the harvest began. Abdul Ghafoor was always good when he spoke about agriculture. He had taken his old job very seriously and when he talked it was always with a sense of pride at man's regulation of nature. The old farmer complained about the shelling which kept him from his work. He had continued weeding until the shells began to explode dangerously near, before joining us in the searing airless bunker. The gnarled and defiant rustic had been just one step ahead of the gunners at Totumdarah and Kulai Surkh. God protected a good Muslim, he said.

'The further you go, the more dangerous it is,' Allah Kador had said among the ruins at Bokoham. He had been right. I had been sad to leave his men but you soon became too absorbed in new worlds to dwell on the old. My escorts changed at every village as we spent five hours marching to the west side of the valley. I was looking forward to meeting Engineer Toorak, one of the leading provincial commanders in Parwan. It was with a sense of achievement that I crossed the rickety wooden bridge over the broiling green Panjshir River into Parwan province. By dusk we were close to the mountains by the town of Jebel Seraj but Toorak and his men, who (I discovered later) lived life constantly on the move between villages, had moved on.

I was roused from a fitful sleep which had been plagued by mosquitoes and led to a large quadrangle enclosing an orchard. Blankets and cushions had been spread on the ground and hundreds of Mujahiddin lounged in the sun. Villagers filed through another gate to the orchard with piles of fresh nan wrapped in bright cloths and blackened kettles of tea. Engineer Toorak was a shy man with a quizzical expression. He was compact and reminded you of an elf. Later, his curious habit of popping up unexpectedly looking rather pleased with himself reinforced that impression. Wherever I went a mysterious chain of communication would inform each commander about me so that they were never really greeting a stranger. They already knew who I was and why I was there before I arrived: a few of my preferences were also transmitted. This telepathy had the quality of the delight of a child at Christmas.

'I think you like boiled eggs,' said the commander, and three duly arrived while he casually examined my face to catch my response.

Abdul Ghafoor was summoned from a distant village and arrived at the end of the afternoon. After we had dispensed with the pleasantries, I asked Toorak how many men he had under his command. 'Oh 20,000 men,' he declared. I settled for the small talk. That evening in a nearby house over a meal of kofta, rice and raw chillis I said to Toorak that I wanted to see some fighting. With most of the commanders, an inclination to please a guest was outweighed by concerns for their safety. It was a stumbling block that many journalists came up against in covering the Afghan war and probably explains why casualties among the Press corps tended to be low. Toorak was amused by the request and began to discuss possible operations with his lieutenants. Mujahiddin began to appear from neighbouring villages bearing RPG launchers and mortars. An air of expectation suffused the gathering as the men checked their weapons.

'Tomorrow you see fighting,' said Toorak.

Then a curious thing happened. I was sitting against the wall of the room which was dimly lit by a hurricane lamp. One of the men gazed at me in an odd way, got up and advanced towards me. Without saying anything he raised his foot shod with a Russian army boot and it crashed against the wall but an inch from my head. I was thankful that I had any face left and more thankful when I examined the squashed remains of an enormous scorpion splattered across the wall. Nobody thought twice about it and even I, who had so assiduously hunted down the harmless cockroaches in Peshawar, shrugged it off. It was an interesting transformation in attitudes. Life was so hard in this country and the day to day business of survival so pressing that there was no time to worry about such modest wildlife. That was a luxury of a more comfortable world.

It was late in the evening when the order to move came. 'Burrow. Harakat,' cried Abdul Ghafoor, 'Commander change his mind and we go now'.

Toorak was chuckling as he slipped freshly-loaded magazines into the pouches on his jacket. Cloud obscured the stars and there was a strong warm wind which made the pantaloons and shirts of the men billow and flap against their bodies. They were heavily burdened with weapons but they moved quickly along the ridges which marked off the fields. There were fifty Mujahiddin and we were heading for Jebel Seraj, but whether Toorak would choose to attack the post there depended on conditions when we arrived. In classic guerrilla fashion the commanders chose when and where to fight. It was one of the few advantages over a more powerful enemy. The journey meant another hairy river crossing. With out boots around our neck and with arms linked we waded the Panjshir which foamed about our chests. I pulled my boots back on over a fresh collection of cuts and silently cursed the lack of bridges while Abdul Ghafoor waited impatiently.

'Mista Mike, you find it difficult. But for the Mujahiddin these difficulties are our happiness.'

A stream of Anglo-Saxon oaths loses its impact when whispered. The wind turned into a gale and whipped up a dust-storm and, as we marched in a broad zig-zag, I lost all sense of direction. We passed silently through Jebel Seraj. There was no light anywhere as we crouched in the shadows of the large inscrutable buildings. Stale nan was passed around and we dipped it in a stream before hungrily eating it. Each time we paused, a bird call or a match lit in a high window would signal us to continue. The town, like all those on the front line, was subversively alive. Towards the outskirts we entered a narrow alley and there, seated at a table, was Toorak. He had a mischievous look about him and he squeezed my hand in a friendly way before explaining that the attack would be further up the main north road. We set off through clouds of mosquitoes which returned as soon as the wind abated and marched for several hours before we came to a farmhouse where we collapsed with our boots on and slept.

We were roused at 4.30 am after two hours' sleep and snatched breakfast before Toorak's final briefing. Outside the farmhouse we were joined by another group of Mujahiddin, about thirty strong, led by one Commander Aqarshareen, whose territory we were now in. Toorak was more sprightly than ever despite being up all night putting the final touches to his plan. There was to be simultaneous attacks on a convoy and the main Russian post at Kulai Surkh. The Aqarshareen group – designated to hit the convoy – took up positions in bombed-out buildings by the side of the road. Incredibly, they were less than 100 metres from a minor government post and Aqarshareen said he hoped to lure the communists out. He was to wait for two hours until the main group, under Toorak, had taken up positions near

the post where there were an estimated 3,000 Russian troops and scores of tanks and vehicles. I set off with the main group through the vineyards and trees of the high ground to the east of the road. Now that it was daylight the devastation brought about by more than three years of near-continuous war became apparent. Villages here were shattered and the landscape pockmarked with craters. Jets and gunships were always present in the blue sky. This was the wasteland of the front line. Yet remarkably many inhabitants survived and continued to tend the land. They were stoical and the cycle of tending the grape crops was an undertaking of quiet pride as much as economic necessity. There was more than a hint of that British capacity for ignoring brutal reality and carrying on as normal.

Scores of villages were in the firing line of a cynical Russian policy designed to demoralise the population and force them into ending their support for the Mujahiddin. As soon as the Mujahiddin attacked one of the posts along the north road, the artillery opened up on the villages. These tactics of terror were designed to brutalise the population into submission. After three and a half years fighting without any lasting success, the Red Army seemed bankrupt of ideas and was reduced to deliberately killing civilians in the vain hope they would abandon their fighting men. The policy was common to all areas I travelled in but was a failure. The more people killed, the greater the hatred for the invader. The Russians failed to

The devastation after three years of almost continuous war.

Fighter waiting for the attack.

understand that the Mujahiddin were a true expression of popular sentiment. The 'popular' movements used by the Russians to export communism were usually a euphemism for small groups of revolutionaries who battened off or terrorised civilian populations. It was inconceivable to the Russians that they were fighting anything different. In a typical raid the Mujahiddin might lose one or two men and a couple wounded but the casualties in the villages were pitiful.

Toorak and his men moved down through the lanes of the hills which overlooked the road. Abdul Ghafoor, myself and four men were left on a hill overlooking the post at Kulai Surkh. We ate grapes and then Abdul Ghafoor wrapped himself in his partouk and slept among the vines. I found a spot behind a low mud wall which afforded a good view of the valley, the north road and the camp. Apart from the silvery rows of huts their neat lines glinting in the sun, and the ranks of dark military vehicles, there was an air of peace about the valley. Even the convoys of bright oil tankers roaring along the road suggested that all was well. But moving invisibly through the carpet of trees below was Toorak and his men. The Afghans were taking the fight to the Russians and that was now the pattern.

It had not always been like this. The invasion of Afghanistan had been a textbook operation but as the armies of the British Empire had discovered the country was easier to invade than to hold. The invasion was a political blunder disguised initially by the slick execution of the operation. In the autumn of 1979 a visit to Afghanistan by Soviet Deputy Defence Minister Ivan Pavlovsky laid the groundwork for the invasion. On 8 December a brigade of crack Soviet troops landed at Bagram air base and moved north to clear Mujahiddin from the Salang Pass through which landborne invasion troops would have to pass. Giant Antonov transports disgorged 800 combat troops at Bagram a week later and army divisions were moved to the Soviet-Afghan border. The invasion by 80,000 troops began on 25 December. As the Antonovs lumbered day and night into the airports, motorised divisions and armour crashed over the border. The invader had secured the major roads and the cities within four days. Amin was killed by a Soviet assassination squad and the Russians' own man Babrak Karmal was installed before the end of the year. The Russians told the world they had been invited into Afghanistan by the government but it was a transparent lie. Karmal did not arrive in Afghanistan until several days after the invasion and so any request by him would be illegal. Would Amin have invited them in to kill him?

The Russians deployed 105th Airborne Divison units at Kabul, Jalalabad and Shindand, south of Herat. The 16th, 66th, 357th and 360th Motorised Rifle Divisions, each supported by hundreds of tanks, were deployed at Herat, Qandahar and Kabul with units of the 66th taking up positions near the Iranian border. Pakistan responded by sending seven army divisions to the North West Frontier Province while China began to send the Zia government large amounts of arms. The invasion saved the communist

138

government from imminent collapse and enabled Moscow's own man to be installed. Russian planners calculated that their armies would play an essentially supporting role, while Afghan troops tackled the Mujahiddin. But it was a fundamental mistake. Not only had they underestimated the depth of the resistance but they did not appreciate that an invasion would turn that resistance into a nationwide revolt. It was the one thing guaranteed to unite the fractious Afghans. Further, the invasion accelerated the process of disintegration of the Afghan army. From a strength of between 80,000 and 100,000 men, it collapsed to less than 30,000 and many of those who remained could not be trusted by the Russians. Desertion and rebellion were widespread and the Russians found themselves in the front line. In the early months of the occupation morale among the soldiers, who had been told they would be welcomed as liberators, was high. The spring offensive in the east was launched. The razing of Azmar in Kunar Province in which at least 1,500 people died, exemplified the ruthless tactics adopted by the Russians and it led to initial successes. These were offset by trouble in the Russian ranks: troops from the central Soviet republics, ethnically akin to many Afghans, showed a marked reluctance to fight. Unrest and desertions to the enemy forced the high command to replace the Tadjiks and Uzbeks with European Russians.

Despite another offensive in the autumn and new tactics involving commando assaults from helicopters in areas softened up by jet strikes which were successful, it was clear to the Russians by the beginning of 1981 that they were engaged in a major war. Resistance was almost universal even if the Mujahiddin tactics were unsophisticated and led to large-scale casualties. Then began the pattern of Russian offensives before which the Mujahiddin learned to retreat before reoccupying areas once the Russians pulled back. A network of posts was established but they were cut off from the population and most were not of a strength to enable them to launch effective operations against the Mujahiddin. By 1983 the resistance was stronger and had developed more sophisticated techniques against the invader. The Russians were reduced to launching their annual spring offensive and smaller offensive against Mujahiddin strongholds during the summer months. But no matter how drastic the casualties inflicted on the resistance, there was never a shortage of Afghans to take the place of those killed. The Russians might clear an area but as soon as they had gone the Mujahiddin returned. The resistance controlled at least 80 per cent of the country and even the cities, held by the Russians, were coming under increasing pressure.

They were now fighting a war against the overwhelming majority of the population. They could prop up the Karmal regime and hold the cities and the major roads but they could not pacify the country. To tackle that they would need perhaps as many as half a million troops instead of the 105,000 they had in Afghanistan by 1983. The Kremlin was paying a heavy political price internationally. Time was now on the side of the Mujahiddin as morale among the poorly-fed Russians deteriorated. The truth of the war was beginning to spread among the Russian people despite the propaganda by the state-controlled media. Officers had terrorised their men with the legends of how the Afghans dealt with their captives. But the Mujahiddin began to help Russian deserters escape to the West. They preferred them to accept Islam and fight alongside the resistance but there would be none of the mutilations articulated by Kipling. As among American troops in Vietnam, the use of drugs became widespread and I came across many cases of troops prepared to exchange their weapons for a little hashish. By the middle of 1983 the Russians seemed bankrupt of military ideas and had resorted to the widespread use of terror. There was nothing for the Red Army, with its glorious record of defending the homeland, to take pride in.

Aqarshareen's group opened up a mile or so away. The peace of the valley was shattered as the sound of heavy machine guns was followed by the whoosh of RPGs. Artillery from the post at Totumdarah opened up on the villages behind. That was the signal for Toorak to launch his attack but the invisible force in the woods below made no move. It was clear why. Above the woods two gunships hovered menacingly as if the enemy knew they were there. While one came down low to search for signs of life, the other flew round in circles a little higher. After thirty minutes the fighting near the Totumdarah post ceased though the shelling continued. The helicopters returned every twenty minutes and hung like great insects over the inscrutable table of green. It was nearly midday when Aqarshareen began a fresh attack. They had not moved from their positions after hitting two trucks in a convoy. When the firing ceased the enemy had assumed they had retreated. 'Communists are stupid,' said Aqarshareen later. Two hours later they had repeated the ambush and claimed two APCs. Now a column of tanks rumbled down the hill from the post at Kulai Surkh and headed for Aqarshareen's positions. The Mujahiddin stood no chance against so many tanks and one of the men in our company ran off almost casually to warn the commander. 'He will get there long before the tanks,' said Abdul Ghafoor leaning against one of the banks in the vineyard his face in the shade of an overhanging vine. Still Toorak made no move and now the gunships were laying smoke trails above the woods, sky markers to guide in a jet strike. The gunships retreated to the northern mountains where they hovered while the MiGs screamed in low and dropped their bombs before banking sharply south. Little silver darts flashing against the yellow and grey peaks.

'Don't worry about Toorak. He is too clever for the Russians,' said Abdul Ghafoor, handing me a bunch of grapes.

The Totumdarah post fell silent and we set off for a village three miles away where the Mujahiddin were meant to regroup. Falling shells barred our way at one point and we sat behind a ridge of earth. The guns were joined by artillery from Kulai Surkh and shells began to fall 100 metres behind us. We made a run for it. The Mujahiddin were laughing as they always seemed to do in the face of danger. Their disregard for danger was unnerving at first and dangerous to your judgement because it became infectious.

The Russian post at Kulai Surkh: Toorak moved through the woods in the foreground.

'Allah O Akbar,' cried one of the men and spat in the direction of the post. The others followed suit.

What the individual says and does had real meaning for his fellows and they were a constant inspiration to each other, even if at times they seemed like children engaged in a jolly jape. I had seen how they coped with pain and I knew that death was an abstract, a door through which you passed from the articles of faith to the glory of God who had witnessed the sacrifice. You understood their contempt for the atheistic communists but wondered where it left you as the shells whispered through the air and exploded nearby. Fear, instinct and adrenalin gave you just enough to keep up with them as they careered through the woods whooping and firing their guns into the air.

Toorak and his men had long moved from the woods when the jets struck. Two of Aqarshareen's men had been wounded but he was pleased with his tally of four vehicles and a score of enemy killed. Toorak's pride was a little dented but it was a sign of the growing maturity of the resistance that commanders knew when to hold back their deepest instincts. The two commanders and their lieutenants were already planning another night march south to be in a position to launch a new attack at dawn. Outside the house where they sat the Mujahiddin were catching up on some sleep in the village square. Villagers stepped among the sleeping men and collected

142

Mujahid, Totumdarah.

tumblers and kettles after the tea they had brought to the fighters.

I found myself in the company of an unpleasant sub-commander and a few of his men walking through the maze of walls outside of the village. We came to an orchard and the sub-commander smashed off the padlock which secured the metal gate. It was a gratuitous act of vandalism in a land where to simply ask is to be granted access to a man's home. As we left the owner of the orchard confronted the sub-commander. He castigated the men and a look of shame suffused their faces. The old man in the turban accused them of failing to live up to the faith. He said they were welcome to anything he owned but that they had humiliated him by denying him the chance to exercise his hospitality. I thought him very brave to berate half a dozen armed men in this way. His words had real impact and most of the young men were reduced to mumbled apologies. Another old man joined the owner of the orchard and with tremendous dignity lectured the men on the way of Mohammed and quoted verses from the *Qoran* until the fighters stood with their heads hung in shame.

We trooped back to the village in silence, only the sub-commander trying to make a joke of the incident. We passed a little boy whose family supported Jamiat. The sub-commander, trying to save face, seized the lad and demanded that he swear allegiance to Hezb. He did it in a half-joking way but even so showed himself a consummate bully. He pulled the lad's coloured cap from his head and tossed it into a stream. Abdul Ghafoor, to his credit, recovered the cap and told the sub-commander to let the boy go. The lad refused to be intimidated: he was still a Jamiat supporter.

Toorak's features may have suggested mischief and gentleness most of the time but I had discovered he was an iron disciplinarian. The no-smoking rule was holy writ and he took pride in the behaviour of his men. Some still smoked but were forced to extreme lengths to do it in secret. More than once I came across sentries posted about a village to warn a few Mujahiddin passing a cigarette around in the square in case the commander came in sight. I had found that the different groups of Mujahiddin reflected the character of their commander. Toorak was a gentleman with a sense of fun who liked nothing better than conversation with intelligent men. He took all aspects of his job very seriously and believed that he and his men should set an example to the population. As a result the behaviour of his men was exemplary and it was a pleasure to keep their company.

Word of the sub-commander's bad manners preceded our arrival in the village and Toorak was waiting impatiently in the square. He verbally mauled the sub-commander and then cuffed him about the head before the rest of the men. Then he relieved him of his command. The now ex-commander was visibly shamed and he knew that the only way to redeem himself was by some act of bravery. His reputation for heroics in the past now meant nothing. By one stupid act he had lost the self-respect and dignity without which the Pathan regards himself as no better than the animals.

Toorak's men were already preparing for the march south as the last rays of sunshine dappled the mountains. Toorak tried to persuade me to go with him but illness had already delayed me and I was anxious to begin the long trek west. Aqarshareen had said that if I stayed with him for two days then he could provide an escort for the mountain crossing into Ghorband. I shook the hands of Toorak and all his men and felt that same tug of emotion and sense of loss as they passed out of sight into the dusk. Now that that cheerful and inquisitive little man had gone I felt lonely in that ruined landscape.

It was three days before I managed to leave: I was delayed an extra night by a sudden and glorious storm which flooded the villages and drove everyone to shelter. Lightning ransacked the mountains and lit up towers of black and boiling cloud while we watched the endless rain turn the courtyard into a mustard-coloured lake. At least it kept the mosquitoes down. I sat in the window recess of a house with Abdul Ghafoor as he explained that he would not be travelling on with me. He wanted to spend more time with his family. Now he talked less of the abstractions of party policy and more about his family and home and I liked him the more for it. Earlier he had translated into English a letter dictated by Aqarshareen. It was an extraordinary missive to the Russian commander at Kulai Surkh, warning him that if he continued to shell the villages he could expect attacks by the resistance to be stepped up. The Mujahiddin had nothing if not cheek.

144

I kept my boots on day and night as the bombardment by jets and artillery was pretty constant. From the tower of a ruined building in the village you could watch the gunships laying their smoke trails above villages and then the jets screaming low through the valley their images seconds ahead of the sound. Then the plumes of white and grey smoke would rise and they too were ahead of the sound of the explosion. It was an eerie exhibition, as if time was slightly out of joint and so, when bombs were dropped nearby and sight and sound were synchronised, everything happening quite suddenly, the fear was heightened. When the jets were gone the gunships would work their way ponderously across the sky to record the damage and if they spotted Mujahiddin would drop suddenly to attack.

The gunship has been the most significant development for use against guerrillas and was first used on a large scale by the Americans in Vietnam. The Russians deployed them in the Angola war of 1975 and they were a significant factor in the Ogaden War in Ethiopia two years later. The brilliant use of gunships by the Russians played a crucial role in the recapture of Jijiga. In the mountainous terrain of Afghanistan against guerrilla forces whose knowledge of and manoeuvrability in the mountains was one of their few advantages, the extensive use of gunships tipped the balance in the invader's favour. Scores of Mi-24 'Hind' gunships were stationed across Afghanistan. Their firepower is awesome, carrying as they do 12.7mm guns

Jet strike in the valley.

mounted in the nose, rocket pods and bombs. In addition it can carry a dozen troops. The Mujahiddin have few weapons to use against them. Anti-aircraft guns were established in mountain areas but after initial successes the Russian pilots learned to avoid those regions. There have also been occasions when the Mujahiddin have brought down low-flying gunships with automatic fire but such successes were rare, highly risky and needed a lot of luck. Despite Russian propaganda about massive weapons aid from the West and the tacit admission by the United States and Great Britain that they were aiding the Mujahiddin, you wondered why shoulder-held anti-aircraft missiles like the American Red-eye or Stinger had never got through. The Mujahiddin were not getting the sort of weapons they needed, the weapons that might tip the balance.

Day and night you lived with the sound of shells exploding somewhere in that huge valley. It was not so much fear you experienced but a gradual unstringing of the nerves so that bizarre rhythms became a part of everyday life: the report of the big guns and the monotonous crump usually in the same place. You listened intently when there was a change in the pattern and then you settled down. At first the best times were those when the guns were silent but then, curiously, you developed a suspicion of those lapses in the bombardment. Anticipation was actually worse than the regularity of the shells flying overhead.

Every night there was the sound of attacks on the communist posts: the urgent sound of automatic fire, the slower machine gun noises and occasionally mortar and RPGs. The string of posts meant that the road stayed open most of the time and the endless convoys were able to bring supplies from the Soviet Union. The artificial economy of the Karmal government was sustained by these supplies. But the Russians and their allies paid a heavy price in keeping the road open. Attacks against the posts and the convoys were always met with the same response: the pump pump of shells directed to all points of the compass. The villages disintegrated further from identifiable ruins to the dust from which its walls were originally made. You glimpsed the nature of shell-shock and felt the more for The Hawk. You cursed the rains which delayed your departure and wondered how the Mujahiddin and villagers coped month after month. But you also sensed the condition of the enemy, penned in their posts, apparently destitute of strategy, and reduced to systematically destroying the villages. The contempt with which the Mujahiddin regarded their enemy seemed justified: the impossible odds they faced a little shorter.

The half-ruined villages I lived in for those four days escaped direct hits but we kept our boots on all the same. The Mujahiddin listened to the patterns of bombardment and were often able to predict where the next shells would land. Perhaps the Russian gunners followed a strict pattern or perhaps it was instinct, but suddenly Mujahiddin and villagers were running for their lives.

'Run Inglestan,' cried the men and we poured through the gaps in the

Minutes before, the author was in this village which was hit by artillery fire.

courtyard wall. We had barely made the perimeter of the village when the
first shells exploded close behind. We dived for cover. Then we were up and
running, adrenalin coursing through the body, across an onion field where
we threw ourselves to the ground every few metres.

'Hey Mista, have one piaz,' called a cheerful character who tossed me an
onion. 'It is good for you to eat.' More shells hit the village which was now
obscured by a pall of smoke.

Now we were wedged into the farmer's little bunker, sodden with sweat
and warding off the thirst with grapes. I took my turn and went to gather
some more bunches, this time from the same place as Abdul Ghafoor had
collected some. 'Mista, mista,' cried the men in horror as they spat the fruit
onto the floor.

They were sour.

147

Full Circle and Due West

The way to Ghorband valley was over soaring mountains. The journey had to be made at night and the obstacles were the north road and the posts on the other side. Then there were the mountains, which you had to climb before sunrise as any movement spotted on the steep and exposed slopes would bring down fire from the posts. One escort would take me as far as the village of Upion in the shadow of the mountains where a second would lead me over the peaks. We got off to an inauspicious start. Having zig-zagged for many kilometres south and west, we followed a long culvert which brought us at dusk to the edge of the road. To our dismay we found a group of Mujahiddin about to launch an attack on a post about a kilometre away. They were an unruly crew who crouched at the side of the culvert smoking hashish. It was no place to try to cut the road, so we set off for another spot further south. There we found another group preparing to move on the posts.

'Don't worry, we will find a good place to cross,' said Nasim, one of the escorts. I liked this gentle unobtrusive man who was rare in that he liked to spend time on his own. At Aqarshareen's camp I had struck up a good rapport with the former student of engineering. As a farewell gesture, Aqarshareen suggested to Nasim that he might like to accompany me as far as Upion. Nasim readily agreed.

We waited at a village and when it was dark set off for the road again. A network of wide streams confronted us and we lost time as I had constantly to tie and untie my shoelaces in the dark while the Mujahiddin merely slipped off their sandals. Nasim insisted on carrying me and my rucksack piggy-back across the stream. It did not seem possible that this slightly-built man could manage such a feat but he did without any trouble. I could feel his body which seemed to be made of steel. We edged closer to the road, crouching to keep below the line of scrub. We were less than 50 metres from the road when one of the groups opened up on the post a kilometre away. Then the second group did likewise in the other direction. Tracer snaked across the sky and the shelling began on the villages. Nasim cursed softly and made the dash across the dense black streak of the road, rolling down the other bank. We followed.

At Upion, high in the foothills, we rested while a new escort arrived.

Nasim banged on several doors but for the first time there was no welcome. Instead, from behind the wooden doors, came fearful, sometimes angry, words, 'Please to go away'. Either this was a village where Hezb was not in control or the population were afraid of harbouring Mujahiddin. Certainly the village was a sitting targer for the post only a few hundred metres away. We finally rested at a smart mosque at the top of the village. From there you could oversee the battle under way at two of the posts and, in the distance, hear a third at Jebel Seraj. I spent a pleasant hour admiring the beautiful glazed blue calligraphy which adorned the interior of the mosque.

Crossing the mountain was murderous. It was steep and covered with loose scree and shards of rock. The climb took us most of the night. There were frequent rock falls and at the summit there was a spot of rock climbing thrown in. One of my new escorts – a tomtit – did nothing but chatter away in Pushtu until I found myself plotting the best spots from which to push him off the cliffs. Below, we left a panorama of blazing guns and tracer. Occasionally a bright flare would illuminate a great swathe of ground, hanging in the sky like some brilliant star. So bright were they that even from that distance they threw our shadows across the mountains and we would flatten ourselves against the rock. I also saw my first towns lit up by electricity, strung out along the north road. Upion had been in darkness but now it was brightly lit up. Once or twice you could spot Mujahiddin running through the streets and then several tanks rumbling out of the post. The Mujahiddin claimed one of the tanks. From that high and freezing perch you felt like a company of gods watching the mortals far below. Then you began the awful slog again. The last 200 metres of the peak was covered in dense cloud so that the world below suddenly disappeared and you carried on blind in a silent eerie world where the only sound was your own breath.

The summit was blanked out. It was 3.45 am and we had made it with an hour to spare before sunrise. We crossed the small and freezing plateau and began the descent. I was looking forward to the comparative peace promised by Ghorband after Totumdarah. The descent proved as hazardous as the climb up the eastern face had been and much of it was on our backsides. I caught up with the four Mujahiddin who were sitting disconsolately where the cloud broke. There was the sound of gunfire below.

'I though there was no power supply to Ghorband,' I said gesturing at the string of towns lit up below.

'No electricity in Ghorband,' said one of them gloomily.

The truth dawned. In the cloud on the summit we had walked a full circle and descended the way we had come. The first rays of dawn were breaking up the dark sky to the east and then the cloud suddenly lifted behind us. We had to climb the last 200 metres again and the night was dissolving rapidly. I cursed their rotten navigation. Light was already giving substance to the world and you hoped that the troops in the posts were too tired after a night's fighting to scan the mountains. Far from it. The communists knew that many of the attacks were launched from over the mountains and the peaks were constantly under observation. We had just made the summit again when shells began to explode along the range. Looking at the plateau in daylight it seemed incredible that we could have turned a full circle in such a tiny area. Ghorband was now before us, thousands of metres below; a haven surrounded by towering peaks. As the sun rose, colour flooded over the high peaks to the west which ended in the snowy fastnesses of the Hindu Kush. My escorts prayed with a shepherd while I smoked a cigarette and watched the blank mountains turn pink and purple in the sunlight.

Four hours laters we were ravenously eating fresh-baked nan and drinking sweet tea in a stone hut at the head of a narrow ravine. The little Mujahiddin outpost served as a jumping-off point for Ghorband fighters crossing the mountains to attack the enemy. Against a rhapsody of early morning bird calls, the sub-commander at the outpost asked me why the West had been so unprepared for the invasion of Afghanistan.

It was a good question. My belief is that the Russians had had a hand in laying enough smokescreens in the region in 1979 to divert attention away from their preparations to invade Afghanistan. Those preparations were almost certainly under way by the autumn of 1979 when it was clear that the communist regime in Kabul was in trouble. The thousands of Russian advisers inside Afghanistan were not enough to save the Taraki regime which was faced with widespread revolt. The coup by Amin in September probably sealed the fate of Afghanistan.

But it was events in neighbouring countries which occupied the attention of the West. In February the US ambassador to Afghanistan had been killed in a mysterious incident in Kabul. In November the United States embassy in Tehran was overrun and 48 hostages seized. Three weeks later the Grand Mosque in Mecca was seized. Then came the sacking of the United States embassy in Pakistan by a student mob. At the time it seemed that this chain of spectacular events was a product of the fissile social and political tendencies of the region. Investigation suggests strongly there was a common thread in most of the events and, according to intelligence sources, that thread can be traced back to Moscow. Some of the attacks were either planned by or encouraged by Moscow. The result was that key United States embassies were knocked out as Moscow prepared to invade.

One source said: 'Volatile forces prevail in the region which is the easiest place on earth for one group to disguise its actions in the name of another organisation. Communists tend to use any name but communist, knowing the antipathy of most Muslims. In the final analysis, just prior to the invasion of Afghanistan the three United States embassies most closely involved in monitoring events in that country – in Afghanistan itself, Iran and Pakistan – had been effectively neutralised. It was a perfect situation for the Soviets to be in prior to the invasion. That they had a hand in bringing about the situation I have no doubt.'

In February ambassador Adolph Dubs was being driven to work at the embassy in Kabul when he was kidnapped and taken to an hotel in Kabul.

Despite pleas by the United States not to take any action that might endangei the diplomat's life, an assault was launched against Room 117 of the Kabul Hotel and the kidnappers and Dubs died in a hail of bullets and explosions. The assault was almost certainly masterminded by Russian advisers and America's subsequent protests were directed pointedly at Moscow as well as Kabul. Who the kidnappers were or what their motives were has never been satisfactorily explained. It is doubtful that Mujahiddin waging war against communism would kidnap an American.

In the same month, a mob led by leftists overran the United States embassy in Tehran. The attack was led by a group trained by Libyan and extremist Palestinians, but staff were released by supporters of Khomeini. In November there was another attack and this time the staff were taken hostage in a crisis which eventually cost James Carter the presidency. The captors presented themselves to the world as Islamic fundamentalists and supporters of Khomeini yet intelligence sources say there was a leftist element in the attack. Analysis of events became complicated in post-revolutionary Iran because of the blurring of political alignments. Muslims, communists and the middle classes were united in their desire to end the reign of the Shah but they differed on the form of government to succeed him. It was the Islamic fundamentalists who prevailed, a development correctly seen by the Tudeh Party and other communists as ultimately dangerous to their health. Some went into hiding while others easily infiltrated religious groups loyal to the theocracy. It was only much later that the mullahs felt in a strong enough position to begin anti-communist purges and witch-hunts.

On 20 November a group of terrorists seized the Grand Mosque in Mecca. The attack on Islam's holiest shrine and synchronised assaults in eastern Saudi Arabia were a direct challenge to the Royal House of Saud. The leader of the well-armed group, which numbered as many as 500, proclaimed himself the Mahdi (the Islamic Messiah, a recurring theme in the history of the faith) and many of his band seemed to have been inspired by the Iranian revolution. But many were later discovered to have been trained in Marxist South Yemen and in Libya, both client states of the Soviet Union. The attack showed a high degree of planning and execution and it took crack units nearly two weeks to end the bloody siege.

An Iranian radio broadcast in which the United States was accused of being behind the attack on the Grand Mosque led to the destruction of the US embassy in Islamabad. The majority of the people in the mob which attacked the embassy were inflamed by religious sentiment. But a substantial minority of students who poured out of the Qaid-i-Azam University and headed for the embassy were communists. I talked to students who took part in the attack. One said: 'The communists would always join in anything anti-American. Most of us were angered by this terrible news and did not care what the motives of the communists were. They were well-organised and seemed to know their way around the place. While many people contented themselves with anti-American slogans, it was the communists who started most of the fires. They were going to destroy the embassy even if it meant frying the Americans inside. They were like commandos. Most of the protestors were carried along by their emotions. The communists undoubtedly manipulated large sections of the protestors. They were very calculating.' Four embassy personnel and two rioters died and the rest of the staff, trapped in a vault in the heart of the complex, only narrowly escaped being burned alive. The embassy was destroyed.

'There is little doubt that highly-organised groups of communists, whose masters are in the Kremlin, showed their hands in 1979,' another intelligence source said. 'Mecca and Islamabad we know for certain contained strong communist elements, guiding elements. Tehran is more marginal but there is strong circumstantial evidence suggestive of communist influence. At the very least it provided a perfect opportunity for subversive elements elsewhere in the region to strike. In turn the accumulation of disorder and fear in the region provided a perfect cover for Soviet intentions in Afghanistan.'

The sub-commander listened carefully, all the time turning his turban carefully in his hand. 'My friend it is not important that people in Europe and America do not care very much about Afghanistan. We will fight the Russians with or without your help. The Afghan people know the truth about the Russian intentions against us and against all countries. But I am wondering if the people of Europe and America understand Russian

The peace of Ghorband.

intentions. The materialism of the West makes you blind to what Russia is doing. Reagan and Thatcher seem strong men (many Afghans refuse to believe that the 'Iron Lady' of Great Britain is actually a woman – a compliment!), but the people think Russia is a long way away. One day you may find Russia is very close. If our people stop fighting then Afghanistan will just be a stepping stone for the Russians.'

Ghorband was peaceful after the front line. The valley rose gently for kilometres to the west and was dominated by the swollen Ghorband River. The storm had wreaked havoc in the valley where whole sections of the road had been swept away by water pouring off the mountains. In one place nearly a kilometre of road had collapsed into the river and disappeared. The river itself was bright orange still from the thousands of tons of earth which it carried along. It happened every year, said one of the Mujahiddin who now formed my escort. He was matter-of-fact about it but there was no resignation in his voice. Such catastrophes were a condition of life in Afghanistan but people remained undaunted. The power and grandeur of nature were reflected in the spirit of the people. Your admiration for the Afghans was renewed every day. Gangs of men stripped to the waist were already rebuilding the road. I felt relieved and happy as we walked the kilometres through the valley, past orchards full of almonds which had just come into season. Wherever there was an abundance the Mujahiddin helped themselves. Eat well, they said to me, in Bamian life was more austere. They laughed. They were not going to Bamian.

We sprawled on carpets laid out on a verandah which overlooked the dusty road and the fields and villages in the loops of the river. At length, Sayyef Rahman, overall commander of Ghorband, appeared. Though not physically striking, he was a sincere and articulate chief (he was also the only Afghan who did not want his photograph taken). I liked his modesty and we spent several hours at the chai khana talking. There was only one communist post in Ghorband and this fact made Sayyef Rahman rather apologetic. He knew I had come from over the mountains where there was a post every few kilometres: in his demesne you could have walked 30 kilometres in either direction in peace. There were sporadic bombing raids and a day's walk away I would see the burned out tanks from an offensive two years before, yet he remained defensive. He brightened when he talked of the post but he had to admit it was manned by Parchamites and not Russians. There was less glory in ambushing government troops than the invader. Ghorband was almost wholly liberated and it acted as a reservoir for Mujahiddin who could be moved over the mountains to the front line. Such expeditions were frequent.

'My job as commander is to fight, to plan the fighting and keep law and order. Perhaps the most important thing is to teach the Islamic way to the people. After the communists have gone we must have Islamic government in Afghanistan. This would mean Islamic teaching in all schools and Islamic law. But we must also have development. I do not see conflict between Islam and development.'

He drank green tea and waved his hand so that dishes of grapes and almonds appeared. Then he talked of the proliferation of political parties in his country in a half-sceptical way. He insisted there were around 100 political parties inside Afghanistan and reeled off dozens of names. There were seven alone specific to the Hazarajat region of central Afghanistan. Did I know there were four communist parties in addition to Parcham and Khalq? Sometimes the parties were important like Hezb or Jamiat or Harakat all of which commanded tens of thousands of followers; sometimes just a village was commanded by someone advocating an obscure variant of Islam. Ah Afghanistan.

I continued west in the company of Sigmatullah, a thoughtful intellectual at whose parents' home I was to stay the night. While dinner was prepared we sat in one of the family orchards while Sigmatullah's young brothers gathered almonds for us to eat. Sigmatullah carefully cracked open the nuts with a small rock and explained why he had joined Hezb and not one of its rivals. There were more intellectuals and professional people in the party, which he considered important in post-communist Afghanistan; the party was founded on Islamic principles and did not merely use Islam as a means to an end as some parties did; the party would not let Afghanistan be dominated by the West; it would carry the Islamic revolution into the Muslim Soviet republics and it had pledged to kill all communists when the

Ghorbandi in a garden of flowers.

government fell. It was the code of vengeance on a terrible scale. Sigmatullah gathered the little pile of almonds and handed them to me with a smile.

In the days spent hiking through Ghorband my appetite returned and I regained some of the weight I had lost. I felt better but I was still weak and the long marches were a strain. For the first time I passed through villages controlled by other parties, mostly the Harakat of Maulavi Mohammed Nabi Mohammedi.

'Only Hezb in this village,' assured the Mujahid as we stood beneath a huge poster bearing the image of Mohammedi.

All I was required to know was that Hezb controlled most of Afghanistan. It was much the same story with all the parties. Eyes would widen at the mention of a rival party chief, as if they were surprised that you had even heard of such an insignificant character. Sometimes the villages in Ghorband boasted more than one party, each with its own political committee and Mujahiddin who patrolled in separate orbits. They lived grudgingly together – of necessity – and regarded the Unity as a hoax perpetrated by fifth columnists in Peshawar. Hezb did not control the country: no party did. Afghanistan was a huge patchwork of parties, some big and some small, who jealously guarded their territory and whose strategy was largely 'what we have, we hold'. Control of territory – and the acquisition of more – was a powerful driving force. Many provinces were dominated by one or other of

Even Ghorband has been hit by the jets.

155

the major parties but they rarely exercised exclusive control. The unspoken truth was that, parallel to the war of resistance, the rival parties were often fighting each other. Just how extensive this internecine strife could be I would find out in the next month. In the tranquility of Ghorband it did not seem possible, but I was heading for what amounted to civil war.

'Mista do not move,' said the Mujahid who edged closer and stamped on a bulbous yellow spider. 'Very dangerous. Andropov no good.' Spiders and scorpions were named after the Russian leader of that time. We were halfway over the ridge of sharp hill and bound for the lush valley of Fendeckestan which bisected Ghorband. From the top of the hot and dusty hills Fendeckestan was a beautiful sight: hundreds of substantial homes, many like fortresses, swathed in green and watered by dozens of streams tumbling off the valley sides. We were taken to a large clearing in the heart of the valley where hundreds of elders were sitting cross-legged in a great rectangle. It was rather like bursting in on a conclave of cardinals but they welcomed us with great curiosity. Presently hundreds of dishes of food were laid before the elders and by the light of a score of hurricane lamps we ate and talked. Representatives of villages from all parts of the valley had been summoned to the jirga to discuss the Jehad and more prosaically the rebuilding of the road. It had been agreed that each village would supply so many men to undertake the venture. Later all the turbaned men prayed together. The young Mujahiddin hovered among the trees and looked on in awe at the men whose gravity and accumulated wisdom ruled the valley.

Fendeckestan was under the command of one Doctor Amirjon but I was not to meet him until the morning. I was left with a sub-commander called Shareen. The word means 'sweet' in Persian but the man was a lout and so were his fighters. We walked the 3 kilometres to his house where the men taunted me about the first Afghan War. 'Mista, you know Doctor Brydon and Macnaghten?' Yes, I did. Were they familiar with General Roberts who hammered the Afghans in the second war? They were not and did not believe it anyway. Then began the lectures on 'Western imperialism'. A sudden attack of dysentery had made me irritable: that is when I was actually in the room and not squatting beneath the stars. I asked them for their definition of imperialism and the best they managed was to equate it with capitalism, and the image for that was 200 years out of date. Hashish was passed around and the litany of platitudes rehearsed again, only more drowsily now. The level of debate was redolent of a score of left-wing conversations in large bed-sits in north London beneath enormous white paper globe lampshades.

Shareen wrestled with his little son. He encouraged the boy to punch him and then sent him sprawling, all the time beckoning him to come forward again. The child was no longer able to suppress his tears. Shareen left his men to carry on the sterile debate. Democracy was meaningless, they said. I pretended to be asleep but they shook me awake. I was reminded of the rancorous left in Great Britain. Little wonder that the intellectual initiative in Britain had been seized by the right. Like these characters, the left did not debate in order to take the argument anywhere, to break new ground, but merely to petrify ideas into shallow orthodoxies sufficient for a mob to chant. The old idealism had become cant. Now in another world that same old rubbish was being dusted down and inflicted on my intelligence. It was a product of Kabul University, an institution I was learning to detest. It had been the second most important source of communist ideology after the military. The rise of the Marxists provoked a corresponding interest in Islamic fundamentalism and the university became virtually polarised. The memories of all these former students were confined to political rallies, demonstrations and plots. One of the men told me with great pride how he helped blow up a laboratory full of pharmacy students most of whom were communists.

'Fascinating,' I said and pretended to be asleep. I wondered if anybody had done any studying at the university. They shook me awake again, so I told them they sounded like a lot of half-baked communists, a thought guaranteed to strain Muslim hospitality but I hoped it might shut them up. It did not, but I was out of the door anyway.

Experience suggested that the world could only get better and so it did. Doctor Amirjon was an urbane middle-aged man whose generous features, walrus moustache and calm air of experience suggested a well-to-do Greek

Ghorband acts as a reservoir of Mujahiddin who cross the mountains to engage the Russians.

restaurateur in Soho. He welcomed me and clasped my hand with his left: his right was in a sling as the result of a bullet wound. The limb was swollen and purple and he had lost much of the feeling in it. He carried a lump of plasticine which he constantly squeezed in his hand to exercise it. Though only 4 kilometres away, it was a different world from that of Shareen whom I had last seen biting open almonds with his teeth. The doctor scratched his pepper and salt hair and led me into his office. I was startled to find that the room was full of leather-bound horsehair sofas and armchairs. It was the first and last time I saw a seat in Afghanistan and the doctor said the great vessels had been brought by the British. Certainly they appeared to have been plucked from a Hampshire rectory but nobody knew how they had come to be transplanted into this wild land. A wave of the hand sent a Mujahid to fetch an interpreter and another gesture resulted in two men lugging a huge unexploded bomb through the door. They chipped away a tiny chunk of the rough textured metallic contents visible through a large split in the casing and laid it on the table. Then they lit it. The tiny chip burst into brilliant flame and gave off a cloud of noxious smoke which scorched the lungs and made the eyes water. I clambered through the window to escape it while the Mujahiddin, who thought it all great fun, crowded through the door. I do not know what nature of bomb it was but I put samples in a matchbox with the intention of having them analysed.

During my stay with Doctor Amirjon I was followed around by a large anti-aircraft gun. It was all to do with the Afghans' delight for being photographed. After some initial courtesy shots, I said flatly that I decided what pictures to take and of whom. The men watched me like hawks and as soon as the camera was in my hand would leap into the picture, rifles clasped firmly across chests. Mujahiddin in a distant landscape would suddenly snap to attention. A pastoral scene with a shepherd would be ruined as half a dozen men shuffled self-consciously into the viewfinder. One day I took a picture of a man praying next to the 12.7 mm DShK-38 anti-aircraft gun on the ramparts of the HQ.

'Mista likes this gun,' said one of the men.

Half a dozen men dismantled it and lugged it down into the courtyard before reassembling it and posing in front of it. Exasperated, I went for a walk along the valley. I turned at the noise of panting behind. The men had hauled the gun after me.

'This is better place for the Mista to take picture,' said one. In the valley below a contingent of men were marching off and, anything to change the subject, I asked where they were going. 'They go to fight. Now you take picture of Mujahiddin.'

I asked why they were heading west instead of south over the mountains. I could tell by the embarrassed silence I had asked the wrong questions. I was interested now.

The next day I climbed the valley to a shady spot to read Shakespeare and then fell asleep. I awoke from a dream about great metallic creations like those in Wells' *The War of the Worlds* to find something similar standing over me.

'What the bloody hell is that doing there?' I shouted at the men who grinned and whistled and pretended not to notice. They had hauled the anti-aircraft weapon all the way up the valley and reassembled it over me. It was not the subtlest of hints but they got their picture taken.

As I moved west, so the dominance of the Pathan people began to give way to more racially mixed communities. There were more Tadjiks and a few Uzbeks; then many Hazaras whose Mongol features mark them out as descendents of Genghis Khan. The Tadjiks dominated the few trades like cobbling or metal working. At Qimchuk the Mujahiddin showed me with great pride the small power station they ran which generated the only electricity in the valley. Each day brought its own little disappointment, best described as the 'motor syndrome'. A few ancient trucks plied the road between Ghorband and Bamian. Each day I was told I would 'take a motor' from the next village and at each village we discovered new sections of the road washed away and the vehicles stranded.

The commander of Darisaidan introduced himself as Qasi Sur Gul. I was taken to the local Mujahiddin HQ, a typical Afghan home. It was large and rectangular with high walls and no windows. Through wooden doors was the courtyard where sheep and chickens roamed and the cooking was usually done. The rooms were all off the courtyard and the windows looked onto it. It was an ancient design which meant that the building could be defended from attack if necessary. An Afghan's home is his castle, often quite literally. Qasi Sur Gul was tall and gawky, with a stern face, and when he walked through the streets with his hands clasped behind his back, a cross between the Duke of Edinburgh and a praying mantis, the people leapt out of his way. He held himself in great esteem. I had not wanted to stay overnight but exigencies of hospitality meant that we could not turn down the invitation. Besides, said Qasi Sur Gul, in the morning he would show me something special.

In Darisaidan the Mujahiddin received one day a week weapons training. Qasi Sur Gul was the teacher. They also spent one day a week receiving Islamic instruction. Qasi Sur Gul was the teacher. He had founded three schools in the village where boys received Islamic lessons. The commander was source and inspiration for everything in his little kingdom. I shocked him by asking why there was no education for girls. He explained it in terms you would use for a particularly dense pupil: girls simply did not need education beyond the duties of the kitchen and the land. Walking through the villages you would see women coming towards you stop and turn their faces to a wall until you had passed. The men are fond of their women and care for them but the fact remains their horizons are limited from birth until death. The men never talk about their women to strangers and so throughout my travels they remained a class of phantoms, and when you actually saw them they turned away. It was one of the more depressing memories.

Qasi Sur Gul was gone when I awoke. We ate some fried nan and set off to rendezvous with the commander. His surprise lived up to its promise. We found him conscientiously inspecting two ranks of his men who were dressed in bizarre uniforms.

'My army,' he said proudly.

They reminded me for some reason of Italian sailors I had seen in old sepia photographs and they looked decidedly unhappy in the gear. Or was it Fred Karno? My companions began to giggle and I had to bite my lip. Afghans do not suit uniforms. Qasi Sur Gul, who was similarly attired, marched them up a hill. I had never seen Afghans looking so miserable. At the top of the hill the commander insisted on putting on a display of drill – Afghans do not suit that either – and then he marched them down again as we waved goodbye. As soon as they were out of sight my companions and I collapsed on the ground laughing.

I had been with my companions, three teenagers, for two days, and we had hit it off. That is, they allowed me a little time to myself for reading, writing and reflection, provided I joined in their high-spirited banter for the rest of the time. I asked them about the Mujahiddin heading west and the eldest, a stocky bearded youth, replied:

'Mista, you go to Bamian. Then you know..'

Further questions were out of order. Besides, one of the others had spotted a snake at the base of cliffs we walked along. Like the Christian, the Muslim has a deep-rooted loathing of serpents. The three of them scrambled down the cliffs and spent an hour stalking, stoning and finally shooting the reptile before bearing it triumphantly up the path. The ghost had been laid.

We reached Ferinjhal at sunset. It was just as well as sunlight did not become it. Ferinjhal was the original one-horse town where sullen men sat on verandahs with their weapons and the only movement you detected was their eyes following you. Dust and a sense of desolation settled in equal parts on new arrivals and though the hospitality of Commander Abdul Khalil Khan was warm and generous, that first impression – a sleepy cowboy town on the Mexican border – never left me. But here at last were the fabled motors, or so they said. I did not actually see one until three days later when I left. Khalil was a Tadjik who with his brothers seemed to run the village. He provided great feasts: hot fresh nan, scrambled egg, salads and mutton followed by purple grapes and pink apples.

Days fell into a pattern of boredom, spent milling around the little dusty square waiting for the motor which never arrived. Each day I would walk the three kilometres from the commander's delightful home high in a valley down to the village square, wait for the fabled motor and then walk back to the house. It was covered in grapevines and each window had little blue shutters so that you thought of the Swiss Alps. I struck up an acquaintance with the blacksmith and took tea in his forge each day while he showed me the farm implements he had made from the metal of Russian tanks. Guns into ploughshares.

A rare sight: a 'motor' used by the Afghans on roads held by the resistance.

One day the smithy introduced me to a relative who had just arrived from the western city of Herat. The flint-eyed man had lost everything he owned in the Russian onslaught against the city in the spring. Thousands of people had died as the jets flattened whole areas of the city and then disease – typhoid, cholera – had set in and hundreds more had died. Because it was so far from the party HQs in Pakistan events in the city had been under-reported. Its trading and commercial links were with Iran which is 100 kilometres from the city. Herat was a powerful symbol for the resistance as the first city to revolt against the communists. In March 1979, mobs hunted down hundreds of communists and their families and butchered them. Soviet advisers were among those flayed alive or mutilated. For nearly a week the rebels held the city until government forces smashed the resistance. Thousands died. Though it is an isolated and small city Herat has a long history of resistance to invaders. In 1838 it was besieged by a Persian army urged on by Russian advisers. A dashing Irish artillery officer, Eldred Pottinger, who happened to be in the city at the time, organised the successful defence of Herat. After the Russian invasion in 1979, a general strike paralysed the city for a week and the resistance began by trying to cut the Herat-Qandahar road. In the spring of 1980 there was a major push against the Mujahiddin. The spring offensive of 1983 led to massive destruction in the city.

But, said the man who had lost two shops and his home, the Mujahiddin who had retreated across the border into Iran were already moving back into the city.

And then the motor appeared in a cloud of dust. The village came to life as the driver, known to all as Uzbek, leapt from the cab of the Mercedes minibus and went from shop to shop helping himself to raisins and cigarettes and cursing those about him. He was a comic, a philosopher and the greatest trader between Parwan and Bamian provinces. I called him Trader. He eyed the crates of fruit destined for shipment to Bamian and ordered those about him to load them. He eyed me in much the same way and shrugged his shoulders before moving down the street to find someone to insult. Trader was a voluble character and there seemed nothing he did not have violent opinions about. He dispensed news which was always welcome and his crazy ideas which were not. He was constantly on the move and traded in anything that came his way. His shrill tones were tempered by the rampant enthusiasm and humour he brought to every topic. Every village looked forward to a visit from Trader.

I had walked some 400 kilometres now and shared the excitement of the Mujahiddin at the prospect of a journey by motor, even in this old wreck which Trader kept going by a combination of genius for mechanical improvisation and the benign sanction of the gods. We set off on the 200 kilometres journey with a dozen men and as many cases of fruit jammed inside the minibus and eight of us and four crates perched precariously on the roof. The initial delight of the alfresco ride gave way to cramp and not a little terror as Trader careered along the rutted road. The cases of fruit shifted alarmingly but the Mujahiddin treated the bone-jarring journey like a charabanc ride. Trader's endless screeching chatter never ceased throughout the entire journey. He ordered everyone out and we walked across the Shibar Pass while the minibus laboured through the loops of the road in first gear. Then we were barrelling down into Bamian where the beautiful sky itself is intimidated by the soaring peaks. To the north the Hindu Kush and south the Koh-i-Baba. We roofriders celebrated by prizing open one of the crates and helping ourselves to bunches of grapes. The next thing we knew we had scoffed about 15 kg and we gazed abashed at the half-empty crate.

Trader was not amused when he inspected his cargo. I was a communist spy, he screamed, and the Mujahiddin were lower than dogs. No, the snakes. His catalogue of insults passed through Darwin's evolutionary scale to the lowest forms of life and then he invented a few of his own, as we passed through the tortured valleys of Bamian. The road followed the Bamian River and now showed an alarming tendency to slope so that the bus tilted frequently toward the precipice. Even though Trader, at the wheel, treated this section with respect, the right-hand wheels suddenly lifted off the ground and we began to tip over. I grabbed an overhanging branch and clung to it as the bus slid away from under me. I hung there expecting the bus to plunge into the boiling river 10 metres below with all hands on board. The bus seemed to be suspended for a moment and then suddenly the Mujahiddin perched on the roof leapt over the right side of the bus and used their weight to pull the vehicle down onto four wheels. I felt vaguely stupid hanging around in a tree.

Trader used the break to exact his price for the grapes we had eaten. He plucked a grenade from the jacket of one of the men and held it up. I feared he might want to blow us up but instead he ordered all of the men into the river while he went 100 metres upstream and lobbed the grenade in. The explosion brought dozens of stunned fish to the surface, which were pulled from the water by the Mujahiddin while Trader cheerfully supervised the operation from the river bank. We completed the journey with our laps full of flapping, twitching and decidedly smelly fish which, Trader screamed, we could cook for his dinner.

12

The Dumb Titans

The westward journey to Bamian had been a pilgrimage for Buddhist monks in ancient times and hippies more recently. I had guessed it would be an extraordinary place and so it turned out to be. I was decanted in the central Bamian valley which was under the control of the Mujahiddin. The entire province was theirs but for two posts at the provincial capital of Bamian. The province had been favoured by the exiled king Zahir Shah who had a summer palace at Comart in the north. The summer retreat was now the HQ of the Hezb provincial commander Tooran Abdur Hadi. My first taste of this regal connection was the two great hounds which bounded up to greet me. They were huge friendly beasts – they looked like a cross between husky dogs and St Bernards – and were of a line specially bred by the ex-king. The Afghans have a pragmatic view of animals and these two were intended to be guard dogs. They merely wanted a bit of attention and, after a few pats on the head, became firm friends. The Mujahiddin seemed vaguely disturbed that the animals had not ripped my throat out.

'The dogs are called Brezhnev and Babrak and I am Abdul Hai,' said the congenial young man in the Chitrali cap. It had been a long hike up the valley south of the main valley. Abdul Hai, brother of Commander Tooran, was a gentle and perceptive man and he commanded an anti-aircraft post at the head of the valley. Sensing the antipathy I had developed for the tomtits assigned to guide me to the camp, he ordered them to remain with the main body of men camped on the floor of the valley in stone huts and led me to the foot of a towering needle of rock.

'This is Kharaghor. It means resting place.' A tiny path wound its way around the tower like a helter-skelter. At the summit of the 150-metre tower of granite was an anti-aircraft dug-out and living quarters hewn from the rock. Across the valley were two other anti-aircraft posts high up among the peaks. Well-crafted pulley systems between the posts and the valley floor enabled food and water to be winched up. You felt pleasantly cut off like a child in a tree den or a scholar with his books. Two days with assorted oddballs, party theoreticians and juvenile pests had left me feeling irascible. Kharaghor was the perfect antidote. The tone of life up on the cool eyrie was set, as always, by the commander. Abdul Hai was gentle and unassuming with a creative flair. There was Abdulwahed who peered into a huge *Qoran* through glasses perched on the end of his nose. He had white hair, beard and eyebrows but age had not dulled his passion for learning and discussion. In any company he would seek out intelligence and engage in debate which went on for hours. It was a pleasure to listen to his soothing voice. He was fluent in Russian and an expert in weaponry. Unfamiliar weapons captured from the enemy were brought from all over the province for Abdulwahed to examine. The cook, said Abdul Hai, closing the Persian-English dictionary, was a 'genie. He can do magic. He never sleeps and we never know where he goes to.'

I spent several blissful days in their company, visiting the posts, inspecting the wreckage of a gunship at the head of the valley, and watching games of volleyball on a court built by the men. The entrance to the camp was marked by an enormous timber triumphal arch so that you were reminded of a boy scout camp. A huge bomb crater had been turned into an ornamental pond with a border of shrubs and a stock of fish. Abdul Hai made ashtrays out of empty cigarette packets (the no-smoking rule was not observed). Dozens of bomb cases had been 'planted' in a little garden next to the pond. No matter what the invader inflicted on these people, they seemed to reply that they would prevail; that they could absorb and even find a use for whatever was thrown at them.

Abdul Hai had a fine voice and would sing softly while making the little ashtrays. The songs sung by the Mujahiddin had led to some confusion on my part. You could hear them – lusty or gentle – in all the hidden valleys of Afghanistan but when you inquired about them of the orthodox party men they would deny that any Mujahid sang songs. Eventually you discovered that song – along with dancing and the listening for pleasure to radio or TV – had been proscribed by the party. Abdul smiled and told me about the songs. One verse ran: 'Come, we go to fight the Russians; our blood will water the flowers of Afghanistan.' Another told of a Mujahid who tells his wife that he is going to fight the enemy and that she will not see him again until the country has been liberated.

'This is how it is for many Mujahiddin,' he said.

Then he produced a cassette recorder and played a remarkable tape. It had been recorded during an air raid on the camp and the valley. Such tapes had become rather fashionable by late 1983; the 'top ten' battles circulated among the groups. To the Afghans technology was to be adapted to their way of life. This tape featured a cacophony of sounds: jets shrieking past, the anti-aircraft guns, bombs, and even automatics chattering ceaselessly. In the midst of the raid the Mujahiddin emerged from their shelters and raised the cry 'Allah O Akbar'. More cries began in the valley below and the posts above. Anyone not manning a weapon was crying 'God is Great' above the din of war until you heard hundreds of voices.

Abdul Hai's brother Commander Tooran had begun the resistance in Bamian. As a senior officer in the Bamian barracks he had led 700 soldiers in revolt. They killed the communists but Tooran had been badly wounded. The loss of leadership at this crucial moment enabled communist reinforcements who had been airlifted in to regain control of the camp. The Russians had later taken over an impregnable hill overlooking the government post at Bamian town. It was a reflection of how little the Russians trusted the government troops.

'Half of the Russian guns are pointed at the Mujahiddin and half at the Karmalite troops,' said Abdul Hai.

His brother had gone on to secure most of the province, driving out communist sympathisers and establishing Mujahiddin groups. They hauled anti-aircraft guns into the mountains to deter air attacks. In 1982 Tooran had personally taken two captured Russians – he gave them Muslim names – to Pakistan and presented them to the world's Press. By 1983 the province was entirely in the hands of two main groups, Hezb and Harakat. The posts were cut off and had to be supplied by air.

But the food was poor in Bamian. There was no fruit which I had used to supplement my diet and we lived on rice and occasionally potatoes. The Genie appeared one day with half a cucumber which he had scrounged in one of the villages. It was the highlight of the meal. On my last day I accompanied Abdul Hai and The Genie to the nearest village. Brezhnev and Babrak came along at my request. Although they had grown unruly, their essential breeding showed and I found it easy to control them. The residents of the village were terrified.

'They think you are genie too because you are friends with dogs,' explained Abdul Hai.

Despite my protests, Abdul Hai had organised the expedition to acquire a chicken so that they could treat their guest. In truth I was hungry and delighted when they insisted. As we walked through the rice fields which stretched down the valley, Abdul Hai told me about himself. He had been an accountant and all he dreamed of was to return to that job. He detested war but it was his duty to fight. Many of the commanders were ambitious and expected important jobs in government after the communists had been defeated. Abdul Hai had no such dreams and I did not doubt him.

The Genie had appeared with a myna bird in a cage and we sat outside a mosque in the village which was adorned with posters of Mauli Mohammed Nabi Mohammedi. Hezb and Harakat lived side by side in the main Bamian valley, he said, feeding the bird with pieces of the whorls of brown bread that tasted of malt. The groups consulted each other although combined assaults on the post were never under single command. A plan would be agreed and then each group would follow its own commander. The idea of the Unity was not scorned here and I was introduced to commanders from Harakat and one from Jamiat. My conclusion later was that this cooperation was a product of necessity. There was a balance of power between the groups in the centre of the province and nobody dared upset it. This was no bad thing and even more encouraging was the real enthusiasm which fighters like Abdul Hai had for the Unity. It was quite different in the north.

Bearing our chicken, we returned to Kharaghor where Abdulwahed stoked the fire. It was a grand meal in splendid company and afterwards Abdul Hai sang for us and the Genie recited little paradoxical verses which set Abdulwahed puzzling until the Genie confessed they were deliberately meaningless. Called upon to sing or recite a poem, I chose the king's battle oration from *Henry V*. I amended the last line thus: 'Cry Allah for Hekmatyar, Afghanistan and Mohammed.' They were delighted and demanded more.

My departure from the eyrie was delayed by a violent attack of the old problem. It meant most of a night squatting on what is without doubt the most hazardous toilet in the world. Convenience dictated that some arrangements be made aloft the needle and public health that it be away from the living quarters. A short path behind a bluff led to the place in question and from the proverbial great height coupled with an exquisite sense of balance you did your business. Necessity not courage forced me to perch thus 150 metres above the valley for most of the night. By dawn I was too exhausted and feverish to stand. Abdul Hai gave me some tablets while The Genie visibly fretted. Abdulwahed threw another rough blanket over me and read favoured verses from the *Qoran* all day. As I sank in and out of the fever I found great comfort in the rhythms of the verses.

'Yaas my friend, welcome to Aingurhun. We have good time together, facking crazy time. Anything you want you ask for. Anything my friend.' With that, Commander Sher Ali grasped a handful of cigarettes from the shelf and thrust them into my hand. The proprietor of the shop looked on in quiet adoration. He would have been honoured if this expansive lion of a man had given his entire shop away. Sher Ali had nothing if not style. He was young and handsome with flashing eyes and a taste for embroidered waistcoats. He was flamboyant and chaotic and so were his men who lived and fought by impulse. Sher Ali's chin was thrust out and his thick moustaches neatly curled at the end. He had all the dash and swashbuckling looks of a young Clark Gable. He helped himself in the shops but forgot to collect the taxes. Before the war he had run an hotel frequented by travellers and hippies at Bandi Amir. As a consequence his language was littered with phrases left by the hippies: far out, too much and facking crazy man!

His base at Aingurhun was modesty itself: two anti-aircraft posts guarding each side of the Bamian Valley and a ground base in a tiny disused water pumping station. It was cold and damp at night (Bamian is 2,500 metres above sea level), but if life was basic at Aingurhun then there were compensations in the turbulent atmosphere.

'Yaas my friend,' growled Sher Ali, 'I show you our guns and then you tell me which is better: Kharaghor or Aingurhun.'

We began the long climb up the mountain. At one of the bunkers Sher Ali burst in to find his men asleep instead of on guard duty. 'Bad mens my

friend. They cheat Sher Ali,' he cried and drove them up the hill with a big stick. Thousands of shell bursts scarred the sides of the valley which came under fire from the posts 6 kilometres away most days. Sher Ali showed off the two anti-aircraft guns located in the nest and began to fire one at the hills across the valley. The last two rounds just cleared the summit and disappeared.

'Facking crazy my friend. I think maybe I just hit Kharaghor camp,' he said shyly and then roared with laughter until the valley rang with the sound.

Bamian was 330 kilometres north-west of Kabul. The ancient route between Balkh and Taxila passed through the valley as did Alexander. To the west was the Hazarajat where the heirs to Genghis Khan swathed in huge black turbans went their own way as they always had. There were no roads into the region and, on the coming to power of the communists, the Hazaras declared themselves independent. Their Mongol legacy and the fact that they were of the minority Muslim sect, the Shias, had always marked them out for discrimination by the dominant Pathans. The Hazaras wanted nothing to do with the rest of the Afghans, never mind the Russians, so they sealed themselves into their mountain fastness, and forgot about the world.

'Hazaras maybe not like Pathans, but they like Sher Ali,' boomed the commander as we rested beneath the antique willows by the river.

Sher Ali and his men with APC knocked out by RPGs.

'Yaas my friend . . .' – Sher Ali, with characteristic disregard for danger, rests on an unexploded bomb.

Breakfast was nan and tea and the best meal of the day. After it, all there was to look forward to was boiled rice, sometimes with a potato. The problem with breakfast was that the Russian artillery often interrupted it. Although the shells always exploded fairly close, in more than three years they had never scored a direct hit. As soon as the first shell struck the men would scatter, some diving into the Bamian River while others covered the ground to the bunker built behind a huge rock. And all of them laughing at this huge joke. I was sheltering in the bunker one morning when I tuned into the World Service of Radio Moscow, designed to imitate the World Service of the BBC. A phrase stuck in my mind: 'The sincere desire of the peace-loving socialist countries to avoid war.' Outside the shells were smashing into the valley side and to the north we heard the deadly fluttering of the gunships.

Sher Ali led me up a side valley and proudly showed me the bean fields owned by his mother. He took me to a stable and showed me his pride and joy, a magnificent white horse. Beneath the sandy coloured bluffs of the valley, hoopoes strutted. In the village a boy played a flute. Two Mujahiddin emptied a partouk full of cheap Afghan jewellery on the ground. These were the taxes. An old man was dancing with a bunch of clover in one hand and a long pole in the other. Then we sat and listened as the old eccentric recited verses from the *Qoran* for an hour. Narwaz – the Afghan snuff taken in the mouth – was passed around. The moment you set foot in Afghanistan the world became unpredictable. Sometimes there was boredom but it was always compensated for by the surprises and delights that came your way.

Sher Ali pleaded the cause of the Unity and spoke in generous terms of the other groups. There was plenty of cooperation between the parties in the central Bamian Valley. But, he added glumly, Tooran was waging war against Harakat in the north. That explained the large movements of Mujahiddin from Ghorband. Sher Ali would not say anything against the provincial commander: loyalty to tribe, family or cause is fundamental in Afghanistan. He made it plain that he believed in cooperation against the principal enemy. It seemed incredible that less than 60 kilometres away all-out war was being fought between two groups which lived side by side in the central valley. It was a reflection of the personalised nature of the war and its loyalties. A Mujahid's loyalty is first to his commander, then the party.

The subject made Sher Ali despondent so he changed it and told me about his life running the hotel favoured by tourists before the war. A natural role for a man who loved company. The Jehad had ended that happy life and the force of his character led him easily into the command of a rumbustious crew of Mujahiddin with his brother Reza Khan as his deputy.

'After the communists are gone I go back to my hotel. I do not want to be commander of this place in peacetime. It is important job but my hotel is better. Maybe my brother will have job of commander. Yaas my friend,' said Sher Ali.

Sher Ali in one of the anti-aircraft gun nests he commands.

Once gaily-coloured buses had made their way from Kabul to Bamian where colossal statues of the Buddha are carved in the sandstone overlooking the town. On board were the hippies. In Bamian they could live cheaply, smoke inexpensive hashish and renounce materialism until their money ran out. Though unintentional, their descent on Afghanistan in great numbers during the 1960s and early 1970s probably influenced the destiny of the country. That period saw the growth of communist ideology. The Soviet Union was playing a skilful game in its influence-through-aid policy. The idealistic impulses of the young were fired by the Marxist ideology which delivered practical help and seemed to point a way forward through development and social justice. What did the West have to offer to counterbalance this? Hippies. To the young and unsophisticated people of Afghanistan, who were searching for new ideas, it appeared that the West was effete, decadent and lazy. Whether the hippies liked it or not they were ambassadors for their countries and young Afghans were not impressed. It resulted in a one-sided debate and, when opposition did finally emerge, it was led by Islamic conservatives. This view is not so far-fetched when you consider that the intellectual debate underway at the time was being conducted among a tiny minority of city-based Afghans. The colourful but aimless bands of hippies represented a political and cultural life apparently bankrupt of ideas. I have no doubt that in their innocence the hippies

The gunner's view.

helped propel Afghanistan into the hands of the communists who would ultimately betray their country to a foreign power.

I was woken each morning by the sound of Sher Ali's booming voice out by the river where he sat while a man with a cut-throat shaved him. One morning he was not there and a different sound, that of an hysterical woman, brought me stumbling from the pumphouse. An old widow had made two waistcoats for the commander who had decided not to buy them at the last moment. Now she had two waistcoats she could not sell and no money. Sher Ali had fled before the confrontation with the old crone and left his men to deal with her. She kept up her wailing for five hours until a messenger from Sher Ali arrived with some money. I found the commander hiding in a copse nearby.

'Ah Afghanistan my friend. Facking crazy.'

There were two characters in the camp that I did not get on with from the start. One was a man called Tadjik whose party piece was to bear his teeth and hiss at you. He had been a Soviet soldier from the republic of Tadjikistan who deserted to the Mujahiddin two years before. He was mentally deranged but the others respected him as a savage fighter. The other was a sub-commander called Hassan, whose hairy Hazara features conjured up all one's images of Genghis Khan, which henceforward I called him. From the start he demanded to know why I did not pray with the Muslims. After each meal the Afghans put out their hands, palm upwards, and say 'grace' before stroking their beards. Genghis demanded I join the others in this custom. I would not have minded but for pride. To have done so would have enabled Genghis to score points. I said I would do so if he repeated, 'For what we are about to receive may the Lord make us truly thankful,' before the meal. He snarled in his contempt. When Sher Ali was away anarchy reigned in the camp. Wild wrestling matches ended in brawls and when the sub-commanders like Genghis tried to stop them getting out of hand the men refused on the valid grounds that it was often their chiefs who had started them. Genghis was, after Sher Ali, the strongest personality in the camp, but his authority was eroded by his tendency to be a passionate advocate of some view rather than the referee in debate.

Towards the end of my stay Genghis mellowed and while at heart he still resented the presence of a non-believer (I overheard him call me 'kafir' and confronted him until he apologised) he was less aggressive. He changed when, during a debate, I argued his cause. For some days there had been rumours that Tooran was going to call on groups from the Bamian Valley to reinforce his army in its war against Harakat. I had already watched hundreds of Ghorband Hezbis pass by heading north. Sher Ali had grown sullen and refused to talk of the possibility. I wondered what would happen if he had to choose between support for the Unity and an order from the provincial commander. One night Genghis declared he would refuse to take his men north and that he would not kill another Afghan under orders from the party. No wonder that his tone was bitter: he had declared nothing less than a renunciation of that iron loyalty which is at the core of Afghan society. It was heresy but at that point the issue did not arise. The issue of the day was how to organise a special feast for their guest. If the Mujahiddin at Kharaghor had managed a chicken, then they were honour-bound to do better.

The first attempt was under the supervision of Sher Ali who declared that I would have 'egg and facking chips, the food that all crazy facking Inglestanis love'. Such was the cultural inheritance of his hotel. Alas, the chip pan exploded and deposited chips over a wide area, leaving me with fried eggs and rice. Sher Ali disappeared and Genghis conferred with some of the others over some new culinary treat.

So it was that a reluctant goat was brought to the camp and tied to a tree. In the afternoon the cooks wrestled it to the ground and slaughtered it with long knives. Just when the beast had been butchered the owner arrived and demanded payment before it was eaten. Sher Ali alone could have saved the situation but he was away and a bitter row developed over money owed by the Mujahiddin. It rapidly degenerated into a brawl but the farmer was adamant and rode off with the meat in a sack. I had retreated to the pumphouse where half a dozen men brought Tadjik in. He was bound with an enormous rope and gagged. They left him like that until the meal arrived. It was dishes of rice – one between three men – each with a potato on top. I have never seen three men look with such undisguised lust at a potato. Upon his return Sher Ali threw up his arms, growled 'Ah Afghanistan' and ordered his horse to be saddled. That night we had goat.

'My friend, which is better? Aingurhun or facking Kharaghor?'

The force of some thirty men were assembled and Sher Ali gave the order to move seconds after the men had shuffled off in their own time. We were going to take a closer look at the town of Bamian and the communist posts. Sher Ali had received intelligence that two soldiers had been killed and several injured at the Afghan army post the night before. I observed that there had been no attacks planned for that night.

'No my friend. This time the Khalqis and the Parchamites kill each other.' It was not just the rivalries between the Mujahiddin groups that marked this war. The Parchamites of Babrak Karmal had long been taking their revenge on the Khalqis for the persecutions carried out by Khalqi leaders Taraki and Amin. The Russians had sought to reconcile the factions within the PDPA but violence still broke out. Beneath the modern forms of national armies, government ministries and the ideas of communism and Islamic fundamentalism, there lay the old ways of Afghanistan. Hospitality, tribal and family loyalties. Vengeance.

We moved down through the gulley near the river and into woods that provided plenty of cover. Half of Sher Ali's men had continued to follow the road despite his cries for them to take the safer route. But they went their own way which was hopelessly exposed to attack from gunships. I was taken to the remains of a gunship and several tanks from the time when the communists hoped to gain more than just a token foothold in the region. We climbed a hill to a village controlled by Harakat which overlooked the broad and fertile valley and the endless corrugations of the mountains beyond. In the centre of the valley was Bamian and the government post. Adjacent to the hill where we stood was another and on top of it the Russian post.

Just beyond the town were the recesses which housed the giant statues of Buddha. Even at that distance they were impressive in terms of their great scale (one is 50 metres tall and the other 30). Yet they were gross and left you with a sense of a philosophy redundant in Afghanistan. Even Genghis Khan had not been able to destroy these figures which speaks volumes. Time and the elements had long since eroded the features of the statues and they stared out across the valley like dumb titans. It seemed appropriate that the Russians should wake up before these empty glories of a philosophy which had long since died out here. Their post on the opposite side of the valley represented a philosophy as beleaguered in time as the troops were in space. The ideas of the left would still hold an appeal but I had long sensed that the rush to Marxism had been halted and reversed. The Marxists were intellectually and morally bankrupt and only those who were gullible or who could ignore or stomach the truth were left. The post on the hill and the gunships in the distance were now the only way forward for Marxism. Its moral claims were shown up as fraudulent; only the committed laboured under the old delusions. Popular sentiment would no longer carry the cause: they were left with subversion, infiltration or brutal power. We were heading for a post-Marxist world. There were the chaps on the hill, at that moment looking faintly absurd, suspicious even of their fellow communists in the camp below.

The reality of life in the Russian Empire meant that the dictators must continue their struggle against the world. Without the enemies of 'Western imperialism', revisionism and capitalism, the subjects of the empire might begin to see through the big lie. Was it just possible that the struggle of the Afghans might mark out their country as the limits of the Russian Empire as it had been for the British Empire? It is in the nature of tyranny that its masters are not products of an intellectual or popular process. They are but the masters of crude power and their use and abuse of that power was all that was left to the rulers of that empire. I wondered if that post on the hill might be the high-water mark for the Russian Empire. In the valley of Bamian two ossified philosophies stared at each other across the green and pleasant fields.

One morning I was washing myself in the icy river, after the shelling, when I noticed Sher Ali's magnificent horse being saddled. The commander had been away for two days after warming to my request to get near to and possibly into Kabul. 'Yaas my friend, I go with you to Kabul. We drink tea in the bazaar and shoot some Russians.' Then he had vanished.

I changed into a clean suit of clothes and set off for the nearest village to buy some cigarettes. The fields were filled with men, women and children at work on the harvest. The blue sky was filled with chaff as men tossed the wheat high into the air. The women squatted by the sheaves of wheat and guarded bundles of bread and kettles of water in an endless landscape of yellow and blue. You felt that this is how it must have been in old England.

The shop in the village was typical of its kind. There were cakes of soap, matches, bags of boiled sweets, large drums of cooking oil, a tank of fuel oil, sacks of grain and boxes of fruit and vegetables. In the midst of the boxes sat the proprietor holding court. The shop was a meeting place and neutral ground for the Mujahiddin of rival parties.

That day I met a former master of Buzkashi, the Afghan national game, who produced his prize possession. It was a winner's medal from some Buzkashi tournament. The game reflects the Afghan temperament, demanding bravery, daring and skill. The head of a sheep in a sack (today a bundle of rags is more common) is the object for dozens of horsemen on a pitch. Anything goes in the free-for-all to secure the sack and ride around two poles placed at either end of the pitch without the sack being wrested from you. The game is most popular in the north but was played in Kabul and other centres. It had been played in Bamian until two years before when a large crowd at a Buzkashi meet was machine-gunned by Russian gunships.

The Buzkashi star embodied the contradictions of Afghanistan. He was a member of Harakat yet the horse he had ridden in the tournaments had been none other than Sher Ali's noble steed. They were friends of long standing. They simply did not discuss the war between their respective parties which was going on in the north.

I did not know it then but even as we spoke of his glorious career as a Buzkashi horseman, Sher Ali was riding that horse at the head of his men. They were heading north to join Tooran in his fight against Harakat. The order had come. When I returned to the camp I found only Genghis sitting in the doorway of the pumphouse. He had stuck to his guns and refused to fight. He and his men had been detailed to remain behind and man the anti-aircraft guns, although at least one of them was being hauled north by Sher Ali. The commander had not said farewell to me, perhaps too embarrassed by the whole business. I knew that this was against his better judgement but I also knew he could not betray his blood. Instead, I chose to picture him travelling in style on his white horse through the mountains, bringing that magic of style, charm and laughter to wherever he passed. 'Where you go now, Inglestan?' asked Genghis.

'North.'

13

Valley of the Shadows

Young men talked guns while their elders articulated wild dreams about taking the fight over the Amu Darya into the Russian Empire. They would take the cities of Samarkand and Bokhara and the Muslim republics of the Soviet Union would revolt. Abdulwahed was more circumspect. He had found a thoughtful young commander and engaged him in conversation. Sayed Abdur Rauf was a diligent commander but some of his Mujahiddin were tomtits. They had just arrived from Ghorband and many of the youngsters were not experienced fighters. They were going to join Tooran in Comart and we had joined them at a dusty village north of the Bamian Valley. That night we slept in a chai khana where the heat from two huge samovars made the room very cosy.

We set off at around 5 am, more than seventy men, to begin the long march up the valley and over the Mountains of the Broken Teeth. Abdulwahed set off at a ridiculous pace for an old man and then I realised he was trying to catch up with Sayed Abdur Rauf to continue their discussion from the night before. We found a village where we could get tea. The people of the valley were poor and some had complained bitterly about having to feed many groups passing north recently. But our host was welcoming and to my delight his toothless wife joined the company. With the exception of Abdulwahed and Sayed Abdur Rauf, the men were too angry or embarrassed to speak. She dominated the conversation and seemed to know as much about weapons and the war as the men. Her opinions about strategy, which she freely gave in a rasping chuckle, were as valid as anybody's. But the men became increasingly restless and gestured to go. These Afghans who were afraid of nobody fled before an old woman. Further up the valley was a swamp full of colourful birds, but there was no time to halt and we continued the long climb through the valley.

It was dark when we reached the snowline and the men gathered clumps of dried gorse to make fires. They inhaled the smoke and urged me to do likewise: it would give us the strength to cover the last few kilometres. It made me cough. It was a vast, silent and cold world at the pass but there was pleasure on the faces of the nomads in their great woollen coats as they welcomed us. They had found someone similarly unhinged to want to spend a night in this freezing emptiness. We crouched around a fire in a stone sheep pen while additional tents were put up. Lamps glowed in the nomads' tents and sheep and cows shuffled about in the darkness. Everything was gilded platinum as a full moon sailed out from behind the peaks. Our hosts brought us bowls of mast (yogurt). They were semi-nomads who travelled through the high pastures in summer but settled in permanent homes in the valleys in winter. They regarded themselves as a race apart, yet they were eager for news of the war. Neither could they escape it at that altitude. Twice that year the jets had bombed them and killed several animals.

The early morning cold made it difficult to handle the bread but it made us hungry too and we ate plenty before setting off. It was obvious that few of the men, particularly the young ones, had seen much action but they swaggered along firing their guns. I found myself in the company of half a dozen louts who first cleaned me out of cigarettes and then pestered me with inane questions. One of the sub-commanders intervened and we walked down the valley together. He was a farmer called Miramat, and most of the year he worked on the land in Ghorband. I asked him how he felt about fighting Harakat and he replied that he did not mind. Harakat supported the restoration of the monarchy which Hezb would never accept. He was fighting for an Islamic republic or nothing. As we marched towards the old country palace at Comart, Miramat said there was nothing to commend the

The journey north.

178

Nomads.

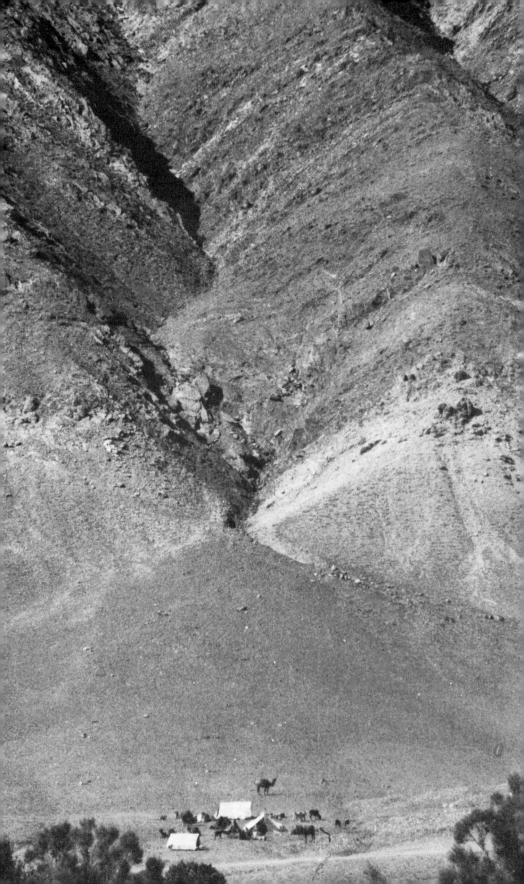

king. All that was past. King Zahir Shah had been in exile in Italy since 1973. You felt sympathy for a monarch who had a reputation for taking an interest in his country's history and culture and who curtailed his own powers under the 1965 constitution. But you also knew he had ruled for forty years and had had his chance. He was now an old man. The monarchists – they included several parties and many people in the West – saw Zahir Shah's return as a compromise. There was even talk that it might suit the Russians, who by 1983 must have realised that the communists in Afghanistan could not survive without their military support. Above all else, the Russians feared an Islamic republic and so it was conceivable that the scourge of monarchist sentiment would support the return of Zahir Shah.

Miramat regarded the idea of compromise as the negation of honour. That, he said, was the difference between the Afghans who were prepared to fight the Russians and the West which was not. He was not desperately impressed by the nuclear extinction argument. 'What has the West done for us?' he asked without reproach.

After the invasion, President Carter announced sanctions against the Soviet Union. The Olympic Games in Moscow was boycotted by American athletes and trade embargoes curtailed the supply of high technology and grain to the Russians. Russian fishermen were barred from American waters and cultural exchanges limited. The United States and Britain tacitly

At the pass.

admitted that the Mujahiddin were being supplied with arms but by 1983 there was no evidence that they were receiving anything but light weapons. Even then many fighters were still armed with ancient 303s. Commentators in the West were preoccupied with the question of whether the invasion meant a return to the cold war and the end of détente. Détente was the euphemism for appeasement. Behind the blandishments and fine words, the Russians saw it as a splendid cover behind which they could continue their policy of subversion. The fundamental ambition of Soviet expansionism did not change a jot: all policy, internal or external, remains subordinate to this. The Kremlin planners calculated well. The waves caused by the invasion could be ridden out and it was not long before the Western allies were arguing over supplies of machinery to help the Russians build the Siberian gas pipeline. A reference to the Press shows how little interest Afghanistan generated after the initial coverage. This was partly a reflection of the difficulties of communications from the country but it also reflects a more depressing reality. Firstly, that the country was always on the outskirts of popular interest in the West; and secondly many of those politicians and diplomats paid to give a damn had virtually written off Afghanistan years before as having fallen into the Soviet 'sphere of influence'. You only had to compare the Press coverage of Afghanistan with Poland – which had not been invaded – to get a measure of how little people cared.

The house at Sayghan.

By nightfall we had reached Sayghan, a broad plain surrounded by mountains worked into ancient shapes by time and the elements. We stopped in a village surrounded by wheatfields. It was the height of the harvest. We were taken to a huge fortress-like house where the local Mujahiddin were quartered. Comart was only half a day's march away and I looked forward to meeting Tooran and possibly Sher Ali. There was an air of despondency about the building with its huge overgrown courtyard. The commander was a pale-faced character dressed in white who sat, lost in his thoughts, in a window sill. I called him the Ghost. He rarely said anything and when he did it was in a whining, bitter tone. His men were little better and the cumulative effect was to render the atmosphere depressing. The food was bad: rice with the consistency of glue and the wing of a bird so old I suspected the species was extinct. I ate little and turned in early.

I was awakened in the middle of the night by the sound of gunfire. 'Lie down Mista,' hissed one of the shadows crouched by the window. He and several others leapt through the window and joined a dozen Mujahiddin heading for the great wooden doors on the other side of the courtyard. The towers at each corner of the building were manned by fighters and you could see the flame of their guns. We were under fire but the building was designed to withstand any attack and it was well supplied with ammunition. I sprinted across the courtyard, fell over a sheep grazing unconcernedly by the moonlight, and climbed one of the towers. There were two men blazing away and two others crouched behind them. As one man ducked to reload, another would take up the position by the slit in the wall. Beyond two feet of mud wall you could hear the bullets striking home like the sound of rain on a window.

'Mista,' laughed one of the Mujahiddin in the darkness, 'Harakat come.'

Below, dozens of Mujahiddin fanned out into the darkness and went on the offensive. Less than 150 metres away the battle raged and went on for most of the night.

Come dawn, the world had returned to normal and the peasants were working in the fields as if nothing had happened. The Ghost, with his watery smile and oriental features, was deep in thought when Abdulwahed, Sayed Abdur Rauf and the men crowded into the main hall of the building. The Ghost whined about the iniquities of the world and his own problems. Abdulwahed was visibly appalled by the man and winced behind his glasses. A Mujahid burst in weeping. The others comforted the young man. One of the men had been killed and two wounded. Sayed Abdur Rauf left the room and the Ghost went on complaining. Abdulwahed could stand it no longer and left. I followed and we shared a cigarette in the courtyard.

Thus began the siege of Sayghan which went on for several days with the occasional burst of fire by day and major attacks by night. By the second day any plans to travel further north had been abandoned as the way had been cut off. The day after it was decided to retreat and Sayed Abdur Rauf assembled his men in twos every 100 metres to begin the march. It was a bitter blow. We had not gone more than two kilometres when we were attacked and had to sprint back to the headquarters in disarray. The Ghost, whose pinched features made him seem capable of any cruelty, seemed more depressed and closeted himself in a room on his own.

The attacks continued and a rumour started that Harakat was bringing up a big gun. I rehearsed all the good things I could remember about the king, just in case. The cigarettes ran out, I had read all the Shakespeare twice and the food was worse than ever. Our retreat had now been overrun by Harakat. We were trapped and surrounded. Abdulwahed was good company but now he spent much of the time with the commanders in long disscusions. Boredom set in. An Uzbek fighter from Mazar-i-Sharif in the north befriended me and we spent many long hours in discussions about why the Russians invaded Afghanistan and where future temptations may lead them.

The invasion of Afghanistan was a calculated gamble to secure an ailing communist government. Only the dogged resistance by the Afghans has obscured the broader ambitions of the Russian Empire. Keeping Afghanistan firmly in the communist camp was the priority of the day but the invasion also opened up new possibilities for expanding the empire. If the Russians are able to consolidate their position in Afghanistan then they will not only be in a position to subvert neighbouring countries but will be able to exert pressure on the Gulf and thereby threaten the West. Exciting tensions in Baluchistan and the Pathan homelands could undermine Pakistan. Were that to happen, India – for long a client of the Soviets – might find itself being sucked ever deeper into the communist camp. Iran, too – alienated from much of the Muslim world and the non-Muslim world for that matter – could also be in trouble. One of the additional considerations made by the Russian planners of the invasion was no doubt that it would serve as a warning to the religious zealots in Iran, not to mention the millions of Muslims in the central Asian republics of the Soviet Union.

It is tempting to see the invasion of Afghanistan as a singular event and not part of some broader strategy, but it would be dangerous and even irresponsible. Their presence in Afghanistan enables the Soviets to put pressure on neighbouring countries which, if they fell, would isolate further the oil-producing nations of the Middle East and further the process of encirclement by the Russian Empire. It is the Afghan resistance which has – for the time being – delayed the Russians from furthering their territorial ambitions.

My Uzbek companion was deeply critical of Hindustan - India — for its failure to denounce the invasion of his country. India's ambitions to be regarded as the pre-eminent nation in the region suffered from the failure of the Gandhi government to condemn the invasion. Afghans felt a strong sense of betrayal by the Gandhi government which accepted the Russian explanation for the invasion. It was suitably rewarded by the Kremlin in terms of arms supplies and aid. Because of its history, India's pronouncements are seen as having a peculiarly moral dimension and are listened to worldwide with some reverence. If India had unequivocally attacked the invasion Moscow would have listened closely. It was little wonder the Kremlin was delighted.

'Hindustan betrayed us but they betrayed themselves too. It suits Gandhi to take weapons from the Russians. She thinks she can use them and she enjoys the pressure that Pakistan is under because they are rivals. But what will Hindustan think if it finds Russian tanks on its border? She has not learned the lesson that we did in Afghanistan when we were friendly with the Russians,' said the Uzbek.

It was strange in that beautiful muted and warm landscape of daytime to conceive of the threat which stalked in the foothills beyond. They waited for night and the next attack. Abdulwahed lost his briskness and grew languid, even sceptical in the presence of the Ghost. It was a bad sign. The Ghost grew more reclusive, apparently resigned, even fatalistic. Then something happened behind closed doors – I never discovered what – and power seemed to shift to Abdulwahed and Sayed Abdur Rauf. Perhaps the Ghost had decided that as they had marched us all into this mess, they should extricate us. We only added to his store of problems.

At any rate the mood changed. A series of messengers came and went and the spirits of the Mujahiddin lifted. Abdulwahed visibly brightened and now I rarely saw him as he was closeted in meeting after meeting. Then, one evening, the wooden doors opened and a great crowd of characters – out of the Bible – walked solemnly in. Nearly twenty of the old bearded men in flowing gowns entered the main hall and settled down with the commanders. They talked for much of the night and all of the next day. Then in the afternoon they shook hands and left.

A truce had been struck with Harakat. The elders had acted as intermediaries. We were to be guaranteed safe passage back the way we had come. We were to get safe escort in return for a pledge from Sayed Abdur Rauf that he would not try to penetrate the region again. It was an humiliating defeat for the commander but he had no choice. Ammunition stocks and food would not last forever. Under the Pushtunwali a party offered a truce is obliged to accept but can lay down stern terms. I felt sympathy for the commander but not for some of the tomtits who treated the business as some sort of a great victory. Personally, I felt angry at having travelled so far to a dead end. The tomtits, sensing my frustration, began to chant 'Mista, you go Comart? You see Tooran?' No, I return south with a crew of fools who have been beaten by Harakat, I told them. A tousle-haired lout muttered 'kafir' so I told him how the Christians had been believers hundreds of years before Mohammed. It was the sort of petty and dismal argument that surfaced amid the frustrations of a journey to nowhere, appalling food and no cigarettes. The youth glared at me and I sensed there would be trouble.

The Soviet Union has already threatened Pakistan with retaliation should it continue to support the Afghan resistance. The Pakistani authorities are only too aware that that threat is less likely to come from direct assult but through the exploitation of the country's Achilles' heel Baluchistan. The minority Baluch have long harboured grievances against Islamabad which has consistently thwarted its ambitions for greater autonomy. Baluch leaders have espoused socialist or communist beliefs and, more importantly, many Baluch feel that Soviet backing is the only way their aspirations will be met. Baluchistan borders southern Afghanistan and extends to the Makran Coast of the Arabian Sea. Furthermore, the Baluch straddle the Pakistan-Iran border, thus posing a threat to Iranian stability. But playing the 'Baluchistan card' would not only be a means whereby the Russians could push a corridor to the Arabian Sea – and the dreamed-of warm water port – it would be a direct challenge to the very stability of Pakistan. Championing the Baluch would no doubt coincide with the resurrection of the Pushtunistan issue by Kabul and the fomenting of trouble in the North West Frontier Province. In addition to these two sensitive areas, the military government of Pakistan faces considerable opposition, some from politicians who would recognise the communists in Afghanistan. The planners in the Kremlin may calculate that the only way to staunch rebel supply lines from Pakistan is to attempt to engineer a government in Islamabad which would proscribe Afghan resistance groups on Pakistan soil.

Early next morning we set off in twos to retrace our footsteps through the long valleys and over the Mountains of the Broken Teeth. At the outskirts of the village we saw the group of elders moving swiftly and with great dignity across the fields to meet us. They would walk ahead of us as a sign to the enemy not to fire. Hundreds of years of experience in this wild and lawless land had evolved this fragile arrangement. The elders walked ahead in silence and we followed. At the river stood another odd assembly. It was a small escort from Harakat and they presented arms as we passed. There was a sense of stiff chivalry about the meeting. A most bizarre fellow now marched ahead of the elders. He was a Harakat commander and he bellowed through an enormous megaphone instructions which echoed about the mountain. He had a long thin moustache and wore riding breeches, jackboots and a heavy and ancient tweed jacket. On his head was a sailor's hat which might have seen service on the head of a pleasure steamer captain. As he cried over and over, 'Do not fire. There is a truce', groups of Harakat fighters emerged from positions high up in the mountains and watched us pass. Without the truce we would not have stood a chance: Harakat had secured the whole valley. They had also taken over the villages and, as our band entered the first, the Harakat commander invited us to stay for lunch. Even in this ridiculous situation everyone had to abide by the code of hospitality, and so we took tea and bread with the enemy, while discussing anything but the rivalry. And all beneath the

Harakat posters which adorned the mosque we were in. Sayed Abdur Rauf's misery was complete, but Abdulwahed put a philosophical gloss on the whole business and winkled out one of the elder Harakatis and engaged him in conversation on some esoteric religious question. Our hosts brought me cigarettes and refused payment.

We shook hands with our hosts and continued the march south. The Harakat commander boomed his orders through the megaphone while the stately elders followed. You sensed the hopelessness of the British forces in their wretched retreat from Kabul in 1842. That desperate march through the snows had been doomed from the start. They were picked off by tribesmen perched in the mountains above, just like the Harakatis were now. There was no way to fight back: you just waited to die. The little oddball with the megaphone and the elders grew in stature as we plodded behind. They were the extent of our horizons and stood between us and death. A rogue commander in the mountains, a breakdown in communications or a belief that this was a ruse. You did not dare to think of anything going wrong.

After about 15 kilometres the Harakat commander stopped, curtly shook everyone's hand and gave me a Hitler salute. I did not return the dubious compliment. Then he and the elders turned and walked back the way we had come. I felt I had glimpsed something from another age. Several ages, all thrown into one bizarre sequence of events. But then the story of Afghanistan is full of parallels with times past. It was popular in the West to make comparisons between the Russians in Afghanistan and the Americans in Vietnam. It is difficult to sustain the comparison: the Soviets did not have to contend with a war thousands of kilometres from home and the attendent supply line logistics; there was no unlimited aid to the enemy as in Vietnam; there was no single charismatic leader of the stature of Ho Chi Minh. Most crucially, the people of the Soviet Union did not have the reality of the war brought to them through the media every day. It was an inaccurate analogy although many Mujahiddin commanders speculated that the Americans were regulating arms supplies so that the resistance had enough to bog the Russians down but not defeat them. It was a cruel and Machiavellian possibility. Naturally, all the American diplomats I talked to denied it and yet the weapons supplied to the resistance made it evident that practical support from the West was less than whole-hearted.

There was another and more alarming feeling I received from American – and some European – diplomats I talked to: a residue of dislike and distrust of anything Muslim. It was a hangover from the hostage crisis.

'There are plenty of my colleagues overseas and in Washington who view the prospect of another Islamic fundamentalist government with about as much enthusiasm as a coronary,' said one American diplomat. 'Many of these people simply talk a language quite alien to the norms of diplomacy. At its worst it is a dialogue of the deaf on both sides. Make no mistake, we want the Soviets out of Afghanistan and then for the Afghans to decide on what form of government they should have. But it is true to say that many in the West view with alarm another Islamic government with fundamentalist sentiments because of the experience with Iran.'

It was inaccurate to call Afghanistan Russia's 'Vietnam'. It was more strikingly similar to the attempt by the British in 1839 to install their own man in Kabul. A great army had marched into Afghanistan and a puppet government had been installed. The most illiterate Afghan could draw the parallels between Babrak Karmal and Shah Shuja. Like the British, the Russian Empire was bogged down and appeared to have lost the military and political initiative. The occasional buying-off of a commander or a tribe still did not amount to pacifying the country. There was little doubt that the Russians could continue to hold the cities and major roads, but there was less doubt that the Mujahiddin would continue to make them pay a heavy price.

'Mista you go to Comart?' intoned the voice, and I turned to find myself surrounded by tomtits. The tousle-haired youth fingered his rifle and eyed me.

'Kafir,' he murmured quietly.

'Arsehole,' I replied. I walked ahead and they kept pace so I dropped behind. They kept going. Late in the afternoon I found them sitting under some trees. I was exhausted and sat down, away from the group, and lit a cigarette.

The tousle-haired one got up and stood before me. 'Mista,' he snapped, 'Burrow, harakat.'

I waved him away but he persisted. He was going to hold sway over the kafir if it was the last thing he did.

'Burrow, harakat,' he screamed, as the others looked on. I gave him a V-sign. He cocked his rifle and aimed it at me. Another did the same. I smiled and swore at them. They pulled the triggers.

They walked off leaving me to contemplate that 1 per cent chance that they just might not have had the safety catches on. Though that familiar sense of mindless exhaustion enabled me to smile and almost not to care anymore, I grew angrier as I drew near the nomads' camp where we were to stay the night. I was sick of guns and tomtits. I was sick of this war and all war. Reason told me that this was the Afghan way and I should judge them by their own standards. For some time I had been dwelling on the difference in the way Islam and Christianity were spread: one by armies and the sword, the other by individuals and persuasion. That was simplistic but it seemed to be the difference between love and coercion. It was not that simple but exhaustion and so much barely subdued contempt robbed you of reason. You wanted to hear of a loving God and not a vengeful one. It was the unreason of illness and fatigue and an angry envy of the Mujahiddin's superhuman strength.

I wrestled the rifles from the tomtits, seized each by the collar and read them the riot act. If they ever dared so much as lift a finger at me I would thrash them within an inch of their lives. The nomads thought it great sport and they and the other men gathered around. Sayed Abdur Rauf demanded to know the full story. I pushed the two offenders to the ground and sat with the commander and Abdulwahed who was chuckling. Sayed Abdur Rauf was furious at their behaviour and said I was at liberty to beat them. I said that I had made my point and the matter should rest. He offered me a large stick with which to thrash them and, when I shook my head, offered to do the job for me. The men had brought dishonour on his group which could only be assuaged by me having my revenge. In the end I had to plead with him not to punish the youths further. I ended that strange and miserable day by offending the commander when I shook the hands of the youths.

There is a postscript to this story. Some days later I found myself alone with the tousle-haired youth and some of the other tomtits. Egged on by the others, he fixed his bayonet and rushed at me in a manner half-joking and half-daring. I took the weapon from him and soundly thrashed him. None of the others intervened and later the commander seemed delighted at the turn of events. Honour had been restored. Ah Afghanistan!

14

Slapstick and Paranoia

'Yaas my friend, we go to Kabul together.' I still thought of Sher Ali's words as I killed time in Bamian Valley, going on the occasional raid against the Karmalite post but mostly bathing in the cool river and lying in the sun. Bamian seemed like a sideshow now and I wanted to go south-east to the capital. But the journey was not on the programme agreed with the party and the commanders procrastinated. Meanwhile, large groups of Mujahiddin from Ghorband passed by, on their way north to join Tooran. I learned that Tooran was under direct instructions from Peshawar to drive out Harakat and try to secure the entire province for Hezb. Officials later denied this but that came as no surprise.

I badgered the commanders, invoking their duties as hosts and suggested the reason they could not get me to Kabul was because the party did not control the territory between. The role of a journalist (their independence too) meant nothing so I employed dirty tricks and played on their obligations to a guest. I was with a number of chiefs after a visit to a village which had recently been bombed, when I finally got my way. Men and boys passed us with massive bundles of scrub which bent them double. Donkeys trotted along braying like old men with ill-fitting dentures and bad chests. A distant figure approached us on a bike. He beamed as he drew closer and leapt from the cycle and began a slow dance before embracing us each in turn. This Terpsichorean Tadjik was also called Sher Ali and he chattered away as he resumed the dance. Then he invited us to stay at his home and we all followed as he danced along. That night after a meal of rice and potatoes, I fell asleep as the gathering grumbled about Kabul.

All were gone when I awoke, save for Sher Ali who told me to hurry and bring my things. Outside, the sound of a motor churned the fresh warm air and a familiar voice raked the valley sides. Trader stood with his hands on his hips. He kissed me on each cheek, insulted me and we roared off in a cloud of dust. The old Mercedes blew two tyres and collided with a wall before we had left the province. He picked up civilians and Mujahiddin, argued with them and set them down.

We dumped the van in the middle of a road and Trader waved his passengers to follow as he set off up through the stepped fields. At the top of the slopes was a home where Trader was greeted by an old friend. Over lunch I noticed the three children of the house had blond hair and distinctly Nordic features. Later Trader told me some of the history. A German girl travelling in Afghanistan had been taken as wife by the man. She produced three children and then one day she had vanished.

Rolling down the hair pins after the Shibar Pass into Parwan, a child hurled a stone at the vehicle and smashed a window. Trader's sense deserted him and he leaned out of the window to scream abuse at the little hooligan and we careered off the road. The culprit had vanished so Trader directed his invective towards his passengers.

Back in the Ghorband the fruit trees were empty and the first leaves had turned brown and were falling. Autumn had started and for the first time in more than four months I felt a twinge of homesickness. In Ferinjhal Commander Khalil smiled thinly when I said I wanted to get to Kabul and the arguments began. While he fretted about how to get me to change my mind, I went for walks with his young son Inyatullah whose pride it was to escort me and explain to all we met that I was 'Inglestan, Mista Inglestan'. He would cry this out to the street and then gaze at me with as much love as you were likely to find in a strange land. Inyatullah would appear in the dusty square and take me by the hand to whichever house Khalil was at tea in that day.

'Kabul very dangerous. Road to Kabul even more dangerous,' he would begin casually. It was a conversational ploy designed to prompt me to decline to go south. He could not deny my request outright so he tried to persuade me to abandon my plans. I would refuse and walk back to the village square with Inyatullah.

It was a strange few days, spent among the falling leaves, walking out to other villages or killing time in the square. One day I noticed a fat and dissolute man watching me. I noticed him for those qualities which are rare in Afghanistan. At length he came and sat next to me and said nothing for twenty minutes.

'You want some hashish,' he hissed at length.

'No,' I hissed back and he was content, or rather resigned.

It was not like the old days, he said, when the tourists came through and money from the drugs trade made him a man of means. Now the tourists were gone and the Mujahiddin said that hashish was bad. The new morality had all but bankrupted him but mostly he missed the old way of life. He now sent his hashish to Pakistan but the wholesale trade was not lucrative and he missed the human contact. The people. He invited me to his home to smoke some hashish with him ('you are my guest; you do not pay') but I declined.

With Inyatullah I walked up through the village and into a small valley to see 'the electrics'. The Mujahiddin were very proud of the electrics and spoke of it with reverence. Inyatullah scampered away to fetch some grapes while I examined the curious Heath Robinson contraption perched on a cliff at the back of a house. A framework of poles supported a cycle wheel which was turned by a waterfall. It drove a dynamo which supplied just enough power

Village, Kabul Province.

for one lightbulb in the house. The scientist, the man of the house, was shy and did not want to meet me. But at night, from the other side of the valley, I watched him sitting in his room beneath the lightbulb deep in thought. I wondered what he thought of the flat earth imams. He seemed inexpressibly lonely.

My excursions took me to see Mujahiddin who a week before had taken part in an action against the Russians across the mountains at Sinjhi Dara. Groups from Ghorband had fought all day to slow down a Russian thrust led by 100 tanks. I was able to ascertain accurate casualty figures: Ferinjhal group 11 dead; Chaud-i-Ghorband group 18 dead; Fendeckestan group 6 dead. At least as many Russians had died and 8 vehicles had been hit. More importantly the invader had withdrawn immediately and the Mujahiddin resumed control of the area. The father of the one of the Mujahiddin killed in the action spoke of his son. 'He died for Islam in the way of the followers of Mohammed. It was a great honour for my son and for me.' I later learned that upon hearing of his son's death the old man had offered himself to Khalil as a replacement fighter.

Inyatullah led me to the house of one of the men who had been wounded in the raid. Gulokhar Khan's dark features were fixed as he related how he had been wounded twice: first the knee had been smashed by a bullet but he had carried on fighting for nine hours until a bullet in the arm rendered him incapable of firing his gun. I said he was brave and he looked at me strangely. There was nothing unusual about it. A Mujahid only stops when he can no longer fire his weapon. There was little conscious bravery about him and the others; their deeds were an extension of their approach to life. In their wild land, nothing daunted the Afghans. Gulokhar Khan and a comrade had spent a night on the freezing mountain before the friend had carried him for eight hours to sanctuary.

Khalil held conference after conference and after each he would summon me and say casually 'Kabul bad place'. Finally he gave in. 'OK you go to Paghman which is by Kabul,' he said grandly as if he had invented the idea. 'But my friend it is very dangerous. Maybe you not want to go,' he added hopefully. I thanked him and packed my rucksack under Inyatullah's sad gaze.

I was delighted yet had come to expect that bad always followed good in this land. Sure enough it did. That night I was plagued by a recurrence of the illness. In each new house I always checked for toilet facilities in case I had to make a visit in the dark. I had found the hole in the floor and scurried there after being woken up by the familiar pain. These primitive loos were sited over the stable. This hole – in fact a chimney outlet used in winter – was sited over a Mujahiddin sleeping chamber. The men were

Inscriptions from the Qoran *adorn the final resting place for the Shaheed.*

anointed from a great height and emerged in the moonlight looking just a little bemused by the antics of Inglestan. Alas, worse was to come. An hour later I was forced to adjourn to the hillside. Manipulating the clods of earth used in lieu of paper, I felt a piercing pain in the nether region. It felt as though somebody had stubbed a cigarette out on my skin. I squashed the small scorpion and lit a cigarette.

Common sense had fled in the face of determination to go south. My first thought was that Khalil would use this as an excuse to cancel his promise so I resolved not to tell anybody about the scorpion sting. I asked casually what the men did when one of them was stung. They said they tried not to let a victim go to sleep because that was dangerous. How big did a scorpion have to be before a sting was fatal? Between forefinger and thumb they indicated as many different sizes as there were men in the room. I had decided already that the insect was not big enough to kill which, on reflection, was merely further evidence that I had lost my marbles in the face of adversity. The Mujahiddin resolved their differences on the mortality rates of scorpion victims by agreeing that no Mujahid would die of a sting anyway.

My journey south was delayed for most of the day and I sat fighting the sleep which threatened to overwhelm me. It was not much of a fight and the next thing I remembered was being violently shaken awake by somewhat puzzled Mujahiddin. 'Mista, burrow, burrow.' My midriff and one leg felt stiff and numb and I had a blinding headache. It was as much as I could do to make the couple of kilometres to the village square.

'Mista, you sick?' inquired the commander looking closely at me.

'Not at all. Never felt better.'

'I think you sick,' he said hopefully.

'With the gracious hospitality of such a brave commander, a man might feel unhappiness at leaving so deep it might be mistaken for sickness.'

I no longer had to bite my tongue at reciting such homilies. In fact I rather enjoyed them and the Mujahiddin did too. It showed breeding and good manners. The utilitarian dreariness of everyday language in the West would horrify them. Khalil shrugged his shoulders and ushered me into the passenger seat of a van which would take me the first 40 kilometres. The prospect of climbing through even the lower reaches of the Koh-i-Baba in my state was daunting.

'You not sick?' asked the commander once more as the engine burst into life. He leaned through the window and stared at me but I shook my head. We set off down the bumpy track and as soon as we had rounded the first bend I told the driver to stop so that I could leap out and be violently ill.

Even by motor the journey was arduous. I had been right about Hezb not controlling all of the territory through which we were travelling. For this reason I had not been given an escort of armed men: my companions were traders who regularly used the road. We passed through a series of checkpoints – Harakat and Jamiat – and at each I was interrogated. Often they toyed with the idea of sending us back to Ghorband but my companions protested and I told them flatly that I would report their actions to their leaders in Peshawar. So we progressed until being flagged down by a Mujahid who appeared from behind rocks waving his Kalashnikov. He climbed into the cab and others appeared who climbed on the back. We must hurry, said the Harakat fighter. There were bandits in the hills and we must reach our destination before nightfall. As if to reinforce his words there was the sound of gunfire behind us. The bandits were Jamiatis, said the Harakat man. I had no doubt that the Jamiatis would have provided an escort and called the Harakatis bandits. I had to remind myself that I was in the care of Hezb and that this was but a gap in their claustrophobic care. You realised the thin dividing line between the gracious hospitality of the code and being fair game for a gunman.

The Harakati was from Qandahar, the country's principal southern city where in 1747 the Afghan kingdom had been proclaimed. It had been Ahmed Shah's capital and the site of his tomb. More recently the garrison had mutinied in 1979 against the communists. In 1982 a major offensive had been launched against the resistance in the city and thousands had died. Yet by the end of the year resistance strength had returned to similar levels.

'How do I know you are not a spy?' began the brawny commander who declined to give his name. I called this ever-watchful man with the huge moustaches and resonant voice Captain Mystery. Though he deliberately shrouded himself in an aura of intrigue, his mind was as sharp as a pin and each question was loaded. Though he spoke good English he insisted on using an interpreter, a vet called Zulmay who doubled up as the local doctor. Captain Mystery, whose features were too broad for him to be called handsome, stared at me with his jet black eyes and repeated the question.

I told him that, my credentials apart, he would have to make his own judgement as dozens of other commanders had done. The commander and his men had arrived at around 9.30 am and we talked until the early hours. The weariness and pain subsided as they subjected me to an inquisition. I sensed there was something behind the endless questions but it was only later that I discovered exactly what. That, and the fact that I was not expected, aroused suspicions all along the route south. I grew tired of the endless questions and for a moment the imagination suggested that the solemn gathering had assembled to pass life or death judgement on me. Such gatherings were normally deliberating how to bring some extra comfort to their guest. Not tonight.

At last the commander seemed satisfied and I fell asleep with the thought that my journey south would be the death of me. It nearly was that night. The guest room was at the top of a four-storey house, most unusual in Afghanistan. As usual I had memorised the layout of the stairs in case of nocturnal necessity. That struck me around 3.30 and I stumbled out of the room into the pitch blackness. I made the first flight of steps and

A tumbling mountain stream on the journey south.

confidently put my foot on the top of the second flight, whereupon I plunged into the inky stairwell. I knew the fall was a long one because, as I fell, I had time to think; firstly that I might fall three storeys and impale myself on the farm implements at the bottom; secondly that it all had the quality of a dream; and lastly, as my clothes billowed about me that I had become a great flying sack of manure. I do not know how long I lay unconscious on the stone steps 4 metres below. It may only have been seconds. I sensed that nothing was broken, which was nothing short of a miracle, and I crawled down the rest of the steps. I was a tangle of conflicting pains but all that mattered then was cleaning my filthy clothes and body. I hobbled down the path and stripped off to wash in the stream. The water, which an hour before had been snow, was a trial. I soaked my clothes and then hid them behind a bush until the morning. As I made my painful way back up the path wearing only my hiking boots, a sentry leaped out from behind a bush and screamed his challenge. He shone a torch on my body and let forth a second ear-piercing scream. 'Genghis bloody Khan,' I muttered and limped off into the darkness while the sentry dissolved into hysterics.

Though the persistence of ill-health depressed me at times, it did get me out of a tight corner on more than one occasion. The following day the concensus among the Mujahiddin seemed to be that no spy could act like such a lunatic. Mujahiddin came from miles around to hear the story; Captain Mystery came early to hear it at first hand. Zulmay appeared to treat my wounds though the business was prolonged as he kept bursting into fits of giggles. I did not mind being the object of fun as all the talk of espionage had been forgotten. I went to look for my clothes and found them already washed and spread out in the sun to dry.

Captain Mystery told me the history of Surkh Parsa, the beautiful wooded valley through which we walked. In the time of Taraki it had had two communist posts but the Mujahiddin had overrun them. Despite attempts by the Russians to reestablish a communist presence the area was still under the control of the Mujahiddin.

'Nearly all my men are ghazi,' said the commander.

I asked what ghazi meant. He said it was a condition of honour achieved if a man 'kill an Inglestani' or another non-believer. I protested at this intolerance and he modified it to the killing of Russians. In a clearing one of the sub-commanders was dishing out the familiar punishment to a young Mujahid who had committed a misdemeanour. Other fighters looked on while the sub-commander solemnly caned the hand of the offender. I had often seen these strange flagellant ceremonies in which the most modest of sticks were used. The audience fell about laughing and the beating ended when the victim burst into tears. The punishment had more to do with humiliation than pain. We walked on through the pretty valley and I grew weary and irritated by the commander's eloquent arrogance: 'Western imperialism' and so on. Universal prejudices and few intellectual resources

Mujahid and donkey.

to back them up. The world was infinitely more subtle than that painted at Kabul University. What was otherwise a most pleasant day came to an end when the commander announced that the Queen was a ruthless dictator and democracy a sham. I was sick of this endless stupidity disguised as political debate and lectured him in front of his men. He disappeared on some pretext and I never saw him again. I had caused grave offence and now I found myself in company of a civilian called Essam and his cousin.

We slept for three hours in a mosque before setting off at 1 am to cross the mountains to Jalraiz. High up in the mountains, where we built a gorse fire to ward off the freezing air, we could hear the tinkling of the bells slung about the necks of the donkeys and horses. From time to time the drovers uttered strange noises and there was a clattering of hoofs on rock somewhere in the distance. In the dark you could only imagine the great struggles which were under way. I was glad of the civilian company for a change. The absence of guns and the talk of the land. We set off up the mountain again, past medieval watchtowers which stood out against the stars. By dawn we had crossed the first mountain but it was freezing and we longed for the sun to rise. It was a grim eighteen-hour journey but there were bright moments: a breakfast of apples and bread in a bitterly cold valley while we chanted phrases to hurry the sun over the snowy peaks; a hair-raising lift in an ancient German army truck; a group of Mujahiddin who ran through a field of yellow flowers to greet us after the painful descent from the mountains.

Jalraiz was packed with hundreds of Mujahiddin from half a dozen provinces. Some had travelled 150 kilometres just for a meeting. Firstly it was to coordinate attacks against Russian positions to mark the fourth anniversary of the invasion in December and secondly to compare notes on offensives against rival parties. Earlier that year hundreds of followers of Harakat and the party of Abdur Rasool Sayyaf, the leader of the Unity no less, had been driven from the area after an offensive. Hezb now controlled even more of the important country surrounding the capital. One commander explained that not only was this important in its own right but that the region provided launching points for an offensive against the capital should the Russians suddenly pull out. I also began to hear the same theory over and over about the role now being played by Masood in the Panjshir. His 'temporary' truce with the Russians had not been rescinded. His Jamiat fighters were being sent to try to take over Hezb villages beyond the Panjshir. The Russians were actually supplying him with arms so that he could try to defeat Hezb which they regarded as their most implacable foe. Islamic fundamentalism was espoused in no purer form than by Hezb and if the Russians could help one party destroy the Hezbis they would. I remained sceptical. This was merely justification for Hezb attacks on its rivals. Strictly Afghan business.

Why did the Russians fear Islamic fundamentalism so much? The answer lies inside the Soviet Union, in the central Asian republics like Uzbekistan and Tadjikistan. Estimates put the number of 'Muslims' in the Soviet Union at 40 million. Their population growth is the highest in the Soviet Union and it is feared that they may actually outnumber the other peoples of the empire by the end of the century. The communists have gone to great lengths to root out Islam from society as it has to suppress all religious thought. One of the many contradictions of Soviet political life is the way it tries to impress Islamic countries with its tolerance of the faith while continuing to stamp it out. All religion threatens the monolithic ideology and has been a target since the revolution. Within two years of the revolution, mosques in central Asia were being razed by the Bolsheviks. It provoked the Basmachi Revolt which lasted ten years and which was put down by the government. The word Basmachi (bandit) has been adapted by the Russians to describe the Afghan resistance. Repression of Islam has been effective although it is far from being eradicated. Limited Muslim representation is tolerated by the state but there is only a fraction of the mosques that once stood in central Asia and copies of the *Qoran* are in short supply. However, many Muslims have gone underground and they meet in secret for prayer. The Afghan resistance has long claimed that it has been taking the fight north of the Amu Darya and attacking Russian positions within the empire. It is wise to treat such claims with caution but I did establish that *Qorans* and Islamic literature are smuggled into and distributed in the cities of Samarkand and Bokhara.

The close questioning began again in Jalraiz. I later discovered that this paranoid interest had been prompted by Russian claims that a British 'spy' had been unmasked in Afghanistan. This rather clumsy fabrication was designed for foreign consumption but the Mujahiddin were on the lookout for spies posing as British journalists. At that time I knew nothing about this 'spy who never was' but I went from camp to camp with a growing sense of persecution. Not that the strangest of characters is not drawn to conflicts like Afghanistan. That Western agents have taken a close interest in the development of the resistance I have no doubts: if I had doubts I would be worried. My only objection is if they pose as journalists which can make life hazardous for real reporters who are vulnerable enough as it is.

On my previous excursion into Afghanistan I had been with three other journalists; a Swiss, an American and a Japanese. There was something odd about the Japanese and the American and I confided my fears in Claude the Swiss photographer. He agreed. Instinct suggested that elements of authenticity were absent: they were not gregarious and did not touch alcohol which for a journalist is a bit like being a fish that cannot swim. By the time we had crossed the border there was nothing we could do, but our suspicions about their bona fides grew. And they were partly correct. Upon our return to the southern Pakistan town of Quetta we had a celebration meal. Over dinner, the American suddenly asked me if I had heard of the Unification Church (The Moonies) and if so what were my views. I was still relating the mass of evidence against this unpleasant cult five minutes later when Claude kicked me under the table.

Refugees begin the long trek to Pakistan.

'Oh,' said the American, 'it's just that my friend and I are members of the church.'

'What if your news editor sends you out on a story unfavourable to the Moonies,' I said having decided that attack was the best defence.

'That is unlikely. The paper is owned by the church.'

We parted with the Japanese saying to the local Mujahiddin that the Moonies would be prepared to 'help with supplies' to the resistance. The oddest sorts cross that frontier.

I set off for the last march to Paghman. We walked through the busy bazaar which was bustling and noisy. The bazaar is central to the life of the Afghan male. Here he could not only buy the staples of sugar, tea and flour but meet friends, gather news and parade himself. The chai khanas were filled with Mujahiddin from far and wide. I spotted some familiar faces who had arrived for the pow-wow on how to dish the rival groups. From amidst the crowd I saw a shy face watching me. It was Abdul Hai from Kharaghor. The man who had spoken so eloquently in favour of the Unity and against fratricide was here to discuss plans for overrunning rival groups. He was friendly but embarrassed.

'My friend, why are you here. I do not think you should be here.'

'No,' I replied sadly, 'neither should you.'

200

15

Back to the Front

It was past midnight when my horse decided that we should part company. The beast was as tired as the two Mujahiddin and myself as we stumbled up the rocky valley beneath the canopy of frozen stars. Far below lay the wooded valleys of Paghman and ahead in the tangle of shadows was the camp of Commander Bilal. The towering peaks were like black plates against the glittering sky. Concentration was difficult now and I was leaving much of the navigation to the horse. The shadow of a tree loomed up and I tried to steer a course down a rocky slope to avoid it. The horse did not think much of that idea and carried on under a stout branch too low to duck. Rider and rucksack hit the ground ignominiously. We were all too weary to laugh.

It was nearly dawn when we reached the little shacks of rock built against the cliffs at the head of the valley. The horse was led away to graze on the sparse scrub, while Bilal peeled an apple for me. He was slight and animated and the way to win his heart was to make him laugh. One of his men had muttered 'kafir' as I passed and being too weary to upbraid him I had joked about England as 'Kafiristan'. Bilal enjoyed it hugely and repeated it a hundred times during my stay. The commander had written a book which combined a study of guerrilla tactics with religious and political philosophy. Conversations with Bilal were just sufficient to distract you from the spartan conditions. The men lived on rice which had to be hauled up the valley by donkey. It was damp and now, in the middle of autumn, bitterly cold at night. Sunshine did not reach the camp until nearly 10am.

'Materialism,' began Bilal after careful thought. 'It is the same in communist countries as in the West. The materialist philosophy is the same. The two sides merely disagree about the best way to materialism. Islam does not choose materialism and therefore does not have to choose between the West and communism. We put God first. Islam first. Developing countries have always had to choose between communism and the West. Even countries of the non-aligned group are often allied with one side or another. Only Islamic countries have a real alternative. To us the communist countries and the West are very similar, though we know the Russians are more dangerous. Our strength is Islam and Allah. Allah protects us and we are happy. If we die fighting for Islam then we are very, very happy.'

·The MiGs streaked across the sky in twos and disappeared behind the peaks, leaving only their sound booming through the valley. High above us the anti-aircraft guns opened up. The distant crump of the bombs followed. The target was the village of Arundhi where we had stopped the day before. The jets circled and again crossed our valley to the south – high and distant to avoid the guns – before plunging into the next valley. Bilal's men were excited and seemed collectively to will the pilots to have a crack at our positions so that they could make a fight of it. But the pilots were familiar with our location and remained tantilisingly out of range. We climbed on a huge rock outcrop the size of a barrage balloon to get a better view. For twenty minutes the jets – I counted six – circled and dived and bombed. When they came into view they barrelled about the sky in dramatic curves and sweeps though they must have known they were out of range. Perhaps it was part of the 'joy' of their war. I later learned that the strike killed eight people and injured a dozen, none of them Mujahiddin. There were two old men, three women and three children. The news was brought up the valley the following day. The messenger stated the facts while Bilal sat listening in silence. They did not pity the dead but honoured them as martyrs. The victims were not innocents in the way we might think of them as innocents. The women too would pick up a gun and fight if their men allowed them.

The fertile land about the capital is largely under Mujahiddin control and subject to constant aerial bombardment.

Each village spawned Mujahiddin and sheltered them too. Most of the countless thousands of villages in the country were controlled by the Mujahiddin. Fighting groups travelled with the nomads. Loathing for and the willingness to fight the invader was nigh universal. When Afghans said to you that they would fight to the last man it was no idle rhetoric.

'Perhaps when they have killed all the women and old men the Russians come and fight the Mujahiddin,' said Bilal.

It rained at night in the valley and afterwards glow-worms would twinkle among the rocks like thousands of cigarette ends. (The analogy probably had something to do with the fact that I had been out of cigarettes for days.) Bilal said that tight security around Kabul made it difficult to smuggle a non-Afghan into the capital but he would give me an escort to try. But it was better that I stay that we might continue our conversation, he said as we snuggled under the coarse wool blanket, woollen hats pulled over our faces to ward off the cold. I was tempted to stay but winter was only weeks away and a permanent sense of weariness had settled within. Curiously, I found it easier to cope with when I was actually on the move and the fatigue was mainly physical. The depredations of illness and hunger had opened the way to a mental strain which was aggravated in the company of fanatics or tomtits. Someone like Bilal was different. He gave me a hat when we parted.

Kabul mirrored the mass of stars above. We gazed for some time on the city below, wedged between the dark mountain ranges. It was a dazzling riot of electricity. We had tried to insinuate ourselves into the suburbs and failed. The Russians had thrown a massive cordon about the outskirts after the fiercest fighting in the capital since the invasion. We tried several points and each time the way was barred by Russian tanks and troops. We retreated to Paghman.

Kabul is a singular place and bears little relationship to the deep conservatism of the countryside. It is surrounded by purple mountains and is 2,000 metres above sea level. It was in the rarefied atmosphere of Kabul that modern ideas germinated while the rest of the country followed the centuries-old traditions. Country people remain suspicious of the capital they see as corrupt and even Godless. Its cosmopolitan tradition stems from its position between India and the old Asian trade routes. Babur loved the city and his tomb is there. But the piety of rural people is offended by such garish examples of modernism as five-star hotels and mysterious organisations like Rotary Clubs. That the invader should deploy its biggest garrison in Kabul confirmed a lot of suspicions in the countryside. Resistance units were increasingly active in the last days of the Amin regime and they have kept up pretty constant pressure on the government and their Russian allies. Government offices and installations – even a bakery known to supply a ministry – come under attack. The Mujahiddin either slip into the city to launch attacks or live there. The writing and distribution of chabanamah (night letters containing Mujahiddin propaganda) was elevated to an art form in the capital.

Not since the days spent in Totumdarah had I seen so much destruction. The huge valley carried the main road north from Kabul to the Soviet Union. Dozens of Russian and government posts had been built to defend the convoys. I now planned to strike north and return to Jebel Seraj where I had left some of my belongings. It meant following the line of the war front. The Mujahiddin were divided as to whether I should be allowed my wishes or be sent back west across the mountains and then north in the comparative safety of Ghorband, before re-crossing the mountains. A Mujahid called Rahman said that I was to be granted my wish to take the direct route.

'Men say to me: Rahman is friend of Mista Mike. Tell if he is crazy or brave man,' said Rahman who tossed me a packet of cigarettes he had secured. 'You crazy or brave?'

At the heart of my decision were two motives: a desire to see more of the front and a horror at the prospect of two crippling mountain climbs which could be avoided.

Rahman and I were squatting in the shade of a ruined building in a ruined village. We listened to distant gun battles at three points. Mujahiddin from the village came to greet us. They escorted us to the remains of a house where the fighters were preparing for a night raid across the valley. The floor of the one habitable room was littered with mines with the strangely satisfying shape of something found on a coral reef. They were being primed along with RPGs and oil rags were being passed between the men stripping their Kalashnikovs. Bullets were being clipped into the curved magazines and spares stuffed into pockets. The village commander, one Zayed, was insistent that I join him on the raid against a post on the outskirts of Kabul. A friend and colleague Robert Cockburn, who had done time covering the tangle of Lebanon, had said just before I left England: 'Play the percentage.' Now the advice drifted up into my mind and I decided to heed it. The risks were too high for no return in terms of photographs. Daylight raids were actually riskier but there was always the possibility of getting a good picture and the mechanical business of operating the camera steadied the nerves. Such is the mangled logic of the trade.

I did not regret my decision: the commander lost two men and four wounded, a high ratio out of a dozen fighters who set out.

The next morning I set off just before dawn to head north to Chaka Dara. Within an hour the sky was glorious: azure with streaks and puffs of cloud. A jig-saw puzzle sky: an English sky. I suddenly longed for home and to know about David Gower's season. The valley was bathed in a pale lemon hue and the air, unsullied by industry, was perfectly sweet. Peace reigned as the men set to work in the fields. The flat roofs of the houses were spread with grapes drying into raisins. Cobs of sweetcorn were piled by the side of the fields. A kilometre away the north road ran straight into the shadow of the mountains and the military posts were spread out on the

Fighters gather under an ancient tree.

foothills on the other side. Everywhere we met groups of armed Mujahiddin just returned from raids or preparing to go on them. A swarthy type complained bitterly that an American journalist had recently written that there was no fighting in Afghanistan. Did he work for the Russians? No, I said. I expect he had merely visited a quiet area and mistakenly assumed it was representative of the whole country. The war had a tendency to flare up in one area and then fade for a time. Or perhaps he had written his piece on a day like this when it was inconceivable that this was a country at war.

'He was a bad journalist,' said the man and seized my hand. 'Come, I show you fight.'

On the west side of the valley, perched high on a hill, was a folly built by King Amanullah. The strange colonnaded building had been used by the king for picnics on Friday, the Muslim day of rest, but was now a bombed-out ruin. The Mujahiddin, with their usual sense of daring and irony, had used the hopelessly exposed building as their HQ until the Russian gunners had got their eye in. Bilal had led his men up a valley and made a new HQ in a village surrounded by orchards. The Russians mounted a massive attack and the rearguard action that Bilal and his men fought was local legend. Of the four villages in the little valley there was little left two years later: only the farmers continued to tend their fields.

Bilal strode out of nowhere, leading a large body of men.

'My friend, where you go now?' he asked.

'To see a fight.'

'Good my friend. I am sorry about Kabul. But you will enjoy this fight. After, it is better that you leave Paghman. My spies come from communist post and say Russian come in Paghman town tomorrow. There will be big fight. I go to Paghman town. You must pass through the town before Russians come.'

With that he marched off and we set off to the centre of the valley. I had met several Afghan soldiers, who would stroll into a Mujahiddin camp, sometimes in uniform, and tell the commander everything they knew. The Russians by now trusted virtually nobody in the Afghan army. Not only were their respective camps always separate, but the Russian command – which dictated strategy – only informed their Afghan counterparts of battle plans at the last moment to try to prevent word leaking out. All along the front, commanders invariably knew in advance of any major strike planned by the Russians. Afghan soldiers usually acted as spies until they were in a position to desert with as many arms as they could bring out. The soldiers I talked to tended to pity their Russian counterparts. They were badly fed and unable to supplement their diet by shopping in the markets for fear of attack. Russian officers kept the best food supplies for themselves. The only comfort for the men was vodka and hashish when they could get it. I was shown many weapons which the Mujahiddin had acquired from Russian soldiers for small amounts of hashish.

'Russians think like donkeys,' said Rahman echoing the favourite phrase used to describe the Russians. 'They give Kalashnikov for hashish. Then they like crazy men when we come to shoot them with their guns.'

We were lying on a bald hill overlooking a series of smaller hills where, incredibly, the Russians had chosen to site two camps. The 'camps' were visible only by the half a dozen tanks and armoured vehicles perched on the summits. Some of the tanks were buried up to their turrets while others lumbered about the gentle slopes, raising huge palls of dust. The men lived in underground bunkers. Rahman peered through field glasses at the vehicles criss-crossing the sides of the hills.

We waited an hour for the attack. It came from two sides of the hill and claimed two tanks, hit by RPGs. Confusion seemed to reign among the T-72 crews which rattled and squeaked about the hillsides in an apparently aimless fashion. From our lofty perspective we knew exactly the Mujahiddin positions among the orchards below the hills. The two vehicles burned on the side of the hill and the air was filled with the sound of automatics. It took the Russians some thirty minutes of rumbling about the hillside finally to locate the Mujahiddin positions. The tanks opened up and blasted holes in the orchards. But they were too late. We could already see two single files of Mujahiddin walking back to the village. Rahman lay on his back chuckling as the Russian tanks kept up the barrage, blasting hundreds of apples into the blue sky. Then he tapped my shoulder and

Gunship over Paghman.

indicated to a point on the horizon. Two gunships from Bagram base were heading our way.

'Gunship come to kill trees too,' he said laughing as we scrambled down the hillside.

The town of Paghman suggested wealth and influence in every street. The buildings were substantial and great walls concealed the most exquisite gardens, now overgrown through neglect. Wealthy Kabulis once maintained weekend retreats in the town. Generals, politicians and the great merchants. A small valley running up into the mountains was filled with streams and trees which concealed fabulous mansions. It was the first evidence of ostentatious wealth I had come across and it was a shock. The gradations of visible wealth were one thing, but these extraordinary buildings were not even in the same league. Rahman told the other Mujahiddin to rest and showed me around the gardens laid out like little Edens. He said grandly that the Mujahiddin had banished the rich exploiters and handed over the homes to the poor. I said he sounded like a dreary socialist and he frowned. He mumbled that all the rich people had been in cahoots with the communists. I did not know whether that was true or not but I did not disbelieve him. Afghanistan boasts the strangest of alliances.

We took lunch in the beautiful home of the local commander. The food was delicious; fresh nan and mutton, salads, soup and mast, followed by

Bombing raid on village near Paghman.

grapes and melon. We sat on exquisite Afghan carpets in a panelled room. The first evidence of the Russian attack came with the chattering of machine guns somewhere in the streets. My host dismissed it. The gunfire got louder and more intense but my host only shrugged his shoulders. I had picked up enough Persian to understand from their conversation that the Russian attack had begun. I grabbed my camera and made for the door as the gunfire came closer. My host seemed hurt that I should abandon his hospitality for such a modest affair as a pitched battle in the next street. He had no intention of allowing his guest to endanger himself. We would finish lunch in the manner of civilised men. Two Mujahiddin leaned against the door and prevented me leaving. The rest of the lunch was eaten in another of those strikingly surreal atmospheres which remain an abiding memory of Afghanistan. The Mujahiddin sat around chatting and joking and asking me about Isa and my thoughts on Islam. Bullets chipped off bits of the wall on the other side of the courtyard and my host asked me if 'Commander' Margaret Thatcher was really a woman? 'Yes,' I said. 'Is that really a war going on outside?' They laughed and said nothing. The meal finished and Rahman suggested we go. My host raised an eyebrow and said we must stay for tea.

After tea we slipped through a back door of the courtyard where we were met by a group of twenty anxious Mujahiddin who had been assembled to get me safely out of the town. I protested that I wanted to stay for the fight but the commander refused. I said it was a waste of men to have such a large group escort me out. He smiled and shook his head. Bilal had said I could stay for the action, I said without blushing.

'I talk to Commander Bilal today. He like you. He say you go,' said the commander, raising his eyebrow.

The men fanned out through the streets and worked a passage up through the valley. By now the fighting seemed to be taking place on all sides. The squeak of the tracks and the grinding of gears came closer. I pleaded with the sub-commander of the group to let me stay but he was adamant. Turning a corner, we were forced to dive for cover as an APC turned into the street 100 metres away. A wounded Mujahid lay in the street firing his rifle. A grenade was thrown from a rooftop at the vehicle. I told the sub-commander that I intended to stay for a few minutes and that he could go to hell.

And that was how I came to be frogmarched out of Paghman. The Afghans will exercise the laws of hospitality and protection whether the guest likes it or not. They do not understand the role of independent journalists and if they do they will not allow you to dishonour them by getting yourself hurt. The impartial observer did not exist: in this world there was no objective truth, only Islam and allegiances. While one man took my rucksack and my cameras, two others pinned my arms and marched me through the streets and refused to unhand me until I promised to behave. A stray bullet whined by so close that I gave in on the grounds that three bodies close together presented an easier target than fleeing individuals.

We ran until I thought my lungs would cave in; up the length of the valley and then across it. the sense of the real world dissolving was heightened by the aberrant architecture of banished wealth. German architects were responsible for the mock gothic turrets and conical towers which sprouted from the luxurious mansions. It seemed like a gigantic parody, a hoax played on the senses as you ran, stumbling through the huge gardens. Most of the buildings were ruined which was just as well because the one thing they spoke of was that they were quite alien to Afghanistan. Here was a ghetto of European homes and no doubt the manners which had once been acted within had been borrowed from there too. If the Afghans felt indignant one could hardly blame them.

I struggled up the steep sides of the barren valley. Below was a canopy of green through which the pointed towers protruded and which muffled the sound of the battle. I paused at the top of the valley until the sub-commander cried menacingly: 'Mista. Burrow. Burrow.' The war receded again.

But it would never be very far away now, on the journey to Chaka Dara. One night I climbed onto the roof of the farmhouse where I was staying and watched the tracer flying through the dark at half a dozen points across the broad valley. The young son of the farmer stood with us and gazed up as if he were watching a grand firework display. Then we went down and ate the mixture of sugar and breadcrumbs worked into a paste which had been prepared for our meal. Our progress through the valley was slow and erratic but the food was varied: interesting dishes like marrow mash with raw chillis and nan stuffed with spiced potatoes, and fried. I stayed in the farmhouse near Isa Khel for two nights and, to my delight, was left alone to read Shakespeare. The Mujahiddin were reserved and amiable and though they did not admit as much there was some difficulty in getting me to the next safe village about 12 kilometres away. At night we all lay in a line shrouded in our partouks like mummies in Cairo Museum. We took breakfast together early and then they would leave. I was not allowed to leave the house so I would sit huddled indoors wrapped in my partouk until the sun made it warm enough to sit in the courtyard.

The camels loped by with their imbecile grins. Ammunition and mortars to make a commander very happy. Talk of difficulties had gone and I was mounted on a brown nag with a backbone like some prehistoric animal. It was another delightful cool and sunny day and we set off, a new escort and myself, for the journey to Chaka Dara. Less than half an hour on the beast without saddle or stirrups, and I could bear it no longer. Two great weals across my backside later became infected and refused to heal. The Mujahiddin laughed and insisted I take the other horse, a grey with saddle.

We passed through low brown hills with villages made of the same soil so that they were camouflaged. Many were badly damaged but everywhere reconstruction work was under way, quietly and without fuss. We stopped and shared tea or a few grapes with gangs of men who patiently explained who among their families had been killed. Of the hundreds of villages I had passed through few had escaped damage but everywhere rows of simple bricks were drying in the sun, having been fashioned from the rubble of the broken homes. It was undramatic but quietly heroic. Life went on, and it was according to the ancient tradition of a people and not according to the standards of the shabby crew which had sold Afghanistan to the empire.

'Now I have new house every year,' said the man with the shovel in one hand and a pot of tea in the other. It was the third time that he had been forced to build a new home.

Islamia stood profile on, his head slightly turned towards me – shy, almost feminine – as if he had just raised his eyes from the ground. He had long lank hair and soft features. In his robes I could only think of a stage version of *Richard III* without the hunchback. He was the commander of the villages of Chaka Dara.

We sat on the roof of a house where the wounded stayed – one man with perforated eardrums and shrapnel in his legs, another with hideous burns to his face and throat. You coped with the sight of serious wounds until the victims were children and all the arguments of a just war vanished. One small boy had had his legs welded together by the heat of bombs dropped on his father's fields, so that he was left with a single misshapen stump and he dragged himself along with a crutch. Another boy, about six, had had his face burned off. His nose was gone and there was a hole in the middle of his face which gave him the appearance of a fish. It was his mouth. An old man with a bullet wound in his stomach had heard I was in the village and climbed the ladder to the roof to seek me out. He hoped I might be a doctor – there were many French doctors in Panjshir, he said – and showed me the suppurating wound, another high on his back where the bullet had left his body. What use was a scribbler now?

A teacher came to sit and talk on the roof. He was the most nervous Afghan I met. He had recently been released, along with 2,000 others, from the notorious Pul-i-Churki jail in Kabul. The freeing of the men was to mark the fifth anniversary of the Saur Revolution. He had been a science teacher until the communists had dragged him from his classroom and thrown him into jail without charge or trial. He had had no political allegiance. During his twenty-five months in jail he was tortured, he said. He had been beaten and he showed me the scars on his shins where the skin had been flayed to the bone. Electric shocks were administered to the genitals, ear lobes and tongue; fingernails were pulled off and cigarettes stubbed out on his body. Most of those released under the amnesty had joined the Mujahiddin. The tens of thousands still in the jails would too, if they survived. Pul-i-Churki had taken on the same significance as the Bastille during the French Revolution.

Islamia's doleful expression masked a profound compassion for the suffering which was everywhere. But there was another side of the man. He could be cheerful and he was proud of his network of Mujahiddin groups. We scrambled from the roof as the artillery began to pound the village 400 metres behind us.

The next day we woke to the same sound which left the lusty cock quavering in mid-note. We set off early for the village where Islamia had his HQ, stopping briefly to watch jets bombing Paghman far to the south. Islamia said that once the Russians knew there was a Western journalist in a certain area they suspended air raids until he had moved on. It seemed an incredible story yet in the weeks I spent in the valley a pattern emerged in which areas I had left were bombed the following day. The villages were half-destroyed and the fields full of craters. We stopped in an orchard and feasted on pears and grapes. Islamia asked me with relish if Bilal had been able to offer me similar fare, knowing full well that life was more spartan in Paghman. I said that as they were members of the same party that it would be no difficulty to send the Mujahiddin of Paghman some fruit to relieve the austerity. But first loyalties tended to be very parochial. Islamia smiled.

Zarbed Sultan was bald and middle-aged and an expert shot with an RPG launcher. He handed me his binoculars to see the convoy of fifty trucks making its way on the distant road through the hills to Kabul. We were joined by a young sub-commander called Engineer Farhad whose English was perfect. Together we toured the villages over several days. Damage was widespread yet life went on: the men working in the fields and the women laying out thousands of cobs of corn in the sun.

One of the excursions we made was to Carismir Gardens which had been laid out by King Zahir Shah. It featured many large buildings – more Germanic architecture – and a mosque set among lawns and groves. However, it was close to the road and two military posts just beyond in the foothills. We approached from the west at a safe distance and sat in the shelter of some trees eating giant sweet peaches. There must be something in the soil which produces such sweet fruit. Just then a Land Rover passed by along the track, before stopping and reversing. The ebullient character at the wheel laughed at our timidity and said he would drive us to the mosque. Although Zarbed Sultan and Farhad had reservations the Mujahiddin thought this would be a great feat of daring. They looked at me and I said, 'Let's go.'

Perhaps it was a combination of good company and a beautiful day that turned my head. The Mujahiddin clambered on the back of the vehicle and cried 'Allah O Akbar' and waved their rifles as the charabanc careered across the lawns in full view of the posts. There was that same air almost of immortality which was infectious and only afterwards did you realise what a lunatic act it had been. Two startled old men with long white beards stopped, then burst into laughter before clambering on the back. Off we went across the undulating green, all as spontaneous as youth in spring, abandoned and foolhardy. More giant peaches appeared and somebody suggested we drive into Kabul, shoot anybody who tried to stop us. 'Allah O Akbar,' they roared. That would be something. Yes, yes, we all cried. To Kabul. Engineer Farhad firmly vetoed the idea and we headed back to the safety of the trees. Perhaps the Russian gunners had been on the hashish, but it was only when we were 2 kilometres away that the first shells began to hit the cool lawns of the king's garden.

I was wakened in the middle of the night by Mujahiddin preparing for an excursion. By the light of torches they were priming mines in the sleeping quarters. They must have known how excited I would be by their tinkering with high explosives a metre from my head in poor light. One of the Mujahiddin kept dropping a home-made bomb that he hoped to try out that night. Finally the men said prayers and trooped out.

They were back before I had risen, having laid the mines near the posts. Farhad was to be my guide north from now and we said goodbye to Islamia and his men. We had not gone far when there was an explosion across the valley. A mine had claimed a tank.

16

Horseman of the Apocalypse

The way was now north but there was a problem at the heart of the valley. The twin towns of Qarabagh and Istalif stood either side of the valley like Scylla and Charybdis: Qarabagh occupied by the Russians and Istalif in the hands of Jamiatis. Navigating a route by night between these two hostile towns meant crossing the well-patrolled main road. To me it seemed that, on balance, it was preferable to making the journey through the mountains.

'No mountains,' said Farhad reassuringly as we sat beneath the apple trees in the orchards that stretched for miles. Farhad sought to please not for the sake of some social code but for its intrinsic joy. He peeled giant pink apples and passed them to the Mujahiddin who sat cleaning their weapons. The engineer was cheerful and urbane and believed it was possible for me to take the direct route north. He was the only one who did. The strong communist presence in the valley meant greater hazards. Now I often moved only at night and was concealed in safe houses by day. When I did travel by day it was always with the tails of my turban pulled across my face like a veil.

We had come from the village of Arghal Chikoo which boasted a communist fort made of red mud. I remembered it as the place where I discovered that my hair was crawling with lice. A particularly haughty intellectual sat in the apple tree next to mine while we spied on the post 200 metres away. He insisted on carrying out a conversation despite my fears that he might alert the enemy. He delivered the lecture on Western imperialism, followed it with a brief and contemptuous analysis of why Christianity was sophisticated idolatry and was demanding to know why I could not pull strings to get him a visa to get into Great Britain, when the shooting started.

'Because we already have enough windbags like you,' I said and leapt from the branches.

He was still whining and making his demands when we settled down for the night at a farmhouse. He refused to believe that British government officials could not simply be bribed into letting him into the country. He laughed when I said that government officials were subject to laws too. I grew so tired of the wretched man that I used a visit to the toilet as a pretext to stay outside in a platinum-lit field for an hour. The men came to say we had to move on immediately. There was talk of informers in the village.

That night we had walked for kilometres in circles until being ushered into a doorway and into a guest room where we fell asleep. I awoke to find myself beneath a large patterned quilt in a room full of hanging plants and a songbird in a cage. After breakfast I was taken to an orchard where Farhad sat peeling apples.

'No mountains,' he cried.

Farhad and myself would recite the two words like some mystical incantation to ward off the doubts and pragmatism of the commanders whose territory we passed through. That pragmatism dictated a detour through the mountains as safer than the risky route direct north. As we drew closer to the bottleneck (Istalif I remembered was noted for its blue glazed pottery; Qarabagh for the 'treacherous' imam who was burned in his own home in 1979), in the centre of the valley, the more persuasion was necessary to obtain escorts and letters of passage. But the more gloomy the prognosis by pessimistic commanders, the more determined Farhad became.

'Qarabagh!' exclaimed the Mujahiddin we met. It was sufficient to confirm their darkest suspicions about advanced education for Afghans and about foreigners in general.

We took the road on the west side of the valley which was high and exposed. We walked in twos and the Mujahiddin concealed their weapons beneath partouks as we were visible through high-powered binoculars from

Communist post at Arghal Chikoo photographed from an apple tree.

posts on the other side of the valley. It was a warm day in the valley with its freshly turned fields and apple orchards and groves of walnuts now ready for harvesting. The children used long poles to dislodge the walnuts and walked along with bundles of apples slung over their shoulders. We stopped in a village with huge trees shading the square and a little pond surrounded by bulrushes. At least 100 Mujahiddin were sprawled in the shade, their guns leant against the tree trunks. The barber was shaving heads and I was tempted to shed my hair and the lice in it, but vanity prevailed and a hope I might find some treatment. Farhad had a friend in the village and there we stopped for a splendid lunch of meat, salad and soup. The friend showed me the water well in his garden which he said had been polluted by chemicals in a bombing raid six months before and which was still unusable. After lunch we hitched a lift on a truck which broke down after a couple of kilometres.

By late afternoon we had arrived in the village of Goldera and Farhad said farewell. He said I would now be escorted through safe villages to Mir Becheh Kut from where I might cross the road between Istalif and Qarabagh. There might be delays but it could be done. He set off south and I walked into the little dusty square. It was pervaded by a sense of the wild west: armed men lounging before little lock-up shops, horses tied up by the side of the road, a sense of aimlessness and concealed violence. My new escorts led me in silence to the home of the village commander where I was admitted to the guest room. I was left alone to admire the view from the window: a panorama of the valley with its dozens of villages.

'Who is the commander of all this area?' demanded the scowling man who entered the room. I told him Islamia at Chaka Dara and he flew into a fury and denounced Islamia as nothing more than a sub-commander.

'For a sub-commander, Islamia carries a hell of a lot of clout around here,' I said. 'As far as I know he is the district commander.'

The man grew angrier and shouted at me in Persian. Another entered the room, a bushy-haired young fellow with a squint, who informed me that I was now in the presence of the district commander: Islamia answered to him. For a horrific moment I feared I might have been taken to the HQ of a rival party, but then I realised that this was some internal wrangle between commanders. In truth I did not give a damn and wanted only rest. The interrogation continued. It was my turn to lose my temper. The young man introduced himself as Doctor Zulmaya and acted as interpreter.

'You have diaries about Afghanistan? You show me diaries.'

I told him to go to hell. The spy story was still doing the rounds. The commander, who refused to tell me his name, asked stiffly who I regarded as the better man: Islamia or him? I normally managed to respond to such arrant vanity with a certain amount of tact. Not this time. His arrogance and rudeness had made me resolve to move on as quickly as possible. I told him that Islamia was the better host. I then proceeded to be as obnoxious as possible to encourage him to send me on my way as quickly as possible. When the subject inevitably turned to religion I bluntly put the case for Jesus

216

being the son of God. They were appalled. On the whole they were a detestable crew, mangled with hate over status and power. In reply to Zulmaya's repeated demands to see my diaries, I extolled the virtues of Islamia's hospitality and his many kindnesses. 'Islamia would never insult me by demanding such a thing,' I said.

The ploy worked: the ill-tempered commander suddenly ordered his men to escort me to the next village. The night march had become my least favourite pastime but, as we trudged over the hills, Goldera receding into the night, I felt a great sense of release. Having been catapulted out into the darkness with barely a goodbye, I found myself bathed in the cold light of a full moon, walking along bright white paths of powdery dust that meandered through the hills. I walked alone and was glad of the solitude. When we came to the solid shapes of the houses in the next village it was late and I was tired. A discussion went on for more than an hour before we were admitted to a house to sleep.

Caution and secrecy dogged my tracks now. I remained in curtained rooms for days and moved only at night, from village to village. In some villages I was moved from house to house, always heavily disguised or at night. The pattern of movement seemed bereft of logic: for every ten kilometres walked we seemed to move one kilometre further north. It was frustrating but still marginally better than the mountain route.

I met several Jamiat Mujahiddin. Even they confirmed that their fellow fighters were moving out of the Panjshir and were trying to take over Hezb areas nearer to Kabul. Their biggest success had been in gaining control of Istalif from Hezb the year before. Some were critical of Masood and said he was pursuing his own ambitions in fighting Hezb at the expense of the common cause. Everywhere I met Hezb commanders who were concerned with fighting off attempts by Jamiat groups to take over. Before entering Afghanistan I had been aware of Hezb's reputation for internal fighting. In Bamian the party had certainly been the aggressor. In this valley two years before they had driven out Mujahiddin whose allegiance had been to a Maoist faction. But in this case I was becoming convinced that Hezb was more sinned against than sinning. I was taken to the main road and watched as a group of armed Mujahiddin were waved through a government checkpoint. Jamiat men, said my escorts, who were free to move about with their weapons. I also met members of rival parties in villages where they lived side by side with Hezb. The groups fought for a number of reasons. One was the personal ambitions of commanders or orders from party HQs in Peshawar. Another reason was skilful intriguing by the communists. Perhaps the main motive was financial. A small community could usually afford to support one group of fighters. Taxes that once went to the government went gladly to the Mujahiddin. But they could not afford to support more than one group in a village. In areas where there were more than one group, considerable strain was placed upon the population and tensions often led to fighting between groups.

We were camped in a bombed out building without decent food or cigarettes. We were close to the main road, though I had lost my bearings in the maze of villages and orchards. That night we would try to cross the road. We set off around 9 pm moving through the lanes and then crawling on all fours through the fields of beans. The burly Pathan in charge was ahead and now he came scrambling back shaking his head in the darkness and putting his hand over my mouth. He pointed through the trees at the black shapes of the tanks. They were no more than 100 metres away. We had almost blundered into a communist patrol. There was no way through. It was a bitter blow but this was no place to argue. We spent most of the night trudging to the west side of the valley.

We had barely gone to sleep at a safe house when we were awoken by men who said I must press on to Chaka Dara, back south. It was too dangerous to attempt another crossing of the road. I must return to Islamia and then make the mountain crossing. I did not see why I could not make the mountain crossing from where we were, but they sidestepped the issue and put me in the care of a group of Mujahiddin who were heading for Pakistan via the route south of Kabul. It was a depressing march, using up precious energy retracing my footsteps, already having wasted a week on the trek north. I had an abscess growing on my big toe. Now there was the mountain crossing to look forward to.

The Mujahiddin I travelled with were in excellent spirits. They were going to Pakistan for the winter and a break from the war. We stopped by a river where they ate handfuls of raisins and nuts. That would be their diet for eight to ten days. The last two days were always the worst, they said, when most of the supplies were exhausted. But the prospect of Peshawar kept them going, said the shaven-headed man who walked with me. Several Jamiatis came to greet us. My companion was their friend. I asked them what they would do if ordered to fight: could they kill a friend who was a member of a rival party? They were enthusiastic in claiming they would not fight but they were not good liars and they grew embarrassed.

I found myself passing through familiar villages. The inhabitants thought that the somewhat eccentric perambulating Inglestani was great sport and joked that they looked forward to meeting me again when I passed through in a week's time. At that point neither I nor they realised that there is many a true word spoken in jest.

Back at Arghal Chikoo the local commander blithely announced that I would have to go back to Paghman where Commander Bilal would provide an escort. The man was trying to pass the buck, I was the buck and I had had enough. Such a detour would have added an extra two or three weeks on the journey to Jebel Seraj. I sat down ahd told the commander that he would have to have me carried. He scratched his head and disappeared. An hour later two men appeared and said they would take me to see someone. We set off up a little river valley full of poplars and through several villages before they left me under a walnut tree. I sat down with some nuts gathered from the floor and estimated ruefully that I had actually travelled some ten kilometres that afternoon – back north. A familiar figure appeared and hugged me. It was Engineer Farhad. He spent half an hour apologising for the failure to get me through and cursed the incompetence of those he had been foolish enough to leave me in the hands of. I said that all I wanted to do was begin the mountain trek as soon as possible.

'No mountains,' he cried.

Farhad said he would send me back north through the valley and that I would take a different route through villages where the people were 'not dogs and fools' to a commander who would get me across the road between the towns. This commander was a great man and would not be put off by a few tanks. I had become reconciled to life lived in an endless circle where nothing was ever achieved, but Farhad seemed the one man who could break the cycle of futility.

So it was that two days later I found myself on that high road on the west side of the valley once again heading north.

The abscess on my toe had made walking difficult and so my companions had acquired a horse. I rode at a leisurely pace along the track above the valley. Less than a kilometre away was a communist post, a drab mud affair across a parched stretch of ground where little dead bushes rolled in the breeze.

The Mujahid who walked next to me suddenly said: 'Your foot still hurting. Still long ride to Mir Becheh Kut.'

That familiar expression – of mangled comprehension, a perfect plan to fit the occasion – spread across his features. I had learned to be wary of that look. It meant trouble. An Afghan inspired by some idea is both irresistible and a menace. Reason and caution wilt before enthusiasm. So it was that my companion leapt onto the horse in front of me and cried: 'I know quick way to Mir Becheh Kut.'

With that he spurred the horse to a gallop and we headed straight for the communist post. I do not know what the guards in the post thought but the effect on me, at least metaphorically, was the same as dysentery. The Mujahid wore his Kalashnikov across his chest and my turban unwound to reveal strictly European features. I was clinging on to a spot south of his midriff and wondering what effect a squeeze might have: would it persuade him to stop or urge him into even greater feats of lunacy. We drew closer to the post and I could see the guards watching us from the ramparts. It was insanity at a gallop and I resigned myself to an unhappy ending. Capture or death, thanks to the momentary insanity of my companion. He was laughing and, sensing my terror, cried that the communists were donkeys and by the time they woke up we would be gone. At the last moment we turned off our disastrous course and galloped along a track through villages and across fields. We startled the Mujahiddin in one village and afterwards he cried that we had just thundered through a Jamiat village.

Russian armoured car.

'Jamiat donkeys too. This good way to Mir Becheh Kut.'

At length we stopped in a village in the very heart of the valley and were taken to a home to eat fatty soup and bread. Our host examined the abscess on my toe and produced a sewing needle. While another held me from behind, my host lanced and drained it as the others looked on intently. I was reminded again of Hollywood drama. Only the Scotch, generously imbibed as anaesthetic, was missing. Afterwards they placed slices of raw onion about my toe and bound it with rags.

It was another two days – spent zig-zagging about the valley – before we fetched up at another village near the north road. So far so good. Farhad had kept his promise and here the men seemed to have a stronger sense of purpose. There was a voluble old man and a young dashing sort, whose enthusiasm for danger was tempered by a facility for planning. The third character was the greediest I had met. At dinner he took great handfuls of soup-soaked nan and stuffed them into his mouth with sucking noises. Then he ate most of the meat and all of the salad. His performance was capped by a record number of cups of tea which he swallowed with a sound akin to a drain in a storm. Afterwards much hashish was smoked and then we went to cross the road.

Earlier we had watched the jets bombing the next village, and in the dark we bumped into two Mujahiddin who had walked the five kilometres to

Villagers near Mir Becheh Kut discuss plans for reconstruction after an air raid.

report on the damage. Three people had been killed and about twenty made homeless. About half would come to our village in the morning to seek shelter with relatives. We crouched by the bank of a dried-up river bed and waited for the scouts to return. I anticipated failure. The road had been a symbol, a great challenge, but that feeling had been superseded by a sense of fatalism. Gunfire started close by and the flares went up. I had not realised just how close the communist post was. One of my companions told me how he and his class-mates had been press-ganged into the army while they were studying at Kabul University. They had been posted to Qandahar airbase and he had waited until he could desert with his weapons. Most of the troops he had met hated the communists. Some were waiting to desert while others acted as spies. Oddly, in its state of disintegration, the army was serving the country. The press-gangs operated in the cities and scoured whole districts for young men. Schools and homes were raided and men pressed into service.

'What the government does not realise is that it is training Mujahiddin,' whispered the figure in the dark. 'They force young boys into the army and teach them not only how to fight but how to hate the government. Then they come to us with their guns.'

We moved on to another village, moving swiftly north along the paths that separated the fields and orchards. There was a large gathering of Mujahiddin in the village and it became clear that they had mounted a major operation to get me across the road. The village was built on a slope and one of the village elders proudly showed me the ingenious early warning system for raids from the communist post. Above the village ran a small river and dozens of little channels criss-crossed the village streets on their way to water the fields. The sluices were opened once a day at 4 pm when the sound of water filled the village. If they were opened at any other time it was a signal from the lookouts that trouble was coming.

We moved off again along the river bed, ever closer to the sound of gunfire. Suddenly the leader of our group turned to me and hissed 'Come on,' before plunging into the undergrowth towards the battle. We crawled the last 100 metres to where the Mujahiddin were firing a mortar towards the communist post. Mujahiddin from my group, delighted by this unplanned excursion into battle, took up positions and blazed away.

'First we kill some communists, then we cross the road,' hissed the commander. I found a boulder the size of a motor car to shelter behind and smoked a cigarette. A Mujahid sat next to me priming an RPG.

'This good fight,' he said.

'Wonderful,' I said.

Bullets were ricocheting off the boulder with monotonous regularity when the commander reappeared and we set off for the road again.

'How you like the fighting?' he asked as we crawled back to the safety of the river bed.

'I'm ecstatic. You must surprise me like that again,' I said.

'Good, good,' he said beaming. 'Before the road there is one more post. Maybe we fight there too.'

Sarcasm is not understood in Afghanistan.

We waited for a long time, less than 100 metres from the road. There was fighting at three posts in the valley but no tanks on the road. I still felt that something would prevent us from making the crossing but then the Mujahiddin were up and running and I could smell the tarmac. We had crossed the Rubicon.

That simple act exorcised the weariness for a while and I was quite happy for the rest of the night march over hills and through swamp, the dark mass of the towns either side. When at last we reached a house we were given food. I had just fallen asleep when I was poked in the ribs.

'Mista. Burrow, harakat. We have a long way to go before dawn.'

17

The Raid

A dozen Mujahiddin came running at me with bayonets. They had appeared suddenly around a corner, fanned out and charged. It had been a trying forty-eight hours. Much of it had been spent marching by night, wading through rivers and stumbling over salt flats trying to keep the oaths down to a roar so that the Russians did not hear you. The most memorable couple of hours had been spent negotiating a way through defunct vineyards, now overgrown. It was a ludicrous episode as half a dozen men tried to walk along the ridges between the tangle of vines, every so often plunging into the superabundant greenery with a strangled scream. We arrived in a safe house at 3.30 am and the commander insisted I take pictures of his men. I explained I needed sunlight and fell asleep. They woke me just after 4 am as the first rays were topping the mountains and dragged me out for a photo session before breakfast. It was only when they lined up in the freezing half-light that I realised what they were up to. I told them not to be so damn stupid and to get me to a cup of tea before I died.

And now I was going to be bayonetted.

The men rushed past and down the street of the village leaving me face to face with Abdul Karim Zayed, commander of the area. He was young, well-organised, active and an egomaniac. I made the mistake of admiring the special Kalashnikov which he carried with its chopped barrel. That set the pattern for my brief and spectacular sojourn with Commander Karim and his men. He loved compliments and received most by the simple expedient of asking for them. He took me on a tour of some of the villages under his command. His appearance was preceded by his 'praetorian guard' which ran ahead. There was no danger to security, but it looked impressive and kept his men on their toes. He made fabulous claims about the number of tanks his men had blown up and Russians killed. He must have sensed my scepticism – he was quite sensitive – because he gave an order which resulted in a huge Mercedes lorry appearing.

Jets were slipping down the sky as Karim took the wheel and we roared off to a village several kilometres away. The planes – one every few minutes – were returning to Bagram air base after bombing raids. Archaeologists had dug up everything from lacquer ware from China to carved ivory from India

'The graveyard of Russian lorries'.

at Bagram, a reflection of its position on the great trade routes. The air base was built under an aid programme by the Russians and they made good use of it during the invasion. Elite airborne units seized Bagram from the outset and it was now the HQ for the Soviet air force.

'One day I show you graveyard of Russian planes,' cried Karim above the roar of the engine and waving at the jets on their final approaches. 'Now I show you graveyard of Russian lorries.'

The jets were so low. What couldn't the Mujahiddin achieve with just a few shoulder-held anti-aircraft missiles?

As if reading my thoughts, Karim cried: 'Tell Commander Thatcher to send rockets for shooting Russian planes. I do to them what I did to these lorries.'

He told me of the great ambush of the year before in which a convoy of lorries had been attacked. The village was an extraordinary sight: dozens of lorries smashed and burned out littered the whole place. It must have been quite a show. Unfortunately much of the village was destroyed in the attack and it was now uninhabitable.

'Yes this was one problem for us,' admitted Karim and we roared off to another village for lunch.

After lunch he suddenly announced that he was going to attack one of the

Burned out oil tanker.

Russian posts that night and that I would be guest of honour on the raid. I thanked him for his kindness but said that I had renounced night raids. I had seen plenty.

'My raids better,' he said gloomily.

I said that I had no doubt that his raids were a marvel to behold but that night raids were out. 'Now daylight raids,' I began.

He brightened. 'You like daylight raids?'

'Yes,' I replied, but asked that no special arrangements be made for me. No unnecessary risks.

'But you are my guest. I make daylight raid for you'.

With that Karim called in one of his sub-commanders and half an hour later I was marching with eight Mujahiddin through the lanes, bound for the north road. Karim, in his flamboyant way, had honoured the code of hospitality.

The group was led by Badur Mohammed, a podgy fellow with a moustache. The RPG bearer was an old balding chap called Sofi Ahmed who loped along with the launcher over his shoulder. There was one other RPG bearer and the rest were armed with Kalashnikovs. It was a typical raid on the road, designed to knock out one or two vehicles. It was my estimate that along the stretch of the main road from Kabul to Jebel Seraj, where there

226

Sweetcorn drying on a roof.

were many such raids each day, the government and the Russians were losing at least fifty vehicles each week.

There was tremendous excitement among the Mujahiddin. Only Badur Mohammed and Sofi Ahmed remained composed. We virtually ran the six kilometres to the villages near the road, as Karim had briefed them to launch the attack before nightfall, lest I lose interest. We stopped in a village and Badur Mohammed and the others consulted with the residents as to the best spot from which to launch an attack that afternoon. They might have been fishermen asking after the best spots on a river bank. We walked another couple of kilometres and Badur Mohammed changed his mind and we walked back again. Suddenly firing started less than a couple of kilometres away and Badur Mohammed feared that it might spoil our excursion. Big attacks often led to the road being closed. But the firing ceased.

At length we came to a narrow path between two high walls, running parallel to and about 100 metres from the road. The men gouged holes in the baked clay which afforded views across the exhausted vineyard to the road. Then they knocked down a large section of the rear wall to enable the RPGs, which throw out a long flame, to be fired. Suddenly Badur Mohammed fell off the shoulders of one of the men and disappeared into a cloud of fine dust. When he emerged he was frantically waving his waistcoat about his head. In

After the harvest, the matter of transporting the crops.

pulling down the wall, he had disturbed a hornets' nest. The ambush was suspended for a while until the humming died down and the men had stopped laughing.

It was dusk when they were all in position; six riflemen and two RPG launchers, each with a peephole through which to see the road. Each waited with his finger on the trigger as along the road passed buses and civilian trucks. The attack itself lasted less than thirty seconds. It was not a normal affair. A tank preceded several trucks and APCs. Sofi Ahmed hit the lead truck with an RPG. It blew up and was engulfed in flames. The second launcher missed. Smoke from the launchers filled the narrow lane where we hid. Normally there was time to get a second and often a third RPG strike in. Not this time. The Mujahiddin blazed away but the return fire was instant and intense. The enemy tended to drive off the other side of the road and take cover. Return fire was usually desultory and ineffective, a token gesture until the Mujahiddin withdrew. The Mujahiddin were satisfied with a couple of hits and the enemy were glad to be alive. The Mujahiddin withdrew almost at leisure. That was how it was with communist troops and usually Russian soldiers. That was not the case when you fired RPGs at some crack Russian unit.

Whoever they were, they were hungry for a fight. The infantry came at us

228

across the vineyard while the tanks and APCs lurched off about the lanes to cut off our escape. Within a few seconds the return fire was so intense that the wall in front of us had begun to disintegrate and the lane was filled with clouds of dust as well as smoke. Mujahiddin, rushing to get out, tripped over others who continued firing through the peepholes. There was confusion for long and dangerous seconds. Badur Mohammed pushed me into the lane down which we had to flee for our lives. Earlier he had referred to it as the lane for 'retreating'.

'Ten times, fifty times we attack Shoravee [Russians] and Karmalite soldiers. They no good. No fighting. Then this time they quite good,' said Badur Mohammed ruefully.

We ran for more than three kilometres, until I was close to collapse and the thirty cigarettes a day felt like a wirebrush drawn across the lungs. And still the enemy kept coming. The Mujahiddin split into two groups, a forward one to stay with me and a rearguard to return fire, until some of the Mujahiddin in the first village came to help. In every lane we ran through and in the orchards or vineyards the bullets flew by until you thought the enemy had surrounded you. The tanks opened up but they were off target. I leapt into a dried-up river bed and flattened myself. I had dropped my cigarettes. The Mujahiddin leapt in after me. One had stopped to pick up the packet.

The firing opened up again and this time it was closer. The enemy were still coming. It was not their style and it was terrifying. Never trust a Russian to do what you want him to do. We set off again. The firing behind would stop for a couple of minutes and then start again, only closer. The bullets whined past and sometimes I looked over my shoulder. The most terrifying thing was that there was nothing to see. Only the trees or a wall or a field. Death was coming from just behind this veil of normality.

I burst out of a grove of trees to find myself running across a perfectly level patch of open ground the size of a cricket pitch. I felt rather cheated that I should come across the only level ground in the whole central mountainous region at a time like this. I had slogged uphill, fallen downhill and stumbled over boulders for nearly four months and now I found myself on what could have been a cricket pitch. The firing came closer and I stopped in my tracks. To go on or double back? I almost began to think about the predicament, which would probably have made me seize up, instead of working by instinct. I ran back and crouched behind a tree.

We had to cross that open ground. Beyond it was a long mud wall at the perimeter of the village and, around that, safety. The four men and myself waited until there was a lull in the firing and then began to sprint across the ground. We had got about half way when the firing, now even closer, began again. Earlier I had spotted a shallow mound – no more than a few centimetres – behind which I reckoned it might be possible for one man to take cover. It was every man for himself so I flattened myself behind it. The other four had the same idea. Five of us lay huddled behind it as the bullets whacked into the wall behind. I felt the man next to me shaking and looked at his face. He was convulsed with laughter.

'Allah O Akbar,' he whispered and began to giggle. 'Allah O Akbar,' the others whispered too, and dissolved into laughter.

We still had to make 50 metres to safety. The other four suddenly burst from the treeline and raced across the open ground, waving us to run too. We did and we all made it with bullets literally flying about our heads. We collapsed against the wall as we rounded the corner. A large group of Mujahiddin were taking up positions in case the Russians tried to enter the village. They did not. But they kept up the tank and artillery bombardment for several hours. It was astonishing that none of us had been hit. The men kept up the cry 'Allah O Akbar' for twenty minutes.

'This was a good fight, Mista Mike. Commander Karim big commander. Now you Mujahid,' said Badur Mohammed as we ate the last of the season's grapes on the walk back to our village. 'You like the fight, I think.'

The truth was that I had enjoyed it. Perhaps that was the 'joy' that fighters feel, a moment on the edge of eternity. Later I felt vaguely ashamed of the feeling and had no desire to repeat it. But at the time I had enjoyed it. We walked home, beneath the stars as the shells blew holes in the fields nearby. But we had all become just a shade immortal then and we barely noticed them.

18

Cauldron without Frontiers

I do not know whether the advent of fear was the result of a negation of reason or the point where it finally asserted itself. I do remember when fear actually appeared.

Mullah Farouk was a thin-faced man who carried a beautiful Walther pistol. After an exhausting day, the intuition and senses were dulled so that when the gaggle of bearded Mujahiddin entered the room it was difficult to guess who was the chief, and so I waited for him to introduce himself. Mullah Farouk did not, but sat in one corner and pulled the pistol from its holster. By the time he was ready to talk I was long asleep.

I fell asleep thinking of Chaurjee village and a carnival at the end of the day. Earlier that day I had been led to a roof overlooking Chaurjee which had once been a large and prosperous village. Now it was utterly ruined. The Mujahiddin who sat around in little groups in the streets below seemed like fully paid up members of a lost cause, amidst the smashed buildings which stretched out all around. It seemed unspeakably mean to take from a people who were so materially poor what little they had. I had seen nothing quite so desolate in all my travels. It was the result of systematic and unremitting bombardment from the Russian posts. Clausewitz and absolute war, Dresden and total war. Little Chaurjee was the heir to that philosophy its inhabitants had never heard of; the strategy of brutal force designed to terrorise the population into submission. You sensed the thoughts of the old men in the party which had abolished God and who were obliged to act like little gods and force the ideology on others lest the whole fraud be exposed. Because of that twisted ideology Chaurjee had to be erased from the landscape.

As we left the village we met a group of Mujahiddin who were preparing for a raid against one of the posts. They wore macabre masks that children wear at Hallowe'en. The commander reasoned that if they came face to face with the enemy it would serve a useful shock value. Dear God, they planned to scare the enemy to death. His men were enthusiastic at the prospect. A few minutes in their company lifted the depression and made the long march easier.

It was dark when we entered the substantial village where Mullah Farouk had his HQ. From some way off we could see lanterns and fires. When we entered the streets we found parades and dancing in the streets. It was part of the three days of celebrations to mark a wedding.

Mullah Farouk came back early the next morning to lead a group to the north road personally so that I might get some pictures. I wanted to get some shots of military vehicles. Mullah Farouk led the way through the area by the road which had been mined.

Now he sat in a corner of the bombed-out room wiping his pistol with a bright cloth. The Mujahiddin were posted about the area while I crouched by the side of the hole in the wall snatching shots of tanks and APCs on the road just 50 metres away. There was no easy escape from the first floor room: you could leap from the window and risk breaking an ankle or negotiate the remains of the staircase. The men were edgy. They regarded a trip to the road without the chance to have a crack at the enemy as faintly sacrilegious.

The fear struck at that moment. I was following the passage of traffic along the road through the viewfinder. A truck load of troops passed on its way to the post in the hills a kilometre away. The corrugated huts glistened in the sun. How skilled the Russians were in building camps, usually for their own people. Through the viewfinder I could see one of the soldiers looking straight at me. Logic told me that he was not actually looking at *me,* merely at the shadow where I crouched. I imagine it was the suppressed fear still lingering from the raid on the road. I found myself trembling uncontrollably. As we sat in the ruin waiting for more military vehicles I sat on my hands so that the others would not see.

It was time to go home.

Mullah Farouk commandeered a Land Rover for the ten-kilometre journey to the next village on my route north. Jebel Seraj was only two days away and it was conceivable that by forcing the pace I might be in Pakistan in two weeks. The incident at the bridge might have been a symbol for the futility of such reckoning. The bridge collapsed and the machine decanted a dozen men into the water. The men lifted the Rover out of the stream and were still joking about the crash over lunch.

Charikar was the provincial capital of Parwan and heavily defended by government and Russian troops. During the First Afghan war the Kohistanis slaughtered Fourth Gurkha Regiment troops garrisoned at Charikar which was partly destroyed by the British during the reprisals. Less than forty years later Abdur Rahman had proclaimed himself Amir there. In 1979 the prison at Charikar was overrun by Mujahiddin and 100 women freed.

Mir-Alim seemed like a saintly old grandfather to the Mujahiddin who fought to free Charikar. He was a man of great presence and few words and he was revered by the men. The communists had turned the town into a fortress so the old man had dug in all around the outskirts. It might have been a symbol for the country. Mujahiddin waiting patiently until the Russians leave or the communists make a mistake.

Armoured personnel carrier en route *to Charikar.*

Mir-Alim led the way and showed me his once substantial home which had been destroyed by the jets. For 100 metres in all directions there were the shattered stumps of trees. After touring the satellite villages of his demesne, we followed the broad irrigation channel – straight as a Roman road – to the outskirts of the town. At a bridge we came to a main road filled with people coming and going to the city gates less than 100 metres away. There was a communist check point, yet a crowd gathered to shake the hands of Mir-Alim and listen as he gently reaffirmed the death sentence on the Godless enemy. The Mujahiddin were everywhere. A system of tunnels which encircled the enemy began here. I was taken on a tour of these Mujahiddin positions. The city limits were marked by a ring of communist posts and fortresses. Everything entering the city was searched. We watched from a specially dug ditch which ran into the tunnel network. The Mujahiddin had the town permanently encircled. Mir-Alim formed a ring with his hands.

'This is how the Mujahiddin are with Charikar. Communists say they control Charikar. Do the men in a prison control that prison? One day. . .'

He brought his hands together with a clap.

The march inevitably took longer than I anticipated. We tramped through the villages and I longed to return to Jebel Seraj and see Engineer Toorak again. Though my health was restored I felt a great weariness which no amount of rest – there was little enough anyway – could shake off.

Bridge just outside Charikar: the resistance has the communist-held city ringed.

We set off early and came to a high ridge above Kohistan. There was a spectacular view all the way from Jebel Seraj to the distant mountains. Bathed in early morning mist, it spoke only of utter peace. But the whole of the ridge was covered in the green and white flags to mark the graves of the Shaheed. Thousands of martyrs. By lunchtime it had grown hot and the jets began to bomb a village about five kilometres distant. We came to a village overlooking the valley. Beneath the trees were three men who squatted and watched the bombing, their backs to us. Engineer Toorak turned round on his heels and smiled. We embraced and he led me to a house where he had a temporary HQ. His hair had grown (so had mine) but he still had that dew-eyed and elfin appearance.

'Tell me about Charles Darwin,' began Toorak after dinner. He had that provocative smile on his face which was an invitation to debate. We always had different views but the debate seemed to reaffirm our friendship. 'So we come from monkeys, Mista Mike,' he said in mock amazement.

We moved from village to village and talked of many things except one – my return to Pakistan. Winter was close now. The mountains would already be very cold and the last huge camel trains from Pakistan were already passing through. The story goes that there are 100 names for Allah and man knows 99 of them. Only the camel knows the other name but he keeps it a secret and that explains his supercilious grin. It was an Arab story but Toorak said he had heard it from an Uzbek merchant.

By not referring to my departure for Pakistan we thus postponed the inevitable. We spent a day walking to Jamalara where Doctor Akhram – handsome and solitary – stood with his black bag in one hand, rifle in the other. There was Ustoz Farid, who had denied his identity before and who now smiled shyly. Abdul Ghafoor appeared and we talked. Four months in Afghanistan had changed him, as it changes everybody. He no longer talked of the party or the people, but of a skirmish or his family. The grand design had given way to humility and suddenly I liked him very much and felt bad about the arguments we had had. I blamed myself and we spent several days apologising to each other for the misunderstandings of months before. It seemed a lifetime ago when I had first come to Jamalara.

One day we walked out to a village which had been bombed. Dead cattle and sheep lay rotting on the approach roads, their faces hideously bloated into masks and the air stinking so that you retched. The headman in the village stood on a mound of rubble and addressed us. He thanked me as a representative of the British people for coming so far to see their humble village. He asked that I return one day when the Russians had been banished and the village rebuilt that they might honour me as a guest. I made a speech about the Afghan people which in my own world, grown cynical, would have been dismissed as sentimental. Among the ruins an old man broke down and wept. It was the more poignant for the absence of grief I had found in Afghanistan and afterwards I asked Abdul Ghafoor to leave me alone for a few moments until I had composed myself.

At length I said to Toorak – in the way of a joke – that I must return to Pakistan.

'Mike, you stay with me for one month. No, one year. You write your book here and we talk of many things. I do not want you to leave still thinking man comes from monkeys.'

It was a pivotal moment in a life. Toorak stood before me, as ever like the diminutive gnome who knows more than he will tell. The air of mystery and magic was stronger than ever and you wanted to stay with him. I felt an inconsolable sadness about leaving such people. Despite the war, the illness and often the mental strain, the prospect of leaving made me sick at heart. If I stayed I doubted if I would ever leave. Toorak took his cue from my silence and was silent. I left the room before the emotion overwhelmed me.

The following day I shook hundreds of outstretched hands in the dusty street outside of Jamalara. In the faces were traces of the fanaticism but there was friendliness, good cheer, nobility and goodness.

'Mike,' cried Toorak as I climbed on the back of the pony and trap which would take me a few kilometres, 'when you first come to me, you ask how many men I have. I say a lie. I tell you 20,000. Really I have 50,000. If you come back I have one more.'

The Mujahiddin were still waving as we turned the bend at the end of the long, straight road. I felt an unspeakable sense of loss. It did not diminish with time.

But the old cycle of hardship and delight turned and, after two days slogging through the mountains, I awoke with a sense of exhilaration. I was now travelling home and familiar pleasures would be restored to me. My companions were four young Mujahiddin all wearing karakul hats, each a farewell present. They were excited at the prospect of Pakistan and would cut a dash in the bazaars wearing their hats. With the karakul kids, I took a mountain 'short cut' to Nijrob and then to Tagob where Commander Ahmedi laid on a special meal and insisted I stay a week or more with him.

We left early the next day. The cycle turned again and I fell sick but the homeward journey made it easy to endure. Afghanistan seemed to be on the move. We passed great camel trains bringing weapons from Pakistan. Thousands of Mujahiddin were arriving after months spent working across the border. They carried great bundles of cash and were now eager for the fight. Although the snows made travel across the border difficult or impossible in winter, the fighting now continued throughout the year. In the early years it had tended to be seasonal, because supplies ran low in winter but the resistance had learned to stock up. Thousands of tons of supplies were pouring into the country. Similarly, thousands of Mujahiddin were migrating to Pakistan, to find work and a rest from the war. We met them

Asking the way during the 'short cut' to Nijrob.

everywhere – a group of fifty in a mosque with all the gay abandon of a works outing – and we would walk and talk and then part.

'I study democracy. I study Marxism. I study Christianity. I did not take Islam from my parents. I study Plato and Bertrand Russell. But I choose Islam,' said the Mujahid who walked with us for most of a day. 'If we can walk for eight days to Peshawar together then I can tell you why Islam is good for you.' But we separated and took different routes.

There were refugees on the move too. Some find life economically impossible in winter in Afghanistan and move their flocks over the border. Others were going for good.

'Are you happy?' cried the karakul kids. I was, but I was too tired to show it as we tackled the first of the mountains. Most days the sun never really made it through the haze and the walking was cool. In the mountains it was bitterly cold even by day. We took a more direct route than on the march into Afghanistan and so we crossed the Kabul River by day. We had very little food and my health had deteriorated so badly by the time we reached Senna Gul's camp in the Laghman Mountains that I had to remain behind while the karakul kids continued.

It was cold in the mountains and the food was poor, mostly rice with a little unrefined sugar to chew. My health grew worse instead of better: rampant dysentery and cut feet that began to fester. The four days to the

New companions on the road to Pakistan.

Fording a stream.

border might as well have been a lifetime. I grew weaker and finally pleaded with Senna Gul to let me travel to the border with a group of merchants who were exporting semi-precious stones. Senna Gul was unhappy about me travelling with 'civilians' but there were no Pakistan-bound Mujahiddin due through for days so he reluctantly arranged for me to travel with the merchants. Then he told me a story.

'One year ago we have American journalist here. He was sick with the same thing. But he died. I do not think he was a good journalist. Good luck, my friend.'

With those strange and disturbing words in my ears, I set off at dusk at the slow and inexorable pace dictated by the pack animals. Long before night fell, the sky was black with the storm that growled and rumbled through the peaks but did not break. The horses were restless and the men worried. They had hoped to descend to the valley a couple of thousand metres below, before the storm broke, but the first large drops of rain were already falling.

The descent was a nightmare. The driving rain made the plates of rock slippery and lethal and the safest way down was on your backside. The gallant horses did their best against gale-force winds, nil visibility and heavy loads that shifted dangerously. The only sound I could hear amidst the raging winds was the tinkle of the bells about their necks and the occasional cry of the drovers cut short and lost in the gale. To keep out of the way of the stumbling horses I found a path parallel to the main one. I heard a pitiful wailing sound and later learned that one of the horses had gone over the cliff. Then the sound was lost in the wind so that you wondered if you had heard anything at all. Two horses out of fourteen went over in the descent.

We reached the foothills. I had no idea how far away the merchants were: the bells always sounded far away even when close. I could see nothing in the storm and then even the sound of the bells disappeared as they rounded a hill. By the time I had rounded the hill they were gone and I was alone in a world of howling winds and darkness. We had been apart for less than two minutes. Lightning illuminated a subsidiary valley and I stumbled up it and it was lightning that showed it to be a dead end. I followed a path to a crest from where much of the broad valley was lit up for an instant. But nothing moved in all that vastness save for the rain.

The worst had happened: I was lost at night in a storm in hostile territory without food or shelter. Even if I survived the night, what would any armed Afghan make of someone jabbering in a foreign language? Even if they did not assume I was a Russian, which would have been logical, any stranger wandering without protection was fair game. The only word to describe my feelings then was despair. In any crisis you are usually your own worst enemy: panic is the common cause of death and though I kept telling myself that it was an hour before irrational terror gave way to a numb realisation that there were options left and choices to be made. The rain stopped and I changed into my spare clothes. They were damp but the wind kept up and they began to dry. I chain-smoked behind a boulder which afforded some protection from the wind. It was bitterly cold and still only 10 pm. The choice was this: risk exposure by spending the night in the open or approach one of the nomads' camps in the valley and stand the chance of being shot. I sensed that I simply would not survive a night in the open and set off for one of the black tents. I did not get within 100 metres of the camp before vicious dogs came bounding up. They set up a fierce howling and made it plain that was as far as I went. I called out a few words in Persian but they were lost in the wind and nothing stirred in the tents. It was the same at a camp two kilometres away. Dogs and silence. I retreated, thankful that I had not been shot. The only thing left was to find somewhere out of the storm. I followed the side of the valley, hoping to find a cave, and eventually came across the ruin of a barn. The best part of three walls were still standing and there was just enough roof left over one corner to keep dry.

I was now confident of surviving the night and my thoughts turned to the morning. I was sure the merchants would send back a search party and it seemed the best thing to do was wait at the spot we had parted company. At dawn I re-traced my steps to that spot and hid among some rocks, fearful of meeting strangers. Men passed along the path but no familiar faces appeared. I was confident I could negotiate my way back to Senna Gul's camp using memory and compass but the thought of back-tracking was too appalling. The first thing to do was beg the protection of a passing Afghan, provided I could convince them I was not a Russian (not the easiest task in a country where 'foreigners' begin at the village limits). One thing I had noticed in my travels was that conversation in your own tongue can disguise as much as illuminate. Here, where language was a barrier, I had learned to read much into a face or manner. That judgement was about to be put to the test.

I stepped out into the open and called to the group of six men who were striding by in single file towards the mountain trail. They were friendly and on their way to the camp of Senna Gul after marching from Pakistan. Logic should have dictated that I accompany them back to the camp but they would not hear of it. One of them would escort me to a village fifteen kilometres away where the merchants probably stayed the night and where, in any event, Mujahiddin passed through. My companion had been walking the usual eighteen hours a day but he thought nothing of such a detour.

I was reunited with the merchants at the village. They had been delayed while they found replacement horses for two which had gone lame. We set off again. Though the pace was slow, it was relentless, and they rarely, if ever, stopped to rest. I found myself in familiar valleys but the merchants largely took a different route. We re-crossed the desert, this time in a freezing rainstorm. The merchants told me that their valuables were entrusted to one

First snows of the winter on the Safed Koh.

man who rode some distance separate from the rest. Russians in gunships regularly raided such groups and stole everything. It was the business of the man carrying the valuables to escape until the Russians had gone.

There was no sleep to be had that night either, as we crowded into a damp and filthy chai khana. There were so many men on the move that the lonely chai khanas were full and in this one there was no room to lie down. We sat huddled in partouks, grateful that it was dry. The first climbs through the Safed Koh began at first light. Now it snowed and the tracks were treacherous. If we were lucky there was one meal of tea and bread a day. Even the imagination became exhausted: joy was no longer a roast beef dinner or the pleasure of friends. It was simply not to have to walk. In the snowbound passes we still met scores of travellers. Most of the Mujahiddin were Jamiatis and I discovered to my chagrin that the merchants were telling them that I had been in Afghanistan as guest of that party. They did not bother to tell me this so that there were suspicious glances when I said I had been with Hezb. A rather noble-looking Jamiati on a beautiful chestnut offered to let me ride his horse and, when I declined, insisted on carrying my pack across his saddle.

'You with Hezb. I with Jamiat. Hezb good. Jamiat good. Any group fighting Russians good. The Unity a good thing.'

He was good company and it seemed that I had travelled hundreds of

The last gruelling barrier.

kilometres to hear his words. I saw him the next day too and he insisted on taking my pack again. We became separated along the trail and I became worried about my pack. Irrationally so. What if he disappeared with my films featuring a rival party? What if he suddenly turned thief? When we met again I retrieved my pack. It was an ignoble and mean response to a typical act of generosity. But with the border so close a hundred suppressed anxieties were beginning to surface. The fears that you only admit afterwards. The qualities of trust and sound judgement were ground under by the strain of illness and exhaustion. To the merchants who favoured no one party I was a bloody nuisance, a liability to their neutrality.

We were within a day's march of the border, gathered about the blazing stoves inside the chai khana. A flurry of snow from the icy world without would blow in every time the door opened. For the first time I felt a hint of excitement at the prospect of actually getting out of the country. I felt that nothing else could go wrong.

One of a large group of unruly Jamiatis who crowded into the chai khana sat next to me and chatted for some time before suddenly demanding: 'You give me one camera.' An hour later he was still refusing to take no for an answer. The merchants were worried by the situation developing in my corner and tried to intervene to no avail. I felt helpless and, despite the snowstorm outside, was ready to resume the march. Those suppressed anxieties came to the surface again. The Jamiati began to rifle my bag until I stopped him. It was a gesture of futility and desperation when we did not have a weapon between us. He laughed and sat back as if to say: I can wait. Once again the world became horribly distorted by illness and exhaustion. The border was just six hours' march away and yet the closer you got the more remote it seemed.

The master of the chai khana was a robust character who regaled his customers with gossip and stories and, slapping me on the back, he extolled the virtues of Inglestanis. I had already resolved to ask for his protection if it came to a showdown, when he suddenly began to quarrel with the Mujahiddin. He told them they would have to leave to make way for refugee women who had no shelter. The argument grew bitter.

'Are you men that you would deny shelter to women and children,' he bawled. 'Are you even Muslims? Inshallah, I already have a room full of women who cannot face the snow and the dark.'

At that, the door opened and in trooped forty women and children out of the snow. They wore bright costumes and jewellery and many were unveiled. They were Turkoman wives and children with broad round faces and expressions of serenity. It was all the more remarkable as they had been walking for more than two weeks. The Mujahiddin – all Pathans – snarled that the Turkomans were 'kafirs'. They are not, and the brave proprietor called in the Jamiat commander and demanded they all leave to make room for the women. The commander nodded and the men trooped out. The appearance of these strangely composed, almost ethereal, people took on the

242

sense of a miracle to me. The innkeeper put a thin cotton curtain across the room to separate men and women. Again there was no room to lie down so we sat huddled before the fires all night. It was my last night in Afghanistan and I will always remember the silhouettes through the curtain, of the women cradling their sleeping children. I shared my last cigarette with the old Turkoman who sat guarding the virtue of the women on our side of the curtain. He said nothing all night and just smiled distantly in the shadows. Despite the discomfort and later the cold there was not a murmur from woman or child. I had never seen such dignity.

I felt that once I crossed the border all would be well. This was a fantasy. I had forgotten the first rule of the region: never return to a place expecting it to be the same as when you left it. I had heard virtually no news for more than four months. The seedy character in the Peshawar hotel who had warned me of the trouble to come in Pakistan had been correct. As one of the organisers he was entitled to be. There had been extensive rioting in Sind and trouble in the North West Frontier Province by the groups opposed to military rule. Parts of the country were in turmoil and it could not have been more inconvenient for me trying to get back to Peshawar. Since the disturbances the police closely watched all movements in and out of the tribal agencies. I had entered without the necessary papers and leaving was going to be a problem.

At the border I bought some pears from the vendors and gazed down at Pakistan far below, disappearing into the haze. The Mujahiddin camp was far below. I was startled to find myself confronted by Pakistani customs officials who were startled to find an Englishman crossing their stretch of the border. I was taken to a fairy tale castle perched on top of one of the peaks where I sat for two hours while they pondered my passport and made telephone calls. The first rule in these situations is to remain calm and it was only exhaustion which rendered me incapable of articulating my anger and frustration. Finally the immaculate customs chief looked down at the dishevelled, jaundiced wreck sitting on his floor and handed me my passport.

'Welcome to Pakistan,' he said.

An hour later I had fulfilled my wildest dreams of sitting down in the Mujahiddin quarters above the armoury with the intention of remaining immobile until I boarded my transport to Parachinar. A Mujahid sat daubing red tincture on my cut feet and prodding the swelling about my ankles.

'Two months ago six Japanese journalists come. They take horses and donkeys and go to Afghanistan. After one night they come back. Finish! Ah Afghanistan,' he murmured.

Hindsight and restored health enabled you to listen with some satisfaction to such stories. At the time I had only mumbled: 'Bloody sensible.'

There should have been peace in crossing the border. But there was not. Instinct was at work and I sensed something was wrong, even before I knew

244

the extent of the trouble in Pakistan. The unease increased when I saw a familiar face at the door.

'Hello my friend,' said Doctor Zulmaya from Goldera. He beamed and spoke volubly about anything that came into his head. Anything that is but what was really on his mind.

'When did you get here?'

'One week ago, Mista Mike.'

'When are you leaving for Peshawar?'

'I do not go to Peshawar. I stay here.'

That was it. Nobody makes the march out of Afghanistan without going on to Peshawar. Unless they are a masochist. The business of the war is conducted in Afghanistan and Peshawar: the camp was just a staging post between the two. He had come specifically to intercept me.

'Mista Mike, you have diaries. I would like to read your diaries.'

'Go to hell.'

I turned over and went to sleep. Hours later when I woke Zulmaya was still sitting there. The false smile was gone and he looked stern.

'Mista Mike, you must show me these diaries.'

I was angry and not a shade desperate. I put to him the following argument which in a room full of armed men may have been a symbol for the liberal view in the modern world.

Into Pakistan.

'Let this be a test of Islamic authority. It is my belief that power corrupts and absolute power corrupts absolutely. You say the exception is power wielded in the name of Islam. You would agree that my belief is certainly true of the Soviet Union and most communist states. There, power is wielded over the individual to an alarming degree. I say that no matter who assumes absolute power – communist or Muslim – that power is abused and the individual must suffer. In this room we have a metaphor. You have absolute power over me, the individual. If you choose to, you can take my diaries by force. I will not hand them over. You must take them by force. If you do take them by force then, as far as I am concerned, I will have had a glimpse of Afghanistan under Islamic control. The choice is yours.'

Doctor Zulmaya got up and left, which was a great relief. I do not think for one moment it was the force of the argument which prompted him to abandon attempts to secure my diaries: I suspect it was a fear of offending a guest. Ah Afghanistan.

That Pakistan was in some turmoil became evident the next day. I was joined by a commander from Badakshan and we hired a car to Parachinar. All along the road, Pakistani troops were digging in. Once they had been dug in to face a possible Russian threat; now the machine gun positions faced Parachinar and their own people. The commander liked this sight.

He beamed roundly as he said: 'I have just come from one war and, look, here is another. Ah Afghanistan. Ah Pakistan.'

I was bundled through the back door of a Mujahiddin house in Parachinar and my worst fears were confirmed. The security crackdown by the authorities had put me and my hosts in a difficult position. Several foreign journalists had already been caught without documents in the tribal agencies and been jailed and had their film confiscated. Five months before you could wander around the tribal lands without passes and nobody took any notice. Now there were roadblocks every few miles. For the first time, the commander I was with actually seemed worried for my safety. It was one more irony.

The commander had been given this job on his side of the border after losing a leg in the war. He limped about on a squeaking artificial limb and seemed more interested in showing it to me than getting me out of this fix. It did not seem possible that after the trials of the last few months my journey should grind to an ignominious halt in Pakistan, just a day's bus ride away from Peshawar. First the commander suggested I stay hidden in Parachinar until the troubles died down. That might have been months, and I shook my head. Then he said they could smuggle me out as baggage in a camel train, but he abandoned it before I had a chance to veto it. He thought that the best way was to summon a party car from Peshawar but even they were checked. Public transport was out of the question. I would be caught. Then we ran out of options. I was stricken by fever again. The diarrhoea and sickness returned and the deliberations as to how to get me to Peshawar did not seem to matter any more.

The world was a surreal enough place without the conversation I had with the sallow commander the next day. The Pakistani authorities blamed much of the troubles on Russian agents smuggled over the border from Afghanistan. The trouble was a prelude to military intervention in Pakistan, so the story ran. There was a fair chance I would be taken for a Russian spy if caught. Even so I could not remain in Parachinar as there were police everywhere, he said. I was to catch the earliest bus the next day in disguise and try to get to Peshawar that way. Then he turned to the subject of his artificial limb which he said did not fit properly. He wanted me to take it to London to be adjusted and send it back. He was adamant and I was in no state to argue.

So it was that with the limb sticking out of my rucksack and one escort, I slipped out of the house before dawn to catch the 5 am bus to Peshawar. The bus was half full and we sat at the back. I had the tail of my turban drawn across my face and the plan was for me to pretend to be asleep on the journey. My escort would do all the talking. Asleep or sick, said the commander. I did not have to pretend to be ill. Sweat soaked me and rampant dysentery destroyed my comfort and dignity. But I could not ask the bus driver to stop every few kilometres. Between Parachinar and Thal we were flagged down six times at police roadblocks. It was still early and they tended to take a perfunctory look at passengers before waving us through.

But at the last roadblock two officers moved down the aisle checking all documents. The game was up, but I barely cared any more. Half-way down the aisle they spotted me and called out what was the matter.

'He is very sick,' said my companion.

A look of alarm spread over their faces. Whatever it was, it looked contagious. They stopped checking passes and left the bus. Perhaps clouds did have a silver lining.

I drifted off and came to beyond Thal. My companion was gone. Then I came to in that same little hotel in Peshawar. I felt startled by waking in a room alone. There were no Mujahiddin and nobody to take decisions on my behalf. The past had the quality of a fabulous dream and the world could never be the same again. I was thrilled at being my own master again with the power of choice. Riches. I took my first decision. To go back to sleep.

Endgame

The cynic in the English pub said: 'I suppose you're going to write about Afghans armed only with rifles, taking on Russian tanks.'

If I have, it is because they did.

But why should the freedom or subjugation of the Afghans matter to the people of the West?

Firstly, it is necessary to dwell on the Soviet position in Afghanistan which can be analysed in two ways: that the invasion was a 'one off' operation designed to stabilise a Marxist regime; or that it was part of a broader strategy.

If the Russian invasion of Afghanistan was merely designed to secure the Marxist government then it can be said only to have succeeded in propping up what the Afghans witheringly refer to as 'The King of Kabulistan'; that is Babrak Karmal. Beyond that, the invasion must be seen as a failure in both military and political terms.

In the field, the Russians have inflicted appalling losses on the Mujahiddin and particularly the civilians. But they have sustained heavy casualties too (one report put the figure in 1983 as 12,000 killed and wounded). The evidence suggests that morale among Soviet forces was low, while the resistance was better armed and organised than at the time of the invasion, even if they still did not receive the types of weapons they needed. The morale of the resistance was high. Indeed, I do not think that 'morale' as we understand it is the best description. The presence of the Russians offends the honour of the Afghans at its deepest levels. Without that honour and the uncompromising necessity to be a Muslim, the Afghan feels he may as well not exist. To accept Marxism is to deny themselves not only a place in this world but in the next world too.

In 1983 the resistance still held at least 80 per cent of the country and even in the cities they were able to pressure the Russians. To even begin to attempt to pacify the country would require probably half a million troops. On the front line it seemed that the Soviet tactics were reduced to trying to bludgeon the civilian population into abandoning its support for the Mujahiddin. Militarily the Soviets, after nearly four years of fighting, were, apart from terror, bankrupt of ideas.

Politically they had failed too. The programme of reforms planned by the communists had long been buried and Karmal's regime reduced to trying to buy off the tribes and declaring its own respect for Islam. But, despite the blandishments from Kabul, it was clear that the regime could not survive without Soviet troops. After nearly four years of occupation I doubt if there was one more communist in the country.

I travelled 1,300 kilometres mostly on foot over more than four months in Afghanistan and spent five weeks in Peshawar talking to refugees and resistance leaders. I talked to hundreds of civilians and Mujahiddin and nowhere did I meet anybody even prepared to countenance compromise with the communists. Not one. It is difficult to meet an Afghan who has not lost a member of his family in the war. Honour dictates that those who have died – in fighting, in air raids, in the prisons – must be avenged. Common sense tells them that a Marxist government would always be inimical to their faith.

If, however, the invasion was part of a bigger game being played by Moscow – no less then the Great Game of Czarist times – then the picture changes. It does not really matter that most of Afghanistan is held by the resistance, provided that the few principal strategic roads and air bases remain in Soviet hands. In 1983 it seemed that the Russians could hold on to their 'forward bases' indefinitely.

Their presence in Afghanistan enables them to put pressure on Iran and Pakistan whenever they choose. Exploitation of the autonomy issue in Baluchistan is just one option available to the Russians at any time. It is highly unlikely that the upheavals in Iran have run their course: Pakistan faces many problems in addition to the Baluch. The Russians – faced with a Muslim population which by the end of the twentieth century may well in numbers outstrip all the other peoples of the empire – saw the Islamic Revolution in Iran and the advance of Islamisation in Pakistan. The third of its southern neighbours, Afghanistan, was in real danger of having a Marxist regime ousted and replaced by an Islamic government. It drove a military wedge through the Islamic resurgence and signalled a warning to other Islamic governments. The invasion also placed them in a position easily to exploit any future weaknesses in a region renowned for turmoil.

Behind these considerations remains the implacable hostility of the Marxists to the West, and that is one reason why the freedom of the Afghans should cause us to give a damn. The Russian Empire moved in 1979 not on a road which ends in Afghanistan but on one designed to weaken and destroy the West. If we care about our own survival, we would be well served to care about the survival of Afghanistan. The military pincer movement aimed at the oil fields is in place and the subversion of the oil states will continue. They too are only waystations on the road to the West and global hegemony. Soviet policy is underpinned by that ambition and has been since Lenin hijacked the Russian revolution.

It is my belief that the central issue of our times is the struggle between freedom and tyranny. Freedom is not a romantic illusion but the best way for men and women to equip themselves for the adventure of the future. The masters of the totalitarian regime which guides the Russian Empire are the heirs to Stalin and Hitler, for whom the future was subordinated to outrageous man-made certainties. The rush to totality in thought and action has marked the twentieth century with the blood of countless tens of millions of people.

The Prophet Mohammed said: 'The best Jehad is to utter the word of truth in front of a tyrant ruler.' The West does not need a nuclear war to show up the lie which is at the heart of Russian totalitarianism because that lie cuts off the Russian Empire from the future. But the West must make greater efforts to counter Russian ambitions and to act decisively. The misguided 'years of trust' under President Carter were followed by a tougher line from President Reagan but by the beginning of 1984 even he had begun to make conciliatory gestures towards Moscow. Yet the Russian troops still occupied Afghanistan and Russians were still being incarcerated in mental hospitals for thoughts deemed unacceptable to the tyrant. Russian calculations that, after an initial period of bluster over the invasion, the West would seek a new pattern of compromise seemed justified. Others would call it appeasement. Further, once it had lulled the West into another false sense of security by preying on fears, Moscow would feel free to continue its aggressive strategy.

The war for the future of the West is being fought far from Europe: the key lies in the Middle East. The Muslim nations on the whole do not want Western troops on their soil but they do have a common cause with our interests. The stumbling block for several decades has been the issue of Palestine. Resolve that and a lot of pieces fall into place. So long as the United States continues to champion without compromise the cause of Israel, even the West's closest Arab allies will remain alienated. Washington does not need to abandon Israel, merely bring the requisite pressure to bear on the unruly infant state to ensure that justice is done to the Palestinians. Unless the Palestinian people receive that justice – in other words their own homeland side by side with Israel – the Muslim world will remain distant from the West, divided among themselves, weak and vulnerable to subversion.

Fear about Islam must be overcome too. The heart of the Islamic Renaissance is not in Iran but in those nations west of the Arabian Gulf which do not regard the whole world as hostile to their faith but who seek a stronger Islamic voice in a world based on mutual respect. A strong belt of Islamic nations south of the Russian Empire, which do not see the West as the backers of an aggressive, expansionist Israel, would be the best guarantee of halting the Russian advance and keeping the oil fields safe.

The West should have the courage of its convictions and make available to the Afghan resistance groups, of whatever shade of political thought, the weapons they need to take on the Russians: that is mainly anti-gunship and anti-aircraft missiles. The Afghans could help themselves by making a concerted effort to promote the Unity. From this could emerge a government in exile which the West should deal with publicly and loudly. The Afghans might also learn from the Palestine Liberation Organisation which has established more than 100 offices around the world to promote its cause. The West must never accept an Afghanistan as part of the Russian Empire.

As for the empire itself: its implosion may well eventually be brought about by the inefficiency and corruption which is an intrinsic part of its dogmatism. The rulers of the empire, despite several generations subject to the relentless propaganda of the state, remain afraid of those individuals prepared to speak the truth 'in front of the tyrant ruler' and ruthlessly seek to suppress those voices.

The West should progressively reduce its trade with the empire and announce on any world forum available, why. Let the masters of the empire match their superior moral tone by demonstrating that a Marxist economy can deliver the goods. That it patently cannot is disguised by more lies. In the developing world, the West should enhance aid and simultaneously attack the tissues of lies perpetrated by Moscow and the international leftist axis. So successful has been the dissemination of the propaganda of untruth that its litany of platitudes is global common currency. If anybody is doubtful about where to start, they might challenge the next person who uses the term 'Western imperialism'.

The underlying reason for caring about the freedom of the Afghan people is because it is indivisible from our own. When we no longer care about the freedom of others, we no longer care for our own. Tyranny will have won.

I do not know where they are now: Murcha, Abdul Ghafoor, Ahmedi, Hash Khan, Juma Gul, Sher Ali, Islamia or any of the others. Or even if they are alive. But I am indebted to them for helping me to glimpse something heroic in a world in which cynicism dulls humanity and which may be the true enemy within.

On a freezing December night back in England, I was walking down Oxford Street with an Afghan Tadjik. He had come to England for medical treatment after his hands were blown off in a battle near the Iranian border. Two pale stumps poked out of the sleeves of his rain mac. I said he should put them in his pockets to keep them warm.

'No, they are very soft now. If I leave them out they will get hard quicker and then the doctor can give me plastic hands. Then I will be able to return to Afghanistan sooner to fight the Jehad.'

Shakespeare said it best:

Nor stony tower, nor walls of beaten brass,
Nor airless dungeon, nor strong links of iron,
Can be retentive to the strength of spirit.

Glossary

Allah O Akbar	'God is great'
APC	Armoured Personnel Carrier
Badal	Vengeance
Basmachi	Bandit
BMP	Russian Infantry Combat Vehicle
Buzkashi	Afghan national game
Chabanamah	Night letters containing Mujahiddin propaganda
Chador	A billowing shapeless gown for women, designed to protect their modesty
Chai khana	Tea house
Feringhi	Foreigners
Ghazi	A fighter for the faith who has killed a non-believer
Hajj	Pilgrimage to Mecca
Imam	Leader of a Muslim community
Inglestani	Englishman
Inshallah	'God willing', with the same connotations as *mañana*
Jehad	A holy war
Jirga	An assembly of tribal elders or representatives
Kafir	Non-Muslim or infidel
Karakul	Breed of sheep with coarse hair from which hats are made
Kofta	Balls of meat
Mahdi	The Islamic Messiah
Mast	Yogurt
Melmestia	Being a good host to all-comers
Mujahid	Warrior of God
Mullah	A Muslim teacher or religious leader
Nan	Type of flat bread
Nanawati	Asylum
Partouk	Shawl
PDPA	People's Democratic Party of Afghanistan, composed of Parcham and Khalq communist parties

Piaz	Onion
Pirahan	Long loose shirt
RPG	Rocket propelled grenade
Salaam alaikum	'Peace be to you'
Satrapy	Province of ancient Persian Empires
Shaheed	Martyrs
Shoravee	Russians
Sufa	Raised platform of earth or baked mud where villagers gather or relax
Tombon	Baggy pantaloons
Vazoo	Washing

Index

Figures in italics refer to page numbers of illustrations.

254